ISBN: 978-0-578-94844-7 (Paperback)
Printed by KINDRED, in China.
First printing, 2021.

KINDRED
448 West 19th Street
Suite 270
Houston, TX 77008

kindredapostle.com

NEW TESTAMENT

Nihil Obstat   Stephen J. Hartdegen, O.F.M.,
                L.S.S.
                Censor Deputatus

Imprimatur   +James A. Hickey, S.T.D., J.C.D.
                Archbishop of Washington
                August 27, 1986

MATTHEW INTRODUCTION

THE
GOSPEL

ACCORDING TO MATTHEW

The position of the Gospel according to Matthew as the first of the four gospels in the New Testament reflects both the view that it was the first to be written, a view that goes back to the late second century A.D., and the esteem in which it was held by the church; no other was so frequently quoted in the noncanonical literature of earliest Christianity. Although the majority of scholars now reject the opinion about the time of its composition, the high estimation of this work remains. The reason for that becomes clear upon study of the way in which Matthew presents his story of Jesus, the demands of Christian discipleship, and the breaking-in of the new and final age through the ministry but particularly through the death and resurrection of Jesus.

The gospel begins with a narrative prologue (Mt 1:1–2:23), the first part of which is a genealogy of Jesus starting with Abraham, the father of Israel (Mt 1:1–17). Yet at the beginning of that genealogy Jesus is designated as "the son of David, the son of Abraham" (Mt 1:1). The kingly ancestor who lived about a thousand years after Abraham is named first, for this is the genealogy of Jesus Christ, the Messiah, the royal anointed one (Mt 1:16). In the first of the episodes of the infancy narrative that follow the genealogy, the mystery of Jesus' person is declared. He is conceived of a virgin by the power of the Spirit of God (Mt 1:18–25). The first of the gospel's fulfillment citations, whose purpose it is to show that he was the one to whom the prophecies of Israel were pointing, occurs here (Mt 1:23): he shall be named Emmanuel, for in him God is with us.

The announcement of the birth of this newborn king of the Jews greatly troubles not only King Herod but all Jerusalem (Mt 2:1–3), yet the Gentile magi are overjoyed to find him and offer him their homage and their gifts (Mt 2:10–11). Thus his ultimate rejection by the mass of his own people and his acceptance by the Gentile nations is foreshadowed. He must be taken to Egypt to escape the murderous plan of Herod. By his sojourn there and his subsequent return after the king's death he relives the Exodus experience of Israel. The words of the Lord spoken through the prophet Hosea, "Out of Egypt I called my son," are fulfilled in him (Mt 2:15); if Israel was God's son, Jesus is so in a way far surpassing the dignity of that nation, as his marvelous birth and the unfolding of his story show (see Mt 3:17; 4:1–11; 11:27; 14:33; 16:16; 27:54). Back in the land of Israel, he must be taken to Nazareth in Galilee because of the danger to his life in Judea, where Herod's son Archelaus is now ruling (Mt 2:22–23). The sufferings of Jesus in the infancy narrative anticipate those of his passion, and if his life is spared in spite of the dangers, it is because his destiny is finally to give it on the cross as "a ransom for many" (Mt 20:28). Thus the word of the angel will be fulfilled, "…he will save his people from their sins" (Mt 1:21; cf. Mt 26:28).

In Mt 4:12 Matthew begins his account of the ministry of Jesus, introducing it by the preparatory preaching of John the Baptist (Mt 3:1–12), the baptism of Jesus that culminates in God's proclaiming him his "beloved Son" (Mt 3:13–17), and the temptation in which he proves his true sonship by his victory over the devil's attempt to deflect him from the way of obedience to the Father (Mt 4:1–11). The central message of Jesus' preaching is the coming of the kingdom of heaven and the need for repentance, a complete change of heart and conduct, on the part of those who are to receive this great gift of God (Mt 4:17). Galilee is the setting for most of his ministry; he leaves there for Judea only in Mt 19:1, and his ministry in Jerusalem, the goal of his journey, is limited to a few days (Mt 21:1–25:46).

In this extensive material there are five great discourses of Jesus, each concluding with the formula "When Jesus finished these words" or one closely similar (Mt 7:28; 11:1; 13:53; 19:1; 26:1). These are an important structure of the gospel. In every case the discourse is preceded by a narrative section, each narrative and discourse together constituting a "book" of the gospel. The discourses are, respectively, the "Sermon on the Mount" (Mt 5:3–7:27), the missionary discourse (Mt 10:5–42), the parable discourse (Mt 13:3–52), the "church order" discourse (Mt 18:3–35), and the eschatological discourse (Mt 24:4–25:46). In large measure the material of these discourses came to Matthew from his tradition, but his work in modifying and adding to what he had received is abundantly evident. No other evangelist gives the teaching of Jesus with such elegance and order as he.

In the "Sermon on the Mount" the theme of righteousness is prominent, and even at this early stage of the ministry the note of opposition is struck between Jesus and the Pharisees, who are designated as "the hypocrites" (Mt 6:2, 5, 16). The righteousness of his disciples must surpass that of the scribes and Pharisees; otherwise, in spite of their alleged following of Jesus, they will not enter into the kingdom of heaven (Mt 5:20). Righteousness means doing the will of the heavenly Father (Mt 7:21), and his will is proclaimed in a manner that is startling to all who have identified it with the law of Moses. The antitheses of the Sermon (Mt 5:21–48) both accept (Mt 5:21–30, 43–48) and reject (Mt 5:31–42) elements of that law, and in the former case the understanding of the law's demands is deepened and extended. The antitheses are the best commentary on the meaning of Jesus' claim that he has come not to abolish but to fulfill the law (Mt 5:17). What is meant by fulfillment of the law is not the demand to keep it exactly as it stood before the coming of Jesus, but rather his bringing the law to be a lasting expression of the will of God, and in that fulfillment there is much that will pass away. Should this appear contradictory to his saying that "until heaven and earth pass away" not even the smallest part of the law will pass (Mt 5:18), that time of fulfillment is not the dissolution of the universe but the coming of the new age, which will occur with Jesus' death and resurrection. While righteousness in the new age will continue to mean conduct that is in accordance with the law, it will be conduct in accordance with the law as expounded and interpreted by Jesus (cf. Mt 28:20, "…all that I have commanded you").

Though Jesus speaks harshly about the Pharisees in the Sermon, his judgment is not solely a condemnation of them. The Pharisees are portrayed as a negative example for his disciples, and his condemnation of those who claim to belong to him while disobeying his word is no less severe (Mt 7:21–23, 26–27).

In Mt 4:23 a summary statement of Jesus' activity speaks not only of his teaching and proclaiming the gospel but of his "curing every disease and illness among the people"; this is repeated almost verbatim in Mt 9:35. The narrative section that follows the Sermon on the Mount (Mt 8:1–9:38) is composed principally of accounts of those merciful deeds of Jesus, but it is far from being simply a collection of stories about miraculous cures. The nature of the community that Jesus will establish is shown; it will always be under the protection of him whose power can deal with all dangers (Mt 8:23–27), but it is only for those who are prepared to follow him at whatever cost (Mt 8:16–22), not only believing Israelites but Gentiles who have come to faith in him (Mt 8:10–12). The disciples begin to have some insight, however imperfect, into the mystery of Jesus' person. They wonder about him whom "the winds and the sea obey" (Mt 8:27), and they witness his bold declaration of the forgiveness of the paralytic's sins (Mt 9:2). That episode of the narrative moves on two levels. When the crowd sees the cure that testifies to the authority of Jesus, the Son of Man, to forgive sins (Mt 9:6), they glorify God "who had given such authority to human beings" (Mt 9:8). The forgiveness of sins is now not the prerogative of Jesus alone but of "human beings," that is, of the disciples who constitute the community of Jesus, the church. The ecclesial character of this narrative section could hardly be more plainly indicated.

The end of the section prepares for the discourse on the church's mission (Mt 10:5–42). Jesus is moved to pity at the sight of the crowds who are like sheep without a shepherd (Mt 9:36), and he sends out the twelve disciples to make the proclamation with which his own ministry began, "The kingdom of heaven is at hand" (Mt 10:7; cf. Mt 4:17), and to drive out demons and cure the sick as he has done (Mt 10:1). Their mission is limited to Israel (Mt 10:5–6) as Jesus' own was (Mt 15:24), yet in Mt 15:16 that perspective broadens and the discourse begins to speak of the mission that the disciples will have after the resurrection and of the severe persecution that will attend it (Mt 10:18). Again, the discourse moves on two levels: that of the time of Jesus and that of the time of the church.

The narrative section of the third book (Mt 11:2–12:50) deals with the growing opposition to Jesus. Hostility toward him has already been manifested (Mt 8:10; 9:3, 10–13, 34), but here it becomes more intense. The rejection of Jesus comes, as before, from Pharisees, who take "counsel against him to put him to death" (Mt 12:14) and repeat their earlier accusation that he drives out demons because he is in league with demonic power (Mt 12:22–24). But they are not alone in their rejection. Jesus complains of the lack of faith of "this generation" of Israelites (Mt 11:16–19) and reproaches the towns "where most of his mighty deeds had been done" for not heeding his call to repentance (Mt 11:20–24). This dark picture is relieved by Jesus' praise of the Father who has enabled "the childlike" to accept him (Mt 11:25–27), but on the whole the story is one of opposition to his word and blindness to the meaning of his deeds. The whole section ends with his declaring that not even the most intimate blood relationship with him counts for anything; his only true relatives are those who do the will of his heavenly Father (Mt 12:48–50).

The narrative of rejection leads up to the parable discourse (Mt 13:3–52). The reason given for Jesus' speaking to the crowds in parables is that they have hardened themselves against his clear teaching, unlike the disciples to whom knowledge of "the mysteries of the kingdom has been granted" (Mt 13:10–16). In Mt 13:36 he dismisses the crowds and continues the discourse to his disciples alone, who claim, at the end, to have understood all that he has said (Mt 13:51). But, lest the impression be given that the church of Jesus is made up only of true disciples, the explanation of the parable of the weeds among the wheat (Mt 13:37–43), as well as the parable of the net thrown into the sea "which collects fish of every kind" (Mt 13:47–49), shows that it is composed of both the righteous and the wicked, and that separation between the two will be made only at the time of the final judgment.

In the narrative that constitutes the first part of the fourth book of the gospel (Mt 13:54–17:27), Jesus is shown preparing for the establishment of his church with its teaching authority that will supplant the blind guidance of the Pharisees (Mt 15:13–14), whose teaching, curiously said to be that of the Sadducees also, is repudiated by Jesus as the norm for his disciples (Mt 16:6, 11–12). The church of Jesus will be built on Peter (Mt 16:18), who will be given authority to bind and loose on earth, an authority whose exercise will be confirmed in heaven (Mt 16:19). The metaphor of binding and loosing has a variety of meanings, among them that of giving authoritative teaching. This promise is made to Peter directly after he has confessed Jesus to be the Messiah, the Son of the living God (Mt 16:16), a confession that he has made as the result of revelation given to him by the heavenly Father (Mt 16:17); Matthew's ecclesiology is based on his high christology.

Directly after that confession Jesus begins to instruct his disciples about how he must go the way of suffering and death (Mt 16:21). Peter, who has been praised for his confession, protests against this and receives from Jesus the sharpest of rebukes for attempting to deflect Jesus from his God-appointed destiny. The future rock upon whom the church will be built is still a man of "little faith" (see Mt 14:31). Both he and the other disciples must know not only that Jesus will have to suffer and die but that they too will have to follow him on the way of the cross if they are truly to be his disciples (Mt 16:24–25).

The discourse following this narrative (Mt 18:1–35) is often called the "church order" discourse, although that title is perhaps misleading since the emphasis is not on the structure of the church but on the care that the disciples must have for one another in respect to guarding each other's faith in Jesus (Mt 18:6–7), to seeking out those who have wandered from the fold (Mt 18:10–14), and to repeated forgiving of their fellow disciples who have offended them (Mt 18:21–35). But there is also the obligation to correct the sinful fellow Christian and, should one refuse to be corrected, separation from the community is demanded (Mt 18:15–18).

The narrative of the fifth book (Mt 19:1–23:39) begins with the departure of Jesus and his disciples from Galilee for Jerusalem. In the course of their journey Jesus for the third time predicts the passion that awaits him at Jerusalem and also his resurrection (Mt 20:17–19). At his entrance into the city he is hailed as the Son of David by the crowds accompanying him (Mt 21:9). He cleanses the temple (Mt 21:12–17), and in the few days of his Jerusalem ministry he engages in a series of controversies with the Jewish religious leaders (Mt 21:23–27; 22:15–22, 23–33, 34–40, 41–46), meanwhile speaking parables against them (Mt 21:28–32, 33–46), against all those Israelites who have rejected God's invitation to the messianic banquet (Mt 22:1–10), and against all, Jew and Gentile, who have accepted but have shown themselves unworthy of it (Mt 22:11–14). Once again, the perspective of the evangelist includes not only the time of Jesus' ministry but that of the preaching of the gospel after his resurrection. The narrative culminates in Jesus' denunciation of the scribes and Pharisees, reflecting not only his own opposition to them but that of Matthew's church (Mt 23:1–36), and in Jesus' lament over Jerusalem (Mt 23:37–39).

In the discourse of the fifth book (Mt 24:1–25:46), the last of the great structural discourses of the gospel, Jesus predicts the destruction of the temple and his own final coming. The time of the latter is unknown (Mt 24:36, 44), and the disciples are exhorted in various parables to live in readiness for it, a readiness that entails faithful attention to the duties of the interim period (Mt 24:45–25:30). The coming of Jesus will bring with it the great judgment by which the everlasting destiny of all will be determined (Mt 25:31–46).

The story of Jesus' passion and resurrection (Mt 26:1–28:20), the climax of the gospel, throws light on all that has preceded. In Matthew "righteousness" means both the faithful response to the will of God demanded of all to whom that will is announced and also the saving activity of God for his people (see Mt 3:15; 5:6; 6:33). The passion supremely exemplifies both meanings of that central Matthean word. In Jesus' absolute faithfulness to the Father's will that he drink the cup of suffering (Mt 26:39), the incomparable model for Christian obedience is given; in his death "for the forgiveness of sins" (Mt 26:28), the saving power of God is manifested as never before. Matthew's portrayal of Jesus in his passion combines both the majestic serenity of the obedient Son who goes his destined way in fulfillment of the scriptures (Mt 26:52–54), confident of his ultimate vindication by God, and the depths of fear and abandonment that he feels in face of death (Mt 26:38–39; 27:46). These two aspects are expressed by an Old Testament theme that occurs often in the narrative, i.e., the portrait of the suffering Righteous One who complains to God in his misery, but is certain of eventual deliverance from his terrible ordeal.

The passion-resurrection of God's Son means nothing less than the turn of the ages, a new stage of history, the coming of the Son of Man in his kingdom (Mt 28:18; cf. Mt 16:28). That is the sense of the apocalyptic signs that accompany Jesus' death (Mt 27:51–53) and resurrection (Mt 28:2). Although the old age continues, as it will until the manifestation of Jesus' triumph at his parousia, the final age has now begun. This is known only to those who have seen the Risen One and to those, both Jews and Gentiles, who have believed in their announcement of Jesus' triumph and have themselves become his disciples (cf. Mt 28:19). To them he is constantly, though invisibly, present (Mt 28:20), verifying the name Emmanuel, "God is with us" (cf. Mt 1:23).

The questions of authorship, sources, and the time of composition of this gospel have received many answers, none of which can claim more than a greater or lesser degree of probability. The one now favored by the majority of scholars is the following.

The ancient tradition that the author was the disciple and apostle of Jesus named Matthew (see Mt 10:3) is untenable because the gospel is based, in large part, on the Gospel according to Mark (almost all the verses of that gospel have been utilized in this), and it is hardly likely that a companion of Jesus would have followed so extensively an account that came from one who admittedly never had such an association rather than rely on his own memories. The attribution of the gospel to the disciple Matthew may have been due to his having been responsible for some of the traditions found in it, but that is far from certain.

The unknown author, whom we shall continue to call Matthew for the sake of convenience, drew not only upon the Gospel according to Mark but upon a large body of material (principally, sayings of Jesus) not found in Mark that corresponds, sometimes exactly, to material found also in the Gospel according to Luke. This material, called "Q" (probably from the first letter of the German word Quelle, meaning "source"), represents traditions, written and oral, used by both Matthew and Luke. Mark and Q are sources common to the two other synoptic gospels; hence the name the "Two-Source Theory" given to this explanation of the relation among the synoptics.

In addition to what Matthew drew from Mark and Q, his gospel contains material that is found only there. This is often designated "M," written or oral tradition that was available to the author. Since Mark was written shortly before or shortly after A.D. 70 (see Introduction to Mark), Matthew was composed certainly after that date, which marks the fall of Jerusalem to the Romans at the time of the First Jewish Revolt (A.D. 66–70), and probably at least a decade later since Matthew's use of Mark presupposes a wide diffusion of that gospel. The post-A.D. 70 date is confirmed within the text by Mt 22:7, which refers to the destruction of Jerusalem.

As for the place where the gospel was composed, a plausible suggestion is that it was Antioch, the capital of the Roman province of Syria. That large and important city had a mixed population of Greek-speaking Gentiles and Jews. The tensions between Jewish and Gentile Christians there in the time of Paul (see Gal 2:1–14) in respect to Christian obligation to observe Mosaic law are partially similar to tensions that can be seen between the two groups in Matthew's gospel. The church of Matthew, originally strongly Jewish Christian, had become one in which Gentile Christians were predominant. His gospel answers the question how obedience to the will of God is to be expressed by those who live after the "turn of the ages," the death and resurrection of Jesus.

THE
PRINCIPAL
DIVISIONS
OF THE
GOSPEL
ACCORDING
TO MATTHEW
ARE THE
FOLLOWING:

I. The Infancy Narrative (1:1–2:23)

II. The Proclamation of the Kingdom (3:1–7:29)

III. Ministry and Mission in Galilee (8:1–11:1)

IV. Opposition from Israel (11:2–13:53)

V. Jesus, the Kingdom, and the Church (13:54–18:35)

VI. Ministry in Judea and Jerusalem (19:1–25:46)

VII. The Passion and Resurrection (26:1–28:20)

MATTHEW CHAPTER 1

I. THE INFANCY NARRATIVE

THE GENEALOGY OF JESUS.[*]

1[a] The book of the genealogy of Jesus Christ, the son of David, the son of Abraham.[*]

2[b] Abraham became the father of Isaac, Isaac the father of Jacob, Jacob the father of Judah and his brothers.[c] **3** Judah became the father of Perez and Zerah, whose mother was Tamar.[d] Perez became the father of Hezron, Hezron the father of Ram, **4**[e] Ram the father of Amminadab. Amminadab became the father of Nahshon, Nahshon the father of Salmon, **5**[f] Salmon the father of Boaz, whose mother was Rahab. Boaz became the father of Obed, whose mother was Ruth. Obed became the father of Jesse, **6**[g] Jesse the father of David the king. David became the father of Solomon, whose mother had been the wife of Uriah. **7**[*][h] Solomon became the father of Rehoboam, Rehoboam the father of Abijah, Abijah the father of Asaph. **8** Asaph became the father of Jehoshaphat, Jehoshaphat the father of Joram, Joram the father of Uzziah. **9** Uzziah became the father of Jotham, Jotham the father of Ahaz, Ahaz the father of Hezekiah. **10** Hezekiah became the father of Manasseh, Manasseh the father of Amos,[*] Amos the father of Josiah. **11** Josiah became the father of Jechoniah and his brothers at the time of the Babylonian exile.

12[i] After the Babylonian exile, Jechoniah became the father of Shealtiel, Shealtiel the father of Zerubbabel, **13** Zerubbabel the father of Abiud. Abiud became the father of Eliakim, Eliakim the father of Azor, **14** Azor the father of Zadok. Zadok became the father of Achim, Achim the father of Eliud, **15** Eliud the father of Eleazar. Eleazar became the father of Matthan, Matthan the father of Jacob, **16** Jacob the father of Joseph, the husband of Mary. Of her was born Jesus who is called the Messiah. **17** Thus the total number of generations from Abraham to David is fourteen generations; from David to the Babylonian exile, fourteen generations; from the Babylonian exile to the Messiah, fourteen generations.[*]

* [1:1–2:23] The infancy narrative forms the prologue of the gospel. Consisting of a genealogy and five stories, it presents the coming of Jesus as the climax of Israel's history, and the events of his conception, birth, and early childhood as the fulfillment of Old Testament prophecy. The genealogy is probably traditional material that Matthew edited. In its first two sections (Mt 1:2–11) it was drawn from Ru 4:18–22; 1 Chr 1–3. Except for Jechoniah, Shealtiel, and Zerubbabel, none of the names in the third section (Mt 1:12–16) is found in any Old Testament genealogy. While the genealogy shows the continuity of God's providential plan from Abraham on, discontinuity is also present. The women Tamar (Mt 1:3), Rahab and Ruth (Mt 1:5), and the wife of Uriah, Bathsheba (Mt 1:6), bore their sons through unions that were in varying degrees strange and unexpected. These "irregularities" culminate in the supreme "irregularity" of the Messiah's birth of a virgin mother; the age of fulfillment is inaugurated by a creative act of God.

Drawing upon both biblical tradition and Jewish stories, Matthew portrays Jesus as reliving the Exodus experience of Israel and the persecutions of Moses. His rejection by his own people and his passion are foreshadowed by the troubled reaction of "all Jerusalem" to the question of the magi who are seeking the "newborn king of the Jews" (Mt 2:2–3), and by Herod's attempt to have him killed. The magi who do him homage prefigure the Gentiles who will accept the preaching of the gospel. The infancy narrative proclaims who Jesus is, the savior of his people from their sins (Mt 1:21), Emmanuel in whom "God is with us" (Mt 1:23), and the Son of God (Mt 2:15).

a. [1:1] Gn 5:1 / 1 Chr 17:11 / Gn 22:18.

* [1:1] The Son of David, the son of Abraham: two links of the genealogical chain are singled out. Although the later, David is placed first in order to emphasize that Jesus is the royal Messiah. The mention of Abraham may be due not only to his being the father of the nation Israel but to Matthew's interest in the universal scope of Jesus' mission; cf. Gn 22:18 ".... in your descendants all the nations of the earth shall find blessing."

b. [1:2–17] Lk 3:23–38.

c. [1:2] Gn 21:3; 25:26; 29:35; 1 Chr 2:1.

d. [1:3] Gn 38:29–30; Ru 4:18; 1 Chr 2:4–9.

e. [1:4] Ru 4:19–20; 1 Chr 2:10–11.

f. [1:5] Ru 4:21–22; 1 Chr 2:11–12.

g. [1:6] 2 Sm 12:24; 1 Chr 2:15; 3:5.

* [1:7] The successor of Abijah was not Asaph but Asa (see 1 Chr 3:10). Some textual witnesses read the latter name; however, Asaph is better attested. Matthew may have deliberately introduced the psalmist Asaph into the genealogy (and in Mt 1:10 the prophet Amos) in order to show that Jesus is the fulfillment not only of the promises made to David (see 2 Sm 7) but of all the Old Testament.

h. [1:7–11] 2 Kgs 25:1–21; 1 Chr 3:10–15.

* [1:10] Amos: some textual witnesses read Amon, who was the actual successor of Manasseh (see 1 Chr 3:14).

i. [1:12–16] 1 Chr 3:16–19.

* [1:17] Matthew is concerned with fourteen generations, probably because fourteen is the numerical value of the Hebrew letters forming the name of David. In the second section of the genealogy (Mt 1:6b–11), three kings of Judah, Ahaziah, Joash, and Amaziah, have been omitted (see 1 Chr 3:11–12), so that there are fourteen generations in that section. Yet the third (Mt 1:12–16) apparently has only thirteen. Since Matthew here emphasizes that each section has fourteen, it is unlikely that the thirteen of the last was due to his oversight. Some scholars suggest that Jesus who is called the Messiah (Mt 1:16b) doubles the final member of the chain: Jesus, born within the family of David, opens up the new age as Messiah, so that in fact there are fourteen generations in the third section. This is perhaps too subtle, and the hypothesis of a slip not on the part of Matthew but of a later scribe seems likely. On Messiah, see note on Lk 2:11.

THE BIRTH OF JESUS.*

18 Now this is how the birth of Jesus Christ came about. When his mother Mary was betrothed to Joseph,* but before they lived together, she was found with child through the holy Spirit. **19** Joseph her husband, since he was a righteous man,* yet unwilling to expose her to shame, decided to divorce her quietly. **20**[j] Such was his intention when, behold, the angel of the Lord* appeared to him in a dream and said, "Joseph, son of David, do not be afraid to take Mary your wife into your home. For it is through the holy Spirit that this child has been conceived in her. **21** She will bear a son and you are to name him Jesus,* because he will save his people from their sins." **22** All this took place to fulfill what the Lord had said through the prophet:

23[*k] "Behold, the virgin shall be with child and bear a son,

and they shall name him Emmanuel,"

which means "God is with us." **24** When Joseph awoke, he did as the angel of the Lord had commanded him and took his wife into his home. **25** He had no relations with her until she bore a son,* and he named him Jesus.[1]

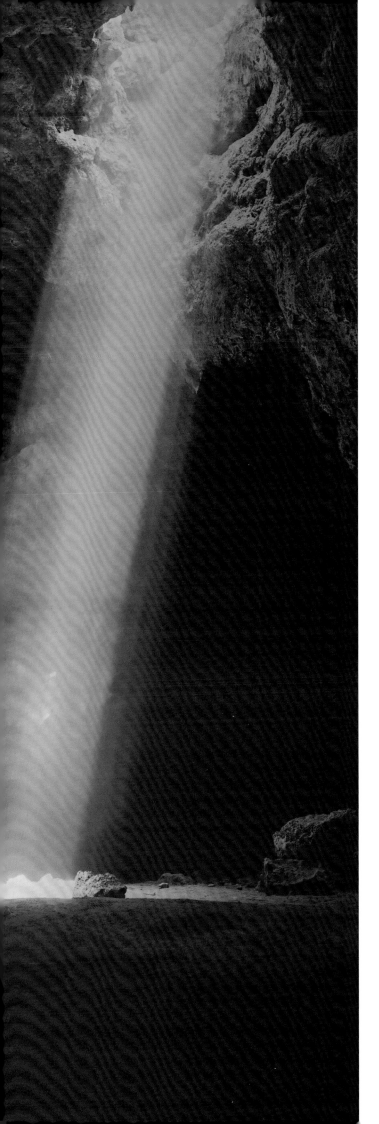

* [1:18–25] This first story of the infancy narrative spells out what is summarily indicated in Mt 1:16. The virginal conception of Jesus is the work of the Spirit of God. Joseph's decision to divorce Mary is overcome by the heavenly command that he take her into his home and accept the child as his own. The natural genealogical line is broken but the promises to David are fulfilled; through Joseph's adoption the child belongs to the family of David. Matthew sees the virginal conception as the fulfillment of Is 7:14.

* [1:18] Betrothed to Joseph: betrothal was the first part of the marriage, constituting a man and woman as husband and wife. Subsequent infidelity was considered adultery. The betrothal was followed some months later by the husband's taking his wife into his home, at which time normal married life began.

* [1:19] A righteous man: as a devout observer of the Mosaic law, Joseph wished to break his union with someone whom he suspected of gross violation of the law. It is commonly said that the law required him to do so, but the texts usually given in support of that view, e.g., Dt 22:20–21 do not clearly pertain to Joseph's situation. Unwilling to expose her to shame: the penalty for proved adultery was death by stoning; cf. Dt 22:21–23.

j. [1:20] 2:13, 19; Lk 1:35.

* [1:20] The angel of the Lord: in the Old Testament a common designation of God in communication with a human being. In a dream: see Mt 2:13, 19, 22. These dreams may be meant to recall the dreams of Joseph, son of Jacob the patriarch (Gn 37:5–11, 19). A closer parallel is the dream of Amram, father of Moses, related by Josephus (Antiquities 2, 9, 3; (par.) 212, 215–16).

* [1:21] Jesus: in first-century Judaism the Hebrew name Joshua (Greek Iēsous) meaning "Yahweh helps" was interpreted as "Yahweh saves."

* [1:23] God is with us: God's promise of deliverance to Judah in Isaiah's time is seen by Matthew as fulfilled in the birth of Jesus, in whom God is with his people. The name Emmanuel is alluded to at the end of the gospel where the risen Jesus assures his disciples of his continued presence, "…I am with you always, until the end of the age" (Mt 28:20).

k. [1:23] Is 7:14 LXX.

* [1:25] Until she bore a son: the evangelist is concerned to emphasize that Joseph was not responsible for the conception of Jesus. The Greek word translated "until" does not imply normal marital conduct after Jesus' birth, nor does it exclude it.

l. [1:25] Lk 2:7.

MATTHEW CHAPTER 2

THE VISIT
OF THE MAGI.*

1 When Jesus was born in Bethlehem of Judea, in the days of King Herod,[*] behold, magi from the east arrived in Jerusalem, **2** saying, "Where is the newborn king of the Jews? We saw his star[*] at its rising and have come to do him homage."^a **3** When King Herod heard this, he was greatly troubled, and all Jerusalem with him. **4** Assembling all the chief priests and the scribes of the people, he inquired of them where the Messiah was to be born.[*]

5^b They said to him, "In Bethlehem of Judea, for thus it has been written through the prophet:

6 'And you, Bethlehem, land of Judah,

are by no means least among the rulers of Judah;

since from you shall come a ruler,

who is to shepherd my people Israel.'"

7 Then Herod called the magi secretly and ascertained from them the time of the star's appearance. **8** He sent them to Bethlehem and said, "Go and search diligently for the child. When you have found him, bring me word, that I too may go and do him homage." **9** After their audience with the king they set out. And behold, the star that they had seen at its rising preceded them, until it came and stopped over the place where the child was. **10** They were overjoyed at seeing the star, **11**^{*c} and on entering the house they saw the child with Mary his mother. They prostrated themselves and did him homage. Then they opened their treasures and offered him gifts of gold, frankincense, and myrrh. **12** And having been warned in a dream not to return to Herod, they departed for their country by another way.

* [2:1–12] The future rejection of Jesus by Israel and his acceptance by the Gentiles are retrojected into this scene of the narrative.

* [2:1] In the days of King Herod: Herod reigned from 37 to 4 B.C. Magi: originally a designation of the Persian priestly caste, the word became used of those who were regarded as having more than human knowledge. Matthew's magi are astrologers.

* [2:2] We saw his star: it was a common ancient belief that a new star appeared at the time of a ruler's birth. Matthew also draws upon the Old Testament story of Balaam, who had prophesied that "A star shall advance from Jacob" (Nm 24:17), though there the star means not an astral phenomenon but the king himself.

a. [2:2] Nm 24:17.

* [2:4] Herod's consultation with the chief priests and scribes has some similarity to a Jewish legend about the child Moses in which the "sacred scribes" warn Pharaoh about the imminent birth of one who will deliver Israel from Egypt and the king makes plans to destroy him.

b. [2:5–6] Mi 5:1; 2 Sm 5:2.

* [2:11] Cf. Ps 72:10, 15; Is 60:6. These Old Testament texts led to the interpretation of the magi as kings.

c. [2:11] Ps 72:10–11, 15; Is 60:6.

THE FLIGHT TO EGYPT.

13 [*] When they had departed, behold, the angel of the Lord appeared to Joseph in a dream and said, "Rise, take the child and his mother, flee to Egypt, [*] and stay there until I tell you. Herod is going to search for the child to destroy him." **14** Joseph rose and took the child and his mother by night and departed for Egypt. **15** [*] He stayed there until the death of Herod, that what the Lord had said through the prophet[d] might be fulfilled, "Out of Egypt I called my son."

[*] [2:13–23] Biblical and nonbiblical traditions about Moses are here applied to the child Jesus, though the dominant Old Testament type is not Moses but Israel (Mt 2:15).

[*] [2:13] Flee to Egypt: Egypt was a traditional place of refuge for those fleeing from danger in Palestine (see 1 Kgs 11:40; Jer 26:21), but the main reason why the child is to be taken to Egypt is that he may relive the Exodus experience of Israel.

[*] [2:15] The fulfillment citation is taken from Hos 11:1. Israel, God's son, was called out of Egypt at the time of the Exodus; Jesus, the Son of God, will similarly be called out of that land in a new exodus. The father-son relationship between God and the nation is set in a higher key. Here the son is not a group adopted as "son of God," but the child who, as conceived by the holy Spirit, stands in unique relation to God. He is son of David and of Abraham, of Mary and of Joseph, but, above all, of God.

d. [2:15] Hos 11:1.

THE MASSACRE OF THE INFANTS.

16 When Herod realized that he had been deceived by the magi, he became furious. He ordered the massacre of all the boys in Bethlehem and its vicinity two years old and under, in accordance with the time he had ascertained from the magi. **17** Then was fulfilled what had been said through Jeremiah the prophet: **18**[*][e] "A voice was heard in Ramah, sobbing and loud lamentation; Rachel weeping for her children, and she would not be consoled, since they were no more."

[*] [2:18] Jer 31:15 portrays Rachel, wife of the patriarch Jacob, weeping for her children taken into exile at the time of the Assyrian invasion of the northern kingdom (722–21 B.C.). Bethlehem was traditionally identified with Ephrath, the place near which Rachel was buried (see Gn 35:19; 48:7), and the mourning of Rachel is here applied to her lost children of a later age. Ramah: about six miles north of Jerusalem. The lamentation of Rachel is so great as to be heard at a far distance.

e. [2:18] Jer 31:15.

THE RETURN FROM EGYPT.

19 When Herod had died, behold, the angel of the Lord appeared in a dream to Joseph in Egypt **20** and said,^f "Rise, take the child and his mother and go to the land of Israel, for those who sought the child's life are dead."* **21** He rose, took the child and his mother, and went to the land of Israel. **22** But when he heard that Archelaus was ruling over Judea in place of his father Herod,* he was afraid to go back there. And because he had been warned in a dream, he departed for the region of Galilee. **23***g He went and dwelt in a town called Nazareth, so that what had been spoken through the prophets might be fulfilled, "He shall be called a Nazorean."

---

f. [2:20] Ex 4:19.

* [2:20] For those who sought the child's life are dead: Moses, who had fled from Egypt because the Pharaoh sought to kill him (see Ex 2:15), was told to return there, "for all the men who sought your life are dead" (Ex 4:19).

* [2:22] With the agreement of the emperor Augustus, Archelaus received half of his father's kingdom, including Judea, after Herod's death. He had the title "ethnarch" (i.e., "ruler of a nation") and reigned from 4 B.C. to A.D. 6.

* [2:23] Nazareth…he shall be called a Nazorean: the tradition of Jesus' residence in Nazareth was firmly established, and Matthew sees it as being in accordance with the foreannounced plan of God. The town of Nazareth is not mentioned in the Old Testament, and no such prophecy can be found there. The vague expression "through the prophets" may be due to Matthew's seeing a connection between Nazareth and certain texts in which there are words with a remote similarity to the name of that town. Some such Old Testament texts are Is 11:1 where the Davidic king of the future is called "a bud" (nēser) that shall blossom from the roots of Jesse, and Jgs 13:5, 7 where Samson, the future deliverer of Israel from the Philistines, is called one who shall be consecrated (a nāzîr) to God.

g. [2:23] 13:54; Mk 1:9; Lk 2:39; 4:34; Jn 19:19.

MATTHEW CHAPTER 3

II. THE PROCLAMATION OF THE KINGDOM

THE PREACHING OF JOHN THE BAPTIST.*

[a]**1** In those days John the Baptist appeared, preaching in the desert of Judea* **2** [and] saying, "Repent,* for the kingdom of heaven is at hand!"[b] **3*** It was of him that the prophet Isaiah[c] had spoken when he said:

"A voice of one crying out in the desert,

'Prepare the way of the Lord,

make straight his paths.'"

4*[d] John wore clothing made of camel's hair and had a leather belt around his waist. His food was locusts and wild honey. **5** At that time Jerusalem, all Judea, and the whole region around the Jordan were going out to him **6** and were being baptized by him in the Jordan River as they acknowledged their sins.* **7** When he saw many of the Pharisees and Sadducees* coming to his baptism, he said to them, "You brood of vipers! Who warned you to flee from the coming wrath?[e] **8** Produce good fruit as evidence of your repentance. **9** And do not presume to say to yourselves, 'We have Abraham as our father.' For I tell you, God can raise up children to Abraham from these stones.[f] **10** Even now the ax lies at the root of the trees. Therefore every tree that does not bear good fruit will be cut down and thrown into the fire. **11**[g] I am baptizing you with water, for repentance, but the one who is coming after me is mightier than I. I am not worthy to carry his sandals. He will baptize you with the holy Spirit and fire.* **12***[h] His winnowing fan is in his hand. He will clear his threshing floor and gather his wheat into his barn, but the chaff he will burn with unquenchable fire."

* [3:1–12] Here Matthew takes up the order of Jesus' ministry found in the gospel of Mark, beginning with the preparatory preaching of John the Baptist.

a. [3:1–12] Mk 1:2–8; Lk 3:2–17.

* [3:1] Unlike Luke, Matthew says nothing of the Baptist's origins and does not make him a relative of Jesus. The desert of Judea: the barren region west of the Dead Sea extending up the Jordan valley.

* [3:2] Repent: the Baptist calls for a change of heart and conduct, a turning of one's life from rebellion to obedience towards God. The kingdom of heaven is at hand: "heaven" (lit., "the heavens") is a substitute for the name "God" that was avoided by devout Jews of the time out of reverence. The expression "the kingdom of heaven" occurs only in the gospel of Matthew. It means the effective rule of God over his people. In its fullness it includes not only human obedience to God's word, but the triumph of God over physical evils, supremely over death. In the expectation found in Jewish apocalyptic, the kingdom was to be ushered in by a judgment in which sinners would be condemned and perish, an expectation shared by the Baptist. This was modified in Christian understanding where the kingdom was seen as being established in stages, culminating with the parousia of Jesus.

b. [3:2] 4:17; 10:7.

* [3:3] See note on Jn 1:23.

c. [3:3] Is 40:3.

* [3:4] The clothing of John recalls the austere dress of the prophet Elijah (2 Kgs 1:8). The expectation of the return of Elijah from heaven to prepare Israel for the final manifestation of God's kingdom was widespread, and according to Matthew this expectation was fulfilled in the Baptist's ministry (Mt 11:14; 17:11–13).

d. [3:4] 11:7–8; 2 Kgs 1:8; Zec 13:4.

* [3:6] Ritual washing was practiced by various groups in Palestine between 150 B.C. and A.D. 250. John's baptism may have been related to the purificatory washings of the Essenes at Qumran.

* [3:7] Pharisees and Sadducees: the former were marked by devotion to the law, written and oral, and the scribes, experts in the law, belonged predominantly to this group. The Sadducees were the priestly aristocratic party, centered in Jerusalem. They accepted as scripture only the first five books of the Old Testament, followed only the letter of the law, rejected the oral legal traditions, and were opposed to teachings not found in the Pentateuch, such as the resurrection of the dead. Matthew links both of these groups together as enemies of Jesus (Mt 16:1, 6, 11, 12; cf. Mk 8:11–13, 15). The threatening words that follow are addressed to them rather than to "the crowds" as in Lk 3:7. The coming wrath: the judgment that will bring about the destruction of unrepentant sinners.

e. [3:7] 12:34; 23:33; Is 59:5.

f. [3:9] Jn 8:33, 39; Rom 9:7–8; Gal 4:21–31.

g. [3:11] Jn 1:26–27, 33; Acts 1:5.

* [3:11] Baptize you with the holy Spirit and fire: the water baptism of John will be followed by an "immersion" of the repentant in the cleansing power of the Spirit of God, and of the unrepentant in the destroying power of God's judgment. However, some see the holy Spirit and fire as synonymous, and the effect of this "baptism" as either purification or destruction. See note on Lk 3:16.

* [3:12] The discrimination between the good and the bad is compared to the procedure by which a farmer separates wheat and chaff. The winnowing fan was a forklike shovel with which the threshed wheat was thrown into the air. The kernels fell to the ground; the light chaff, blown off by the wind, was gathered and burned up.

h. [3:12] 13:30; Is 41:16; Jer 15:7.

THE BAPTISM OF JESUS.*

13[i] Then Jesus came from Galilee to John at the Jordan to be baptized by him. **14**[*] John tried to prevent him, saying, "I need to be baptized by you, and yet you are coming to me?" **15** Jesus said to him in reply, "Allow it now, for thus it is fitting for us to fulfill all righteousness." Then he allowed him. **16**[*j] After Jesus was baptized, he came up from the water and behold, the heavens were opened [for him], and he saw the Spirit of God descending like a dove [and] coming upon him. **17** And a voice came from the heavens, saying, "This is my beloved Son,* with whom I am well pleased."[k]

* [3:13–17] The baptism of Jesus is the occasion on which he is equipped for his ministry by the holy Spirit and proclaimed to be the Son of God.

i. [3:13–17] Mk 1:9–11; Lk 3:21–22; Jn 1:31–34.

* [3:14–15] This dialogue, peculiar to Matthew, reveals John's awareness of Jesus' superiority to him as the mightier one who is coming and who will baptize with the holy Spirit (Mt 3:11). His reluctance to admit Jesus among the sinners whom he is baptizing with water is overcome by Jesus' response. To fulfill all righteousness: in this gospel to fulfill usually refers to fulfillment of prophecy, and righteousness to moral conduct in conformity with God's will. Here, however, as in Mt 5:6; 6:33, righteousness seems to mean the saving activity of God. To fulfill all righteousness is to submit to the plan of God for the salvation of the human race. This involves Jesus' identification with sinners; hence the propriety of his accepting John's baptism.

* [3:16] The Spirit…coming upon him: cf. Is 42:1.

j. [3:16] Is 42:1.

* [3:17] This is my beloved Son: the Marcan address to Jesus (Mk 1:11) is changed into a proclamation. The Father's voice speaks in terms that reflect Is 42:1; Ps 2:7; Gn 22:2.

k. [3:17] 12:18; 17:5; Gn 22:2; Ps 2:7; Is 42:1.

MATTHEW CHAPTER 4

THE TEMPTATION OF JESUS.

1 *[a] Then Jesus was led by the Spirit into the desert to be tempted by the devil. **2**[b] He fasted for forty days and forty nights,* and afterwards he was hungry. **3** The tempter approached and said to him, "If you are the Son of God, command that these stones become loaves of bread." **4** * He said in reply, "It is written:[c]

'One does not live by bread alone,

but by every word that comes forth from the mouth of God.'"

5 * Then the devil took him to the holy city, and made him stand on the parapet of the temple, **6** and said to him, "If you are the Son of God, throw yourself down. For it is written:

'He will command his angels concerning you'

and 'with their hands they will support you,

lest you dash your foot against a stone.'"[d]

7 Jesus answered him, "Again it is written, 'You shall not put the Lord, your God, to the test.'"[e] **8** Then the devil took him up to a very high mountain, and showed him all the kingdoms of the world in their magnificence, **9** and he said to him, "All these I shall give to you, if you will prostrate yourself and worship me."* **10** At this, Jesus said to him, "Get away, Satan! It is written:

'The Lord, your God, shall you worship

and him alone shall you serve.'"[f]

11 Then the devil left him and, behold, angels came and ministered to him.

* [4:1–11] Jesus, proclaimed Son of God at his baptism, is subjected to a triple temptation. Obedience to the Father is a characteristic of true sonship, and Jesus is tempted by the devil to rebel against God, overtly in the third case, more subtly in the first two. Each refusal of Jesus is expressed in language taken from the Book of Deuteronomy (Dt 8:3; 6:13, 16). The testings of Jesus resemble those of Israel during the wandering in the desert and later in Canaan, and the victory of Jesus, the true Israel and the true Son, contrasts with the failure of the ancient and disobedient "son," the old Israel. In the temptation account Matthew is almost identical with Luke; both seem to have drawn upon the same source.

a. [4:1–11] Mk 1:12–13; Lk 4:1–13.

b. [4:2] Ex 24:18; Dt 8:2.

* [4:2] Forty days and forty nights: the same time as that during which Moses remained on Sinai (Ex 24:18). The time reference, however, seems primarily intended to recall the forty years during which Israel was tempted in the desert (Dt 8:2).

* [4:4] Cf. Dt 8:3. Jesus refuses to use his power for his own benefit and accepts whatever God wills.

c. [4:4] Dt 8:3.

* [4:5–7] The devil supports his proposal by an appeal to the scriptures, Ps 91:11a, 12. Unlike Israel (Dt 6:16), Jesus refuses to "test" God by demanding from him an extraordinary show of power.

d. [4:6] Ps 91:11–12.

e. [4:7] Dt 6:16.

* [4:9] The worship of Satan to which Jesus is tempted is probably intended to recall Israel's worship of false gods. His refusal is expressed in the words of Dt 6:13.

f. [4:10] 16:23; Dt 6:13.

THE BEGINNING OF THE GALILEAN MINISTRY.*

12[g] When he heard that John had been arrested, he withdrew to Galilee. **13** He left Nazareth and went to live in Capernaum by the sea, in the region of Zebulun and Naphtali,[h] **14** that what had been said through Isaiah the prophet might be fulfilled:

15 "Land of Zebulun and land of Naphtali,[i]

the way to the sea, beyond the Jordan,

Galilee of the Gentiles,

16 the people who sit in darkness

have seen a great light,

on those dwelling in a land overshadowed by death

light has arisen."[j]

17[*] From that time on, Jesus began to preach and say,[k] "Repent, for the kingdom of heaven is at hand."

---

* [4:12–17] Isaiah's prophecy of the light rising upon Zebulun and Naphtali (Is 8:22–9:1) is fulfilled in Jesus' residence at Capernaum. The territory of these two tribes was the first to be devastated (733–32 B.C.) at the time of the Assyrian invasion. In order to accommodate Jesus' move to Capernaum to the prophecy, Matthew speaks of that town as being "in the region of Zebulun and Naphtali" (Mt 4:13), whereas it was only in the territory of the latter, and he understands the sea of the prophecy, the Mediterranean, as the sea of Galilee.

g. [4:12–13] Mk 1:14–15; Lk 4:14, 31.

h. [4:13] Jn 2:12.

i. [4:15–16] Is 8:23 LXX; 9:1.

j. [4:16] Lk 1:79.

* [4:17] At the beginning of his preaching Jesus takes up the words of John the Baptist (Mt 3:2) although with a different meaning; in his ministry the kingdom of heaven has already begun to be present (Mt 12:28).

k. [4:17] 3:2.

THE CALL OF THE FIRST DISCIPLES.*

18 As he was walking by the Sea of Galilee, he saw two brothers, Simon who is called Peter, and his brother Andrew, casting a net into the sea; they were fishermen. **19** He said to them, "Come after me, and I will make you fishers of men." **20** At once they left their nets and followed him. **21** He walked along from there and saw two other brothers, James, the son of Zebedee, and his brother John. They were in a boat, with their father Zebedee, mending their nets. He called them, **22** and immediately they left their boat and their father and followed him.

*[4:18–22] The call of the first disciples promises them a share in Jesus' work and entails abandonment of family and former way of life. Three of the four, Simon, James, and John, are distinguished among the disciples by a closer relation with Jesus (Mt 17:1; 26:37).

l. [4:18–22] Mk 1:16–20; Lk 5:1–11.

* [4:20] Here and in Mt 4:22, as in Mark (Mk 1:16–20) and unlike the Lucan account (Lk 5:1–11), the disciples' response is motivated only by Jesus' invitation

MINISTERING TO A GREAT MULTITUDE.*

23 He went around all of Galilee, teaching in their synagogues,* proclaiming the gospel of the kingdom, and curing every disease and illness among the people.[m] **24**[*] His fame spread to all of Syria, and they brought to him all who were sick with various diseases and racked with pain, those who were possessed, lunatics, and paralytics, and he cured them. **25**[n] And great crowds from Galilee, the Decapolis,* Jerusalem, and Judea, and from beyond the Jordan followed him.

* [4:23–25] This summary of Jesus' ministry concludes the narrative part of the first book of Matthew's gospel (Mt 3–4). The activities of his ministry are teaching, proclaiming the gospel, and healing; cf. Mt 9:35.

*[4:23] Their synagogues: Matthew usually designates the Jewish synagogues as their synagogue(s) (Mt 9:35; 10:17; 12:9; 13:54) or, in address to Jews, your synagogues (Mt 23:34), an indication that he wrote after the break between church and synagogue.

m. [4:23] 9:35; Mk 1:39; Lk 4:15, 44.

* [4:24] Syria: the Roman province to which Palestine belonged.

n. [4:25] Mk 3:7–8; Lk 6:17–19.

* [4:25] The Decapolis: a federation of Greek cities in Palestine, originally ten in number, all but one east of the Jordan.

MATTHEW CHAPTER 5

THE SERMON ON THE MOUNT.

1* When he saw the crowds,* he went up the mountain, and after he had sat down, his disciples came to him. **2** He began to teach them, saying:

* [5:1–7:29] The first of the five discourses that are a central part of the structure of this gospel. It is the discourse section of the first book and contains sayings of Jesus derived from Q and from M. The Lucan parallel is in that gospel's "Sermon on the Plain" (Lk 6:20–49), although some of the sayings in Matthew's "Sermon on the Mount" have their parallels in other parts of Luke. The careful topical arrangement of the sermon is probably not due only to Matthew's editing; he seems to have had a structured discourse of Jesus as one of his sources. The form of that source may have been as follows: four beatitudes (Mt 5:3–4, 6, 11–12), a section on the new righteousness with illustrations (Mt 5:17, 20–24, 27–28, 33–48), a section on good works (Mt 6:1–6, 16–18), and three warnings (Mt 7:1–2, 15–21, 24–27).

* [5:1–2] Unlike Luke's sermon, this is addressed not only to the disciples but to the crowds (see Mt 7:28).

THE BEATITUDES*

3 "Blessed are the poor in spirit,*

for theirs is the kingdom of heaven.[a]

4 *Blessed are they who mourn,[b]

for they will be comforted.

5 *Blessed are the meek,[c]

for they will inherit the land.

6 Blessed are they who hunger and thirst for righteousness,*

for they will be satisfied.

7 Blessed are the merciful,

for they will be shown mercy.[d]

8 *Blessed are the clean of heart,[e]

for they will see God.

9 Blessed are the peacemakers,

for they will be called children of God.

10 Blessed are they who are persecuted for the sake of righteousness,*

for theirs is the kingdom of heaven.[f]

11 Blessed are you when they insult you and persecute you and utter every kind of evil against you [falsely] because of me.[g] **12** *Rejoice and be glad, for your reward will be great in heaven.[h] Thus they persecuted the prophets who were before you.

* [5:3–12] The form Blessed are (is) occurs frequently in the Old Testament in the Wisdom literature and in the psalms. Although modified by Matthew, the first, second, fourth, and ninth beatitudes have Lucan parallels (Mt 5:3 // Lk 6:20; Mt 5:4 // Lk 6:21b; Mt 5:6 // Lk 6:21a; Mt 5:11–12 // Lk 5:22–23). The others were added by the evangelist and are probably his own composition. A few manuscripts, Western and Alexandrian, and many versions and patristic quotations give the second and third beatitudes in inverted order.

* [5:3] The poor in spirit: in the Old Testament, the poor ('anāwîm) are those who are without material possessions and whose confidence is in God (see Is 61:1; Zep 2:3; in the NAB the word is translated lowly and humble, respectively, in those texts). Matthew added in spirit in order either to indicate that only the devout poor were meant or to extend the beatitude to all, of whatever social rank, who recognized their complete dependence on God. The same phrase poor in spirit is found in the Qumran literature (1QM 14:7).

a. [5:3–12] Lk 6:20–23.

* [5:4] Cf. Is 61:2, "(The Lord has sent me)…to comfort all who mourn." They will be comforted: here the passive is a "theological passive" equivalent to the active "God will comfort them"; so also in Mt 5:6, 7.

b. [5:4] Is 61:2–3; Rev 21:4.

* [5:5] Cf. Ps 37:11, "…the meek shall possess the land." In the psalm "the land" means the land of Palestine; here it means the kingdom.

c. [5:5] Gn 13:15; Ps 37:11.

* [5:6] For righteousness: a Matthean addition. For the meaning of righteousness here, see note on Mt 3:14–15.

d. [5:7] 18:33; Jas 2:13.

* [5:8] Cf. Ps 24:4. Only one "whose heart is clean" can take part in the temple worship. To be with God in the temple is described in Ps 42:3 as "beholding his face," but here the promise to the clean of heart is that they will see God not in the temple but in the coming kingdom.

e. [5:8] Ps 24:4–5; 73:1.

* [5:10] Righteousness here, as usually in Matthew, means conduct in conformity with God's will.

f. [5:10] 1 Pt 2:20; 3:14; 4:14.

g. [5:11] 10:22; Acts 5:41.

* [5:12] The prophets who were before you: the disciples of Jesus stand in the line of the persecuted prophets of Israel. Some would see the expression as indicating also that Matthew considered all Christian disciples as prophets.

h. [5:12] 2 Chr 36:16; Heb 11:32–38; Jas 5:10.

THE SIMILES OF SALT AND LIGHT.*

13[i] "You are the salt of the earth. But if salt loses its taste, with what can it be seasoned? It is no longer good for anything but to be thrown out and trampled underfoot.* 14 You are the light of the world. A city set on a mountain cannot be hidden.[j] 15 Nor do they light a lamp and then put it under a bushel basket; it is set on a lampstand, where it gives light to all in the house.[k] 16 Just so, your light must shine before others, that they may see your good deeds and glorify your heavenly Father.[l]

* [5:13–16] By their deeds the disciples are to influence the world for good. They can no more escape notice than a city set on a mountain. If they fail in good works, they are as useless as flavorless salt or as a lamp whose light is concealed.

i. [5:13] Mk 9:50; Lk 14:34–35.

* [5:13] The unusual supposition of salt losing its flavor has led some to suppose that the saying refers to the salt of the Dead Sea that, because chemically impure, could lose its taste.

j. [5:14] Jn 8:12.

k. [5:15] Mk 4:21; Lk 8:16; 11:33.

l. [5:16] Jn 3:21.

TEACHING ABOUT THE LAW.

17[*] "Do not think that I have come to abolish the law or the prophets. I have come not to abolish but to fulfill. **18** Amen, I say to you, until heaven and earth pass away, not the smallest letter or the smallest part of a letter will pass from the law, until all things have taken place.[m] **19** Therefore, whoever breaks one of the least of these commandments and teaches others to do so will be called least in the kingdom of heaven. But whoever obeys and teaches these commandments will be called greatest in the kingdom of heaven.[*]

20 I tell you, unless your righteousness surpasses that of the scribes and Pharisees, you will not enter into the kingdom of heaven.

[*] [5:17–20] This statement of Jesus' position concerning the Mosaic law is composed of traditional material from Matthew's sermon documentation (see note on Mt 5:1–7:29), other Q material (cf. Mt 18; Lk 16:17), and the evangelist's own editorial touches. To fulfill the law appears at first to mean a literal enforcement of the law in the least detail: until heaven and earth pass away nothing of the law will pass (Mt 5:18). Yet the "passing away" of heaven and earth is not necessarily the end of the world understood, as in much apocalyptic literature, as the dissolution of the existing universe. The "turning of the ages" comes with the apocalyptic event of Jesus' death and resurrection, and those to whom this gospel is addressed are living in the new and final age, prophesied by Isaiah as the time of "new heavens and a new earth" (Is 65:17; 66:22). Meanwhile, during Jesus' ministry when the kingdom is already breaking in, his mission remains within the framework of the law, though with significant anticipation of the age to come, as the following antitheses (Mt 5:21–48) show.

m. [5:18] Lk 16:17.

[*] [5:19] Probably these commandments means those of the Mosaic law. But this is an interim ethic "until heaven and earth pass away."

TEACHING
ABOUT ANGER.*

21 "You have heard that it was said to your ancestors,[n] 'You shall not kill; and whoever kills will be liable to judgment.'* **22*** But I say to you, whoever is angry* with his brother will be liable to judgment,[o] and whoever says to his brother, 'Raqa,' will be answerable to the Sanhedrin, and whoever says, 'You fool,' will be liable to fiery Gehenna. **23** Therefore, if you bring your gift to the altar, and there recall that your brother has anything against you,[p] **24** leave your gift there at the altar, go first and be reconciled with your brother, and then come and offer your gift. **25** Settle with your opponent quickly while on the way to court with him.[q] Otherwise your opponent will hand you over to the judge, and the judge will hand you over to the guard, and you will be thrown into prison. **26** Amen, I say to you, you will not be released until you have paid the last penny.

---

* [5:21–48] Six examples of the conduct demanded of the Christian disciple. Each deals with a commandment of the law, introduced by You have heard that it was said to your ancestors or an equivalent formula, followed by Jesus' teaching in respect to that commandment, But I say to you; thus their designation as "antitheses." Three of them accept the Mosaic law but extend or deepen it (Mt 5:21–22; 27–28; 43–44); three reject it as a standard of conduct for the disciples (Mt 5:31–32; 33–37; 38–39).

n. [5:21] Ex 20:13; Dt 5:17.

* [5:21] Cf. Ex 20:13; Dt 5:17. The second part of the verse is not an exact quotation from the Old Testament, but cf. Ex 21:12.

* [5:22–26] Reconciliation with an offended brother is urged in the admonition of Mt 5:23–24 and the parable of Mt 5:25–26 (//Lk 12:58–59). The severity of the judge in the parable is a warning of the fate of unrepentant sinners in the coming judgment by God.

* [5:22] Anger is the motive behind murder, as the insulting epithets are steps that may lead to it. They, as well as the deed, are all forbidden. Raqa: an Aramaic word rēqā' or rēqâ probably meaning "imbecile," "blockhead," a term of abuse. The ascending order of punishment, judgment (by a local council?), trial before the Sanhedrin, condemnation to Gehenna, points to a higher degree of seriousness in each of the offenses. Sanhedrin: the highest judicial body of Judaism. Gehenna: in Hebrew gê-hinnōm, "Valley of Hinnom," or gê ben-hinnōm, "Valley of the son of Hinnom," southwest of Jerusalem, the center of an idolatrous cult during the monarchy in which children were offered in sacrifice (see 2 Kgs 23:10; Jer 7:31). In Jos 18:16 (Septuagint, Codex Vaticanus) the Hebrew is transliterated into Greek as gaienna, which appears in the New Testament as geenna. The concept of punishment of sinners by fire either after death or after the final judgment is found in Jewish apocalyptic literature (e.g., Enoch 90:26) but the name geenna is first given to the place of punishment in the New Testament.

o. [5:22] Jas 1:19–20.

p. [5:23] Mk 11:25.

q. [5:25–26] 18:34–35; Lk 12:58–59.

TEACHING ABOUT ADULTERY

27* "You have heard that it was said,r 'You shall not commit adultery.' 28 But I say to you, everyone who looks at a woman with lust has already committed adultery with her in his heart. 29* If your right eye causes you to sin, tear it out and throw it away.s It is better for you to lose one of your members than to have your whole body thrown into Gehenna. 30 And if your right hand causes you to sin, cut it off and throw it away. It is better for you to lose one of your members than to have your whole body go into Gehenna.

* [5:27] See Ex 20:14; Dt 5:18.

r. [5:27] Ex 20:14; Dt 5:18.

* [5:29–30] No sacrifice is too great to avoid total destruction in Gehenna.

s. [5:29–30] 18:8–9; Mk 9:43–47.

TEACHING ABOUT DIVORCE.

31[*] "It was also said, 'Whoever divorces his wife must give her a bill of divorce.'^t **32** But I say to you, whoever divorces his wife (unless the marriage is unlawful) causes her to commit adultery, and whoever marries a divorced woman commits adultery.^u

* [5:31–32] See Dt 24:1–5. The Old Testament commandment that a bill of divorce be given to the woman assumes the legitimacy of divorce itself. It is this that Jesus denies. (Unless the marriage is unlawful): this "exceptive clause," as it is often called, occurs also in Mt 19:9, where the Greek is slightly different. There are other sayings of Jesus about divorce that prohibit it absolutely (see Mk 10:11–12; Lk 16:18; cf. 1 Cor 7:10, 11b), and most scholars agree that they represent the stand of Jesus. Matthew's "exceptive clauses" are understood by some as a modification of the absolute prohibition. It seems, however, that the unlawfulness that Matthew gives as a reason why a marriage must be broken refers to a situation peculiar to his community: the violation of Mosaic law forbidding marriage between persons of certain blood and/or legal relationship (Lv 18:6–18). Marriages of that sort were regarded as incest (porneia), but some rabbis allowed Gentile converts to Judaism who had contracted such marriages to remain in them. Matthew's "exceptive clause" is against such permissiveness for Gentile converts to Christianity; cf. the similar prohibition of porneia in Acts 15:20, 29. In this interpretation, the clause constitutes no exception to the absolute prohibition of divorce when the marriage is lawful.

t. [5:31] 19:3–9; Dt 24:1.

u. [5:32] Lk 16:18; 1 Cor 7:10–11.

TEACHING ABOUT OATHS.

33[*][v] "Again you have heard that it was said to your ancestors, 'Do not take a false oath, but make good to the Lord all that you vow.' **34**[w] But I say to you, do not swear at all;[*] not by heaven, for it is God's throne; **35** nor by the earth, for it is his footstool; nor by Jerusalem, for it is the city of the great King. **36** Do not swear by your head, for you cannot make a single hair white or black. **37**[*] Let your 'Yes' mean 'Yes,' and your 'No' mean 'No.' Anything more is from the evil one.

[*] [5:33] This is not an exact quotation of any Old Testament text, but see Ex 20:7; Dt 5:11; Lv 19:12. The purpose of an oath was to guarantee truthfulness by one's calling on God as witness.

v. [5:33] Lv 19:12; Nm 30:3.

w. [5:34–37] Ps 48:3; Sir 23:9; Is 66:1; Jas 5:12.

[*] [5:34–36] The use of these oath formularies that avoid the divine name is in fact equivalent to swearing by it, for all the things sworn by are related to God.

[*] [5:37] Let your 'Yes' mean 'Yes,' and your 'No' mean 'No': literally, "let your speech be 'Yes, yes,' 'No, no.'" Some have understood this as a milder form of oath, permitted by Jesus. In view of Mt 5:34, "Do not swear at all," that is unlikely. From the evil one: i.e., from the devil. Oath-taking presupposes a sinful weakness of the human race, namely, the tendency to lie. Jesus demands of his disciples a truthfulness that makes oaths unnecessary.

TEACHING ABOUT RETALIATION.

38 * "You have heard that it was said,[x] 'An eye for an eye and a tooth for a tooth.' **39**[y] But I say to you, offer no resistance to one who is evil. When someone strikes you on [your] right cheek, turn the other one to him as well. **40** If anyone wants to go to law with you over your tunic, hand him your cloak as well. **41** Should anyone press you into service for one mile,* go with him for two miles.[z] **42** Give to the one who asks of you, and do not turn your back on one who wants to borrow.[a]

* [5:38–42] See Lv 24:20. The Old Testament commandment was meant to moderate vengeance; the punishment should not exceed the injury done. Jesus forbids even this proportionate retaliation. Of the five examples that follow, only the first deals directly with retaliation for evil; the others speak of liberality.

x. [5:38] Ex 21:24; Lv 24:19–20.

y. [5:39–42] Lk 6:29–30.

* [5:41] Roman garrisons in Palestine had the right to requisition the property and services of the native population.

z. [5:41] Lam 3:30.

a. [5:42] Dt 15:7–8.

LOVE OF ENEMIES.*

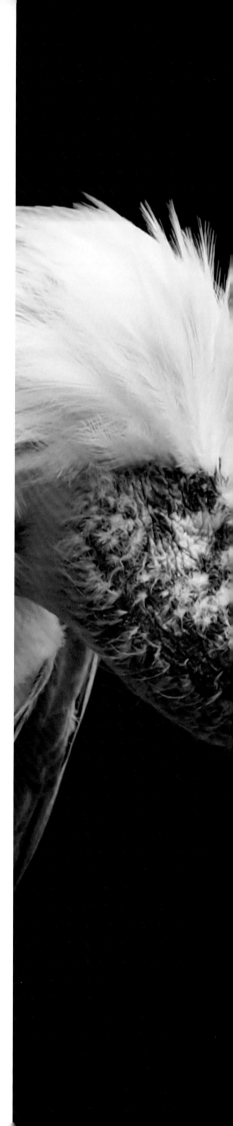

43[b] "You have heard that it was said, 'You shall love your neighbor and hate your enemy.'[c] **44** But I say to you, love your enemies, and pray for those who persecute you, **45** that you may be children of your heavenly Father, for he makes his sun rise on the bad and the good, and causes rain to fall on the just and the unjust. **46** For if you love those who love you, what recompense will you have? Do not the tax collectors* do the same? **47** And if you greet your brothers only, what is unusual about that? Do not the pagans do the same?* **48** So be perfect,* just as your heavenly Father is perfect.[d]

* [5:43–48] See Lv 19:18. There is no Old Testament commandment demanding hatred of one's enemy, but the "neighbor" of the love commandment was understood as one's fellow countryman. Both in the Old Testament (Ps 139:19–22) and at Qumran (1QS 9:21) hatred of evil persons is assumed to be right. Jesus extends the love commandment to the enemy and the persecutor. His disciples, as children of God, must imitate the example of their Father, who grants his gifts of sun and rain to both the good and the bad.

b. [5:43–48] Lk 6:27, 32–36.

c. [5:43] Lv 19:18.

* [5:46] Tax collectors: Jews who were engaged in the collection of indirect taxes such as tolls and customs. See note on Mk 2:14.

* [5:47] Jesus' disciples must not be content with merely usual standards of conduct; see Mt 5:20 where the verb "surpass" (Greek perisseuō) is cognate with the unusual (perisson) of this verse.

* [5:48] Perfect: in the gospels this word occurs only in Matthew, here and in Mt 19:21. The Lucan parallel (Lk 6:36) demands that the disciples be merciful.

d. [5:48] Lv 11:44; 19:2; Dt 18:13; Jas 1:4; 1 Pt 1:16; 1 Jn 3:3.

MATTHEW CHAPTER 6

TEACHING ABOUT ALMSGIVING.*

1 "[But] take care not to perform righteous deeds in order that people may see them;[a] otherwise, you will have no recompense from your heavenly Father. 2 When you give alms, do not blow a trumpet before you, as the hypocrites* do in the synagogues and in the streets to win the praise of others. Amen, I say to you, they have received their reward.[b] 3 But when you give alms, do not let your left hand know what your right is doing, 4 so that your almsgiving may be secret. And your Father who sees in secret will repay you.

* [6:1–18] The sermon continues with a warning against doing good in order to be seen and gives three examples, almsgiving (Mt 6:2–4), prayer (Mt 6:5–15), and fasting (Mt 6:16–18). In each, the conduct of the hypocrites (Mt 6:2) is contrasted with that demanded of the disciples. The sayings about reward found here and elsewhere (Mt 5:12, 46; 10:41–42) show that this is a genuine element of Christian moral exhortation. Possibly to underline the difference between the Christian idea of reward and that of the hypocrites, the evangelist uses two different Greek verbs to express the rewarding of the disciples and that of the hypocrites; in the latter case it is the verb apechō, a commercial term for giving a receipt for what has been paid in full (Mt 6:2, 5, 16).

a. [6:1] 23:5.

* [6:2] The hypocrites: the scribes and Pharisees, see Mt 23:13, 15, 23, 25, 27, 29. The designation reflects an attitude resulting not only from the controversies at the time of Jesus' ministry but from the opposition between Pharisaic Judaism and the church of Matthew. They have received their reward: they desire praise and have received what they were looking for.

b. [6:2] Jn 12:43.

TEACHING ABOUT PRAYER.

5 "When you pray, do not be like the hypocrites, who love to stand and pray in the synagogues and on street corners so that others may see them. Amen, I say to you, they have received their reward. 6 But when you pray, go to your inner room, close the door, and pray to your Father in secret. And your Father who sees in secret will repay you. 7* In praying, do not babble like the pagans, who think that they will be heard because of their many words.* 8 Do not be like them. Your Father knows what you need before you ask him.

* [6:7–15] Matthew inserts into his basic traditional material an expansion of the material on prayer that includes the model prayer, the "Our Father." That prayer is found in Lk 11:2–4 in a different context and in a different form.

* [6:7] The example of what Christian prayer should be like contrasts it now not with the prayer of the hypocrites but with that of the pagans. Their babbling probably means their reciting a long list of divine names, hoping that one of them will force a response from the deity.

THE LORD'S PRAYER.

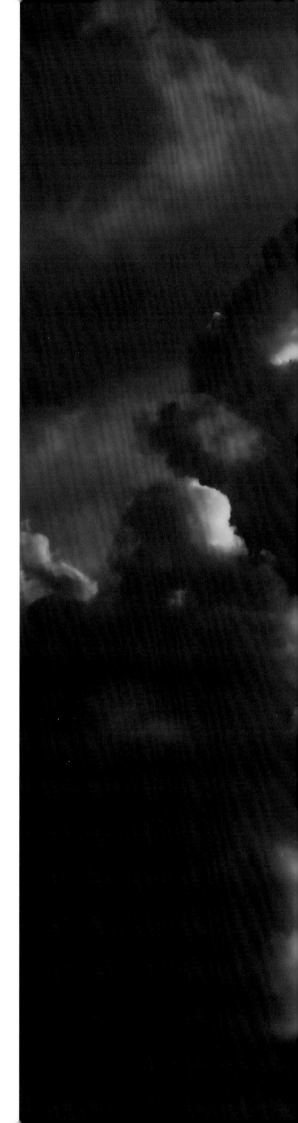

9[*] "This is how you are to pray:[c]

Our Father in heaven,[*]

hallowed be your name,

10 your kingdom come,[*]

your will be done,

on earth as in heaven.[d]

11[*e] Give us today our daily bread;

12 and forgive us our debts,[*]

as we forgive our debtors;[f]

13 and do not subject us to the final test,[*]

but deliver us from the evil one.[g]

14[*] If you forgive others their transgressions, your heavenly Father will forgive you.[h] **15** But if you do not forgive others, neither will your Father forgive your transgressions.[i]

* [6:9–13] Matthew's form of the "Our Father" follows the liturgical tradition of his church. Luke's less developed form also represents the liturgical tradition known to him, but it is probably closer than Matthew's to the original words of Jesus.

c. [6:9–13] Lk 11:2–4.

* [6:9] Our Father in heaven: this invocation is found in many rabbinic prayers of the post-New Testament period. Hallowed be your name: though the "hallowing" of the divine name could be understood as reverence done to God by human praise and by obedience to his will, this is more probably a petition that God hallow his own name, i.e., that he manifest his glory by an act of power (cf. Ez 36:23), in this case, by the establishment of his kingdom in its fullness.

* [6:10] Your kingdom come: this petition sets the tone of the prayer, and inclines the balance toward divine rather than human action in the petitions that immediately precede and follow it. Your will be done, on earth as in heaven: a petition that the divine purpose to establish the kingdom, a purpose present now in heaven, be executed on earth.

d. [6:10] 26:42.

* [6:11] Give us today our daily bread: the rare Greek word epiousios, here daily, occurs in the New Testament only here and in Lk 11:3. A single occurrence of the word outside of these texts and of literature dependent on them has been claimed, but the claim is highly doubtful. The word may mean daily or "future" (other meanings have also been proposed). The latter would conform better to the eschatological tone of the whole prayer. So understood, the petition would be for a speedy coming of the kingdom (today), which is often portrayed in both the Old Testament and the New under the image of a feast (Is 25:6; Mt 8:11; 22:1–10; Lk 13:29; 14:15–24).

e. [6:11] Prv 30:8–9.

* [6:12] Forgive us our debts: the word debts is used metaphorically of sins, "debts" owed to God (see Lk 11:4). The request is probably for forgiveness at the final judgment.

f. [6:12] 18:21–22; Sir 28:2.

* [6:13] Jewish apocalyptic writings speak of a period of severe trial before the end of the age, sometimes called the "messianic woes." This petition asks that the disciples be spared that final test.

g. [6:13] Jn 17:15; 2 Thes 3:3.

* [6:14–15] These verses reflect a set pattern called "Principles of Holy Law." Human action now will be met by a corresponding action of God at the final judgment.

h. [6:14] 18:35; Sir 28:1–5; Mk 11:25.

i. [6:15] Jas 2:13.

TEACHING ABOUT FASTING.

16 "When you fast,[*] do not look gloomy like the hypocrites. They neglect their appearance, so that they may appear to others to be fasting. Amen, I say to you, they have received their reward. **17** But when you fast, anoint your head and wash your face, **18** so that you may not appear to others to be fasting, except to your Father who is hidden. And your Father who sees what is hidden will repay you.

[*] [6:16] The only fast prescribed in the Mosaic law was that of the Day of Atonement (Lv 16:31), but the practice of regular fasting was common in later Judaism; cf. Didache 9:1.

TREASURE IN HEAVEN.

19[*] "Do not store up for yourselves treasures on earth, where moth and decay destroy, and thieves break in and steal.[j] **20** But store up treasures in heaven, where neither moth nor decay destroys, nor thieves break in and steal. **21** For where your treasure is, there also will your heart be.[k]

[*] [6:19–34] The remaining material of this chapter is taken almost entirely from Q. It deals principally with worldly possessions, and the controlling thought is summed up in Mt 6:24: the disciple can serve only one master and must choose between God and wealth (mammon). See further the note on Lk 16:9.

j. [6:19] Jas 5:2–3.

k. [6:20–21] Lk 12:33–34.

THE LIGHT OF THE BODY.*

22 "The lamp of the body is the eye. If your eye is sound, your whole body will be filled with light; **23** but if your eye is bad, your whole body will be in darkness. And if the light in you is darkness, how great will the darkness be.[1]

---

* [6:22–23] In this context the parable probably points to the need for the disciple to be enlightened by Jesus' teaching on the transitory nature of earthly riches.

I. [6:22–23] Lk 11:34–36.

GOD AND MONEY.

24 * "No one can serve two masters.^m He will either hate one and love the other, or be devoted to one and despise the other. You cannot serve God and mammon.

* [6:24] Mammon: an Aramaic word meaning wealth or property.
m. [6:24] Lk 16:13.

DEPENDENCE ON GOD. *

25[n] "Therefore I tell you, do not worry about your life, what you will eat [or drink], or about your body, what you will wear. Is not life more than food and the body more than clothing? **26** Look at the birds in the sky; they do not sow or reap, they gather nothing into barns, yet your heavenly Father feeds them. Are not you more important than they?[o] **27** Can any of you by worrying add a single moment to your life-span?* **28** Why are you anxious about clothes? Learn from the way the wild flowers grow. They do not work or spin. **29** But I tell you that not even Solomon in all his splendor was clothed like one of them. **30*** If God so clothes the grass of the field, which grows today and is thrown into the oven tomorrow, will he not much more provide for you, O you of little faith? **31** So do not worry and say, 'What are we to eat?' or 'What are we to drink?' or 'What are we to wear?' **32** All these things the pagans seek. Your heavenly Father knows that you need them all. **33** But seek first the kingdom [of God] and his righteousness,* and all these things will be given you besides. **34** Do not worry about tomorrow; tomorrow will take care of itself. Sufficient for a day is its own evil.

* [6:25–34] Jesus does not deny the reality of human needs (Mt 6:32), but forbids making them the object of anxious care and, in effect, becoming their slave.

n. [6:25–33] Lk 12:22–31.

o. [6:26] Ps 145:15–16; 147:9.

* [6:27] Life-span: the Greek word can also mean "stature." If it is taken in that sense, the word here translated moment (literally, "cubit") must be translated literally as a unit not of time but of spatial measure. The cubit is about eighteen inches.

* [6:30] Of little faith: except for the parallel in Lk 12:28, the word translated of little faith is found in the New Testament only in Matthew. It is used by him of those who are disciples of Jesus but whose faith in him is not as deep as it should be (see Mt 8:26; 14:31; 16:8 and the cognate noun in Mt 17:20).

* [6:33] Righteousness: see note on Mt 3:14–15.

MATTHEW CHAPTER 7

JUDGING OTHERS.

1[*][a] "Stop judging,[*] that you may not be judged.[b]
2 For as you judge, so will you be judged, and the measure with which you measure will be measured out to you.[c] **3** Why do you notice the splinter in your brother's eye, but do not perceive the wooden beam in your own eye? **4** How can you say to your brother, 'Let me remove that splinter from your eye,' while the wooden beam is in your eye? **5** You hypocrite,[*] remove the wooden beam from your eye first; then you will see clearly to remove the splinter from your brother's eye.

[*] [7:1–12] In Mt 7:1 Matthew returns to the basic traditional material of the sermon (Lk 6:37–38, 41–42). The governing thought is the correspondence between conduct toward one's fellows and God's conduct toward the one so acting.

a. [7:1–5] Lk 6:37–38, 41–42.

[*] [7:1] This is not a prohibition against recognizing the faults of others, which would be hardly compatible with Mt 7:5, 6 but against passing judgment in a spirit of arrogance, forgetful of one's own faults.

b. [7:1] Rom 2:1–2; 1 Cor 4:5.

c. [7:2] Wis 12:22; Mk 4:24.

[*] [7:5] Hypocrite: the designation previously given to the scribes and Pharisees is here given to the Christian disciple who is concerned with the faults of another and ignores his own more serious offenses.

PEARLS BEFORE SWINE.

6 "Do not give what is holy to dogs,[*] or throw your pearls before swine, lest they trample them underfoot, and turn and tear you to pieces.[d]

---

[*] [7:6] Dogs and swine were Jewish terms of contempt for Gentiles. This saying may originally have derived from a Jewish Christian community opposed to preaching the gospel (what is holy, pearls) to Gentiles. In the light of Mt 28:19 that can hardly be Matthew's meaning. He may have taken the saying as applying to a Christian dealing with an obstinately impenitent fellow Christian (Mt 18:17).

d. [7:6] Prv 23:9.

THE ANSWER TO PRAYERS.

7[e] "Ask and it will be given to you; seek and you will find; knock and the door will be opened to you.[f] 8 For everyone who asks, receives; and the one who seeks, finds; and to the one who knocks, the door will be opened.[g] 9 Which one of you would hand his son a stone when he asks for a loaf of bread,[*] 10 or a snake when he asks for a fish? 11 If you then, who are wicked, know how to give good gifts to your children, how much more will your heavenly Father give good things to those who ask him.[h]

e. [7:7–11] Mk 11:24; Lk 11:9–13.

f. [7:7] 18:19.

g. [7:8] Lk 18:1–8; Jn 14:13.

* [7:9–10] There is a resemblance between a stone and a round loaf of bread and between a serpent and the scaleless fish called barbut.

h. [7:11] 1 Jn 5:14–15.

THE GOLDEN RULE.

12[*] "Do to others whatever you would have them do to you.[i] This is the law and the prophets.

[*] [7:12] See Lk 6:31. This saying, known since the eighteenth century as the "Golden Rule," is found in both positive and negative form in pagan and Jewish sources, both earlier and later than the gospel. This is the law and the prophets is an addition probably due to the evangelist.

i. [7:12] Lk 6:31.

THE NARROW GATE.

13[*] "Enter through the narrow gate;[*] for the gate is wide and the road broad that leads to destruction, and those who enter through it are many.^j **14** How narrow the gate and constricted the road that leads to life. And those who find it are few.

* [7:13–28] The final section of the discourse is composed of a series of antitheses, contrasting two kinds of life within the Christian community, that of those who obey the words of Jesus and that of those who do not. Most of the sayings are from Q and are found also in Luke.

* [7:13–14] The metaphor of the "two ways" was common in pagan philosophy and in the Old Testament. In Christian literature it is found also in the Didache (1–6) and the Epistle of Barnabas (18–20).

j. [7:13] Lk 13:24.

15 "Beware of false prophets, who come to you in sheep's clothing, but underneath are ravenous wolves.[k] **16**[l] By their fruits you will know them. Do people pick grapes from thornbushes, or figs from thistles? **17** Just so, every good tree bears good fruit, and a rotten tree bears bad fruit. **18** A good tree cannot bear bad fruit, nor can a rotten tree bear good fruit. **19** Every tree that does not bear good fruit will be cut down and thrown into the fire. **20** So by their fruits you will know them.[m]

---

* [7:15–20] Christian disciples who claimed to speak in the name of God are called prophets (Mt 7:15) in Mt 10:41; Mt 23:34. They were presumably an important group within the church of Matthew. As in the case of the Old Testament prophets, there were both true and false ones, and for Matthew the difference could be recognized by the quality of their deeds, the fruits (Mt 7:16). The mention of fruits leads to the comparison with trees, some producing good fruit, others bad.

k. [7:15] 2 Pt 2:1.

l. [7:16–17] 12:33; Lk 6:43–44.

m. [7:20] 3:10.

THE TRUE DISCIPLE.

21 "Not everyone who says to me, 'Lord, Lord,' will enter the kingdom of heaven,[*] but only the one who does the will of my Father in heaven.[n] **22** Many will say to me on that day,[o] 'Lord, Lord, did we not prophesy in your name? Did we not drive out demons in your name? Did we not do mighty deeds in your name?'[p] **23** Then I will declare to them solemnly, 'I never knew you.[*] Depart from me, you evildoers.'[q]

[*] [7:21–23] The attack on the false prophets is continued, but is broadened to include those disciples who perform works of healing and exorcism in the name of Jesus (Lord) but live evil lives. Entrance into the kingdom is only for those who do the will of the Father. On the day of judgment (on that day) the morally corrupt prophets and miracle workers will be rejected by Jesus.

n. [7:21] Is 29:13; Lk 6:46.

o. [7:22–23] Lk 13:26–27.

p. [7:22] 25:11–12.

[*] [7:23] I never knew you: cf. Mt 10:33. Depart from me, you evildoers: cf. Ps 6:9.

q. [7:23] Ps 5:5; 6:9.

THE TWO FOUNDATIONS.

24 * "Everyone who listens to these words of mine and acts on them will be like a wise man who built his house on rock.ʳ **25** The rain fell, the floods came, and the winds blew and buffeted the house.ˢ But it did not collapse; it had been set solidly on rock. **26** And everyone who listens to these words of mine but does not act on them will be like a fool who built his house on sand. **27** The rain fell, the floods came, and the winds blew and buffeted the house. And it collapsed and was completely ruined."

28 * When Jesus finished these words, the crowds were astonished at his teaching, **29** *ᵗ for he taught them as one having authority, and not as their scribes.

* [7:24–27] The conclusion of the discourse (cf. Lk 6:47–49). Here the relation is not between saying and doing as in Mt 7:15–23 but between hearing and doing, and the words of Jesus are applied to every Christian (everyone who listens).

r. [7:24–27] Lk 6:47–49.

s. [7:25–26] Prv 10:25.

* [7:28–29] When Jesus finished these words: this or a similar formula is used by Matthew to conclude each of the five great discourses of Jesus (cf. Mt 11:1; 13:53; 19:1; 26:1).

* [7:29] Not as their scribes: scribal instruction was a faithful handing down of the traditions of earlier teachers; Jesus' teaching is based on his own authority. Their scribes: for the implications of their, see note on Mt 4:23.

t. [7:29] Mk 1:22; Lk 4:32.

MATTHEW CHAPTER 8

III. MINISTRY AND MISSION IN GALILEE*

THE CLEANSING OF A LEPER

1[a] When Jesus came down from the mountain, great crowds followed him. **2** And then a leper[*] approached, did him homage, and said, "Lord, if you wish, you can make me clean." **3** He stretched out his hand, touched him, and said, "I will do it. Be made clean." His leprosy was cleansed immediately. **4**[*] Then Jesus said to him, "See that you tell no one, but go show yourself to the priest, and offer the gift that Moses prescribed;[b] that will be proof for them."

[*] [8:1–9:38] This narrative section of the second book of the gospel is composed of nine miracle stories, most of which are found in Mark, although Matthew does not follow the Marcan order and abbreviates the stories radically. The stories are arranged in three groups of three, each group followed by a section composed principally of sayings of Jesus about discipleship. Mt 9:35 is an almost verbatim repetition of Mt 4:23. Each speaks of Jesus' teaching, preaching, and healing. The teaching and preaching form the content of Mt 5–7; the healing, that of Mt 8–9. Some scholars speak of a portrayal of Jesus as "Messiah of the Word" in Mt 5–7 and "Messiah of the Deed" in Mt 8–9. That is accurate so far as it goes, but there is also a strong emphasis on discipleship in Mt 8–9; these chapters have not only christological but ecclesiological import.

a. [8:1–4] Mk 1:40–44; Lk 5:12–14.

[*] [8:2] A leper: see note on Mk 1:40.

[*] [8:4] Cf. Lv 14:2–9. That will be proof for them: the Greek can also mean "that will be proof against them." It is not clear whether them refers to the priests or the people.

b. [8:4] Lv 14:2–32; Lk 17:14.

THE HEALING OF A CENTURION'S SERVANT.*

5[c] When he entered Capernaum,* a centurion approached him and appealed to him, **6** saying, "Lord, my servant is lying at home paralyzed, suffering dreadfully." **7** He said to him, "I will come and cure him." **8** The centurion said in reply,* "Lord, I am not worthy to have you enter under my roof; only say the word and my servant will be healed. **9** For I too am a person subject to authority, with soldiers subject to me. And I say to one, 'Go,' and he goes; and to another, 'Come here,' and he comes; and to my slave, 'Do this,' and he does it." **10** When Jesus heard this, he was amazed and said to those following him, "Amen, I say to you, in no one in Israel* have I found such faith. **11**[d] I say to you,* many will come from the east and the west, and will recline with Abraham, Isaac, and Jacob at the banquet in the kingdom of heaven, **12** but the children of the kingdom will be driven out into the outer darkness, where there will be wailing and grinding of teeth." **13** And Jesus said to the centurion, "You may go; as you have believed, let it be done for you." And at that very hour [his] servant was healed.

* [8:5–13] This story comes from Q (see Lk 7:1–10) and is also reflected in Jn 4:46–54. The similarity between the Q story and the Johannine is due to a common oral tradition, not to a common literary source. As in the later story of the daughter of the Canaanite woman (Mt 15:21–28) Jesus here breaks with his usual procedure of ministering only to Israelites and anticipates the mission to the Gentiles.

c. [8:5–13] Lk 7:1–10; Jn 4:46–53.

* [8:5] A centurion: a military officer commanding a hundred men. He was probably in the service of Herod Antipas, tetrarch of Galilee; see note on Mt 14:1.

* [8:8–9] Acquainted by his position with the force of a command, the centurion expresses faith in the power of Jesus' mere word.

* [8:10] In no one in Israel: there is good textual attestation (e.g., Codex Sinaiticus) for a reading identical with that of Lk 7:9, "not even in Israel." But that seems to be due to a harmonization of Matthew with Luke.

d. [8:11–12] 13:42, 50; 22:13; 24:51; 25:30; Lk 13:28–29.

* [8:11–12] Matthew inserts into the story a Q saying (see Lk 13:28–29) about the entrance of Gentiles into the kingdom and the exclusion of those Israelites who, though descended from the patriarchs and members of the chosen nation (the children of the kingdom), refused to believe in Jesus. There will be wailing and grinding of teeth: the first occurrence of a phrase used frequently in this gospel to describe final condemnation (Mt 13:42, 50; 22:13; 24:51; 25:30). It is found elsewhere in the New Testament only in Lk 13:28.

THE CURE OF PETER'S MOTHER-IN-LAW.*

14[e] Jesus entered the house of Peter, and saw his mother-in-law lying in bed with a fever. **15** He touched her hand, the fever left her, and she rose and waited on him.[f]

* [8:14–15] Cf. Mk 1:29–31. Unlike Mark, Matthew has no implied request by others for the woman's cure. Jesus acts on his own initiative, and the cured woman rises and waits not on "them" (Mk 1:31) but on him.

e. [8:14–16] Mk 1:29–34; Lk 4:38–41.

f. [8:15] 9:25.

OTHER HEALINGS.

16 When it was evening, they brought him many who were possessed by demons, and he drove out the spirits by a word[*] and cured all the sick, **17** to fulfill what had been said by Isaiah the prophet:[*g]

"He took away our infirmities

and bore our diseases."

[*] [8:16] By a word: a Matthean addition to Mk 1:34; cf. 8:8.

g. [8:17] Is 53:4.

[*] [8:17] This fulfillment citation from Is 53:4 follows the MT, not the LXX. The prophet speaks of the Servant of the Lord who suffers vicariously for the sins ("infirmities") of others; Matthew takes the infirmities as physical afflictions.

THE WOULD-BE FOLLOWERS OF JESUS.*

18[h] When Jesus saw a crowd around him, he gave orders to cross to the other side.* **19**[i] A scribe approached and said to him, "Teacher,* I will follow you wherever you go." **20** Jesus answered him, "Foxes have dens and birds of the sky have nests, but the Son of Man* has nowhere to rest his head." **21** Another of [his] disciples said to him, "Lord, let me go first and bury my father." **22*** But Jesus answered him, "Follow me, and let the dead bury their dead."

* [8:18–22] This passage between the first and second series of miracles about following Jesus is taken from Q (see Lk 9:57–62). The third of the three sayings found in the source is absent from Matthew.

h. [8:18] Mk 4:35.

* [8:18] The other side: i.e., of the Sea of Galilee.

i. [8:19–22] Lk 9:57–60.

* [8:19] Teacher: for Matthew, this designation of Jesus is true, for he has Jesus using it of himself (Mt 10:24, 25; 23:8; 26:18), yet when it is used of him by others they are either his opponents (Mt 9:11; 12:38; 17:24; 22:16, 24, 36) or, as here and in Mt 19:16, well-disposed persons who cannot see more deeply. Thus it reveals an inadequate recognition of who Jesus is.

* [8:20] Son of Man: see note on Mk 8:31. This is the first occurrence in Matthew of a term that appears in the New Testament only in sayings of Jesus, except for Acts 7:56 and possibly Mt 9:6 (//Mk 2:10; Lk 5:24). In Matthew it refers to Jesus in his ministry (seven times, as here), in his passion and resurrection (nine times, e.g., Mt 17:22), and in his glorious coming at the end of the age (thirteen times, e.g., Mt 24:30).

* [8:22] Let the dead bury their dead: the demand of Jesus overrides what both the Jewish and the Hellenistic world regarded as a filial obligation of the highest importance. See note on Lk 9:60.

THE CALMING OF THE STORM AT SEA.

23 *j He got into a boat and his disciples followed him. **24** Suddenly a violent storm* came up on the sea, so that the boat was being swamped by waves; but he was asleep. **25**k They came and woke him, saying, "Lord, save us!* We are perishing!" **26** He said to them, "Why are you terrified, O you of little faith?"* Then he got up, rebuked the winds and the sea, and there was great calm. **27** The men were amazed and said, "What sort of man is this, whom even the winds and the sea obey?"

---

* [8:23] His disciples followed him: the first miracle in the second group (Mt 8:23–9:8) is introduced by a verse that links it with the preceding sayings by the catchword "follow." In Mark the initiative in entering the boat is taken by the disciples (Mk 4:35–41); here, Jesus enters first and the disciples follow.

j. [8:23–27] Mk 4:35–40; Lk 8:22–25.

* [8:24] Storm: literally, "earthquake," a word commonly used in apocalyptic literature for the shaking of the old world when God brings in his kingdom. All the synoptics use it in depicting the events preceding the parousia of the Son of Man (Mt 24:7; Mk 13:8; Lk 21:11). Matthew has introduced it here and in his account of the death and resurrection of Jesus (Mt 27:51–54; 28:2).

k. [8:25–26] Ps 107:28–29.

* [8:25] The reverent plea of the disciples contrasts sharply with their reproach of Jesus in Mk 4:38.

* [8:26] You of little faith: see note on Mt 6:30. Great calm: Jesus' calming the sea may be meant to recall the Old Testament theme of God's control over the chaotic waters (Ps 65:8; 89:10; 93:3–4; 107:29).

THE HEALING OF THE GADARENE DEMONIACS.

28[l] When he came to the other side, to the territory of the Gadarenes,[*] two demoniacs who were coming from the tombs met him. They were so savage that no one could travel by that road. **29** They cried out, "What have you to do with us,[*] Son of God? Have you come here to torment us before the appointed time?" **30** Some distance away a herd of many swine was feeding.[*] **31** The demons pleaded with him, "If you drive us out, send us into the herd of swine."[m] **32** And he said to them, "Go then!" They came out and entered the swine, and the whole herd rushed down the steep bank into the sea where they drowned. **33** The swineherds ran away, and when they came to the town they reported everything, including what had happened to the demoniacs. **34** Thereupon the whole town came out to meet Jesus, and when they saw him they begged him to leave their district.

l. [8:28–34] Mk 5:1–17; Lk 8:26–37.

* [8:28] Gadarenes: this is the reading of Codex Vaticanus, supported by other important textual witnesses. The original reading of Codex Sinaiticus was Gazarenes, later changed to Gergesenes, and a few versions have Gerasenes. Each of these readings points to a different territory connected, respectively, with the cities Gadara, Gergesa, and Gerasa (modern Jerash). There is the same confusion of readings in the parallel texts, Mk 5:1 and Lk 8:26; there the best reading seems to be "Gerasenes," whereas "Gadarenes" is probably the original reading in Matthew. The town of Gadara was about five miles southeast of the Sea of Galilee, and Josephus (Life 9:42) refers to it as possessing territory that lay on that sea. Two demoniacs: Mark (5:1–20) has one.

* [8:29] What have you to do with us?: see note on Jn 2:4. Before the appointed time: the notion that evil spirits were allowed by God to afflict human beings until the time of the final judgment is found in Enoch 16:1 and Jubilees 10:7–10.

* [8:30] The tending of pigs, animals considered unclean by Mosaic law (Lv 11:6–7), indicates that the population was Gentile.

m. [8:31] Lk 4:34, 41.

MATTHEW CHAPTER 9

THE HEALING OF A PARALYTIC.

1 *a He entered a boat, made the crossing, and came into his own town. **2** And there people brought to him a paralytic lying on a stretcher. When Jesus saw their faith, he said to the paralytic, "Courage, child, your sins are forgiven."b **3** At that, some of the scribes* said to themselves, "This man is blaspheming." **4** Jesus knew what they were thinking, and said, "Why do you harbor evil thoughts? **5** Which is easier, to say, 'Your sins are forgiven,' or to say, 'Rise and walk'? **6*** But that you may know that the Son of Man has authority on earth to forgive sins"—he then said to the paralytic, "Rise, pick up your stretcher, and go home."c **7** He rose and went home. **8*** When the crowds saw this they were struck with awe and glorified God who had given such authority to human beings.

* [9:1] His own town: Capernaum; see Mt 4:13.

a. [9:1–8] Mk 2:3–12; Lk 5:18–26.

b. [9:2] Lk 7:48.

* [9:3] Scribes: see note on Mk 2:6. Matthew omits the reason given in the Marcan story for the charge of blasphemy: "Who but God alone can forgive sins?" (Mk 2:7).

* [9:6] It is not clear whether But that you may know...to forgive sins is intended to be a continuation of the words of Jesus or a parenthetical comment of the evangelist to those who would hear or read this gospel. In any case, Matthew here follows the Marcan text.

c. [9:6] Jn 5:27.

* [9:8] Who had given such authority to human beings: a significant difference from Mk 2:12 ("They...glorified God, saying, 'We have never seen anything like this'"). Matthew's extension to human beings of the authority to forgive sins points to the belief that such authority was being claimed by Matthew's church.

THE CALL OF MATTHEW.[*]

9 As Jesus passed on from there,[d] he saw a man named Matthew[*] sitting at the customs post. He said to him, "Follow me." And he got up and followed him. **10** While he was at table in his house,[*] many tax collectors and sinners came and sat with Jesus and his disciples.[e] **11** The Pharisees saw this and said to his disciples, "Why does your teacher[*] eat with tax collectors and sinners?" **12** He heard this and said, "Those who are well do not need a physician, but the sick do.[*] **13** Go and learn the meaning of the words,[f] 'I desire mercy, not sacrifice.'[*] I did not come to call the righteous but sinners."

[*] [9:9–17] In this section the order is the same as that of Mk 2:13–22.

d. [9:9–13] Mk 2:14–17; Lk 5:27–32.

[*] [9:9] A man named Matthew: Mark names this tax collector Levi (Mk 2:14). No such name appears in the four lists of the twelve who were the closest companions of Jesus (Mt 10:2–4; Mk 3:16–19; Lk 6:14–16; Acts 1:13 [eleven, because of the defection of Judas Iscariot]), whereas all four list a Matthew, designated in Mt 10:3 as "the tax collector." The evangelist may have changed the "Levi" of his source to Matthew so that this man, whose call is given special notice, like that of the first four disciples (Mt 4:18–22), might be included among the twelve. Another reason for the change may be that the disciple Matthew was the source of traditions peculiar to the church for which the evangelist was writing.

[*] [9:10] His house: it is not clear whether his refers to Jesus or Matthew. Tax collectors: see note on Mt 5:46. Table association with such persons would cause ritual impurity.

e. [9:10] 11:19; Lk 15:1–2.

[*] [9:11] Teacher: see note on Mt 8:19.

[*] [9:12] See note on Mk 2:17.

f. [9:13] 12:7; Hos 6:6.

[*] [9:13] Go and learn…not sacrifice: Matthew adds the prophetic statement of Hos 6:6 to the Marcan account (see also Mt 12:7). If mercy is superior to the temple sacrifices, how much more to the laws of ritual impurity.

THE QUESTION ABOUT FASTING.

14[g] Then the disciples of John approached him and said, "Why do we and the Pharisees fast [much], but your disciples do not fast?" **15** Jesus answered them, "Can the wedding guests mourn as long as the bridegroom is with them? The days will come when the bridegroom is taken away from them, and then they will fast.[*] **16** No one patches an old cloak with a piece of unshrunken cloth,[*] for its fullness pulls away from the cloak and the tear gets worse. **17** People do not put new wine into old wineskins. Otherwise the skins burst, the wine spills out, and the skins are ruined. Rather, they pour new wine into fresh wineskins, and both are preserved."

g. [9:14–17] Mk 2:18–22; Lk 5:33–39.

[*] [9:15] Fasting is a sign of mourning and would be as inappropriate at this time of joy, when Jesus is proclaiming the kingdom, as it would be at a marriage feast. Yet the saying looks forward to the time when Jesus will no longer be with the disciples visibly, the time of Matthew's church. Then they will fast: see Didache 8:1.

[*] [9:16–17] Each of these parables speaks of the unsuitability of attempting to combine the old and the new. Jesus' teaching is not a patching up of Judaism, nor can the gospel be contained within the limits of Mosaic law.

THE OFFICIAL'S DAUGHTER AND THE WOMAN WITH A HEMORRHAGE.

18[*] While he was saying these things to them,[h] an official[*] came forward, knelt down before him, and said, "My daughter has just died. But come, lay your hand on her, and she will live." **19** Jesus rose and followed him, and so did his disciples. **20** A woman suffering hemorrhages for twelve years came up behind him and touched the tassel[*] on his cloak. **21** She said to herself, "If only I can touch his cloak, I shall be cured."[i] **22** Jesus turned around and saw her, and said, "Courage, daughter! Your faith has saved you." And from that hour the woman was cured.

23 When Jesus arrived at the official's house and saw the flute players and the crowd who were making a commotion, **24** he said, "Go away! The girl is not dead but sleeping."[*] And they ridiculed him. **25** When the crowd was put out, he came and took her by the hand, and the little girl arose. **26** And news of this spread throughout all that land.

[*] [9:18–34] In this third group of miracles, the first (Mt 9:18–26) is clearly dependent on Mark (Mk 5:21–43). Though it tells of two miracles, the cure of the woman had already been included within the story of the raising of the official's daughter, so that the two were probably regarded as a single unit. The other miracles seem to have been derived from Mark and Q, respectively, though there Matthew's own editing is much more evident.

h. [9:18–26] Mk 5:22–43; Lk 8:41–56.

[*] [9:18] Official: literally, "ruler." Mark calls him "one of the synagogue officials" (Mk 5:22). My daughter has just died: Matthew heightens the Marcan "my daughter is at the point of death" (Mk 5:23).

[*] [9:20] Tassel: possibly "fringe." The Mosaic law prescribed that tassels be worn on the corners of one's garment as a reminder to keep the commandments (see Nm 15:37–39; Dt 22:12).

i. [9:21] 14:36; Nm 15:37.

[*] [9:24] Sleeping: sleep is a biblical metaphor for death (see Ps 87:6 LXX; Dn 12:2; 1 Thes 5:10). Jesus' statement is not a denial of the child's real death, but an assurance that she will be roused from her sleep of death.

THE HEALING OF TWO BLIND MEN.*

27[j] And as Jesus passed on from there, two blind men followed [him], crying out, "Son of David, have pity on us!"[k] **28** When he entered the house, the blind men approached him and Jesus said to them, "Do you believe that I can do this?" "Yes, Lord," they said to him. **29** Then he touched their eyes and said, "Let it be done for you according to your faith." **30** And their eyes were opened. Jesus warned them sternly, "See that no one knows about this." **31** But they went out and spread word of him through all that land.

* [9:27–31] This story was probably composed by Matthew out of Mark's story of the healing of a blind man named Bartimaeus (Mk 10:46–52). Mark places the event late in Jesus' ministry, just before his entrance into Jerusalem, and Matthew has followed his Marcan source at that point in his gospel also (see Mt 20:29–34). In each of the Matthean stories the single blind man of Mark becomes two. The reason why Matthew would have given a double version of the Marcan story and placed the earlier one here may be that he wished to add a story of Jesus' curing the blind at this point in order to prepare for Jesus' answer to the emissaries of the Baptist (Mt 11:4–6) in which Jesus, recounting his works, begins with his giving sight to the blind.

j. [9:27–31] 20:29–34.

* [9:27] Son of David: this messianic title is connected once with the healing power of Jesus in Mark (Mk 10:47–48) and Luke (Lk 18:38–39) but more frequently in Matthew (see also Mt 12:23; 15:22; 20:30–31).

k. [9:27] 15:22.

THE HEALING OF A MUTE PERSON.

32[l] As they were going out,[*] a demoniac who could not speak was brought to him, **33** and when the demon was driven out the mute person spoke. The crowds were amazed and said, "Nothing like this has ever been seen in Israel."[m] **34**[*] But the Pharisees said,[n] "He drives out demons by the prince of demons."

l. [9:32–34] 12:22–24; Lk 11:14–15.

* [9:32–34] The source of this story seems to be Q (see Lk 11:14–15). As in the preceding healing of the blind, Matthew has two versions of this healing, the later in Mt 12:22–24 and the earlier here.

m. [9:33] Mk 2:12; 7:37.

* [9:34] This spiteful accusation foreshadows the growing opposition to Jesus in Mt 11 and 12.

THE COMPASSION OF JESUS.

35[*][o] Jesus went around to all the towns and villages, teaching in their synagogues, proclaiming the gospel of the kingdom, and curing every disease and illness. **36**[p] At the sight of the crowds, his heart was moved with pity for them because they were troubled and abandoned,[*] like sheep without a shepherd. **37**[*][q] Then he said to his disciples, "The harvest is abundant but the laborers are few; **38** so ask the master of the harvest to send out laborers for his harvest."

[*] [9:35] See notes on Mt 4:23–25; Mt 8:1–9:38.

o. [9:35] 4:23; Lk 8:1.

p. [9:36] Nm 27:17; 1 Kgs 22:17; Jer 50:6; Ez 34:5; Mk 6:34.

[*] [9:36] See Mk 6:34; Nm 27:17; 1 Kgs 22:17.

[*] [9:37–38] This Q saying (see Lk 10:2) is only imperfectly related to this context. It presupposes that only God (the master of the harvest) can take the initiative in sending out preachers of the gospel, whereas in Matthew's setting it leads into Mt 10 where Jesus does so.

q. [9:37–38] Lk 10:2; Jn 4:35.

MATTHEW CHAPTER 10

THE MISSION OF THE TWELVE.

1^{*} Then he summoned his twelve disciples^{*} and gave them authority over unclean spirits to drive them out and to cure every disease and every illness.^a **2** The names of the twelve apostles^{*} are these: first, Simon called Peter, and his brother Andrew; James, the son of Zebedee, and his brother John; **3** Philip and Bartholomew, Thomas and Matthew the tax collector; James, the son of Alphaeus, and Thaddeus; **4** Simon the Cananean, and Judas Iscariot who betrayed him.

* [10:1–11:1] After an introductory narrative (Mt 10:1–4), the second of the discourses of the gospel. It deals with the mission now to be undertaken by the disciples (Mt 10:5–15), but the perspective broadens and includes the missionary activity of the church between the time of the resurrection and the parousia.

* [10:1] His twelve disciples: although, unlike Mark (Mk 3:13–14) and Luke (Lk 6:12–16), Matthew has no story of Jesus' choosing the Twelve, he assumes that the group is known to the reader. The earliest New Testament text to speak of it is 1 Cor 15:5. The number probably is meant to recall the twelve tribes of Israel and implies Jesus' authority to call all Israel into the kingdom. While Luke (Lk 6:13) and probably Mark (Mk 4:10, 34) distinguish between the Twelve and a larger group also termed disciples, Matthew tends to identify the disciples and the Twelve. Authority…every illness: activities the same as those of Jesus; see Mt 4:23; Mt 9:35; 10:8. The Twelve also share in his proclamation of the kingdom (Mt 10:7). But although he teaches (Mt 4:23; 7:28; 9:35), they do not. Their commission to teach comes only after Jesus' resurrection, after they have been fully instructed by him (Mt 28:20).

a. [10:1–4] Mk 3:14–19; Lk 6:13–16; Acts 1:13.

* [10:2–4] Here, for the only time in Matthew, the Twelve are designated apostles. The word "apostle" means "one who is sent," and therefore fits the situation here described. In the Pauline letters, the place where the term occurs most frequently in the New Testament, it means primarily one who has seen the risen Lord and has been commissioned to proclaim the resurrection. With slight variants in Luke and Acts, the names of those who belong to this group are the same in the four lists given in the New Testament (see note on Mt 9:9). Cananean: this represents an Aramaic word meaning "zealot." The meaning of that designation is unclear (see note on Lk 6:15).

5[b] Jesus sent out these twelve[*] after instructing them thus, "Do not go into pagan territory or enter a Samaritan town. **6**[c] Go rather to the lost sheep of the house of Israel. **7** As you go, make this proclamation: 'The kingdom of heaven is at hand.'[d] **8**[*] Cure the sick, raise the dead, cleanse lepers, drive out demons. Without cost you have received; without cost you are to give. **9**[e] Do not take gold or silver or copper for your belts; **10**[f] no sack for the journey, or a second tunic, or sandals, or walking stick. The laborer deserves his keep. **11**[g] Whatever town or village you enter, look for a worthy person in it, and stay there until you leave. **12** As you enter a house, wish it peace. **13** If the house is worthy, let your peace come upon it; if not, let your peace return to you.[*] **14**[*h] Whoever will not receive you or listen to your words—go outside that house or town and shake the dust from your feet. **15** Amen, I say to you, it will be more tolerable for the land of Sodom and Gomorrah on the day of judgment than for that town.[i]

b. [10:5–15] Mk 6:7–13; Lk 9:1–6.

[*] [10:5–6] Like Jesus (Mt 15:24), the Twelve are sent only to Israel. This saying may reflect an original Jewish Christian refusal of the mission to the Gentiles, but for Matthew it expresses rather the limitation that Jesus himself observed during his ministry.

c. [10:6] 15:24.

d. [10:7] 3:2; 4:17.

[*] [10:8–11] The Twelve have received their own call and mission through God's gift, and the benefits they confer are likewise to be given freely. They are not to take with them money, provisions, or unnecessary clothing; their lodging and food will be provided by those who receive them.

e. [10:9–10] Mk 6:8–9; Lk 9:3; 10:4.

f. [10:10] Lk 10:7; 1 Cor 9:14; 1 Tm 5:18.

g. [10:11–15] Mk 6:10–11; Lk 9:4–5; 10:5–12.

[*] [10:13] The greeting of peace is conceived of not merely as a salutation but as an effective word. If it finds no worthy recipient, it will return to the speaker.

[*][10:14] Shake the dust from your feet: this gesture indicates a complete disassociation from such unbelievers.

h. [10:14] Acts 13:51; 18:6.

i. [10:15] 11:24; Gn 19:1–29; Jude 7.

THE COMMISSIONING OF THE TWELVE.

COMING PERSECUTIONS.

16[j] "Behold, I am sending you like sheep in the midst of wolves; so be shrewd as serpents and simple as doves. 17[*] But beware of people,[k] for they will hand you over to courts and scourge you in their synagogues,[l] 18 and you will be led before governors and kings for my sake as a witness before them and the pagans. 19 When they hand you over, do not worry about how you are to speak or what you are to say. You will be given at that moment what you are to say.[m] 20 For it will not be you who speak but the Spirit of your Father speaking through you. 21[*n] Brother will hand over brother to death, and the father his child; children will rise up against parents and have them put to death. 22 You will be hated by all because of my name, but whoever endures to the end[*] will be saved. 23 When they persecute you in one town, flee to another. Amen, I say to you, you will not finish the towns of Israel before the Son of Man comes.[*] 24[o] No disciple is above his teacher, no slave above his master. 25 It is enough for the disciple that he become like his teacher, for the slave that he become like his master. If they have called the master of the house Beelzebul,[*] how much more those of his household!

j. [10:16] Lk 10:3.

* [10:17] The persecutions attendant upon the post-resurrection mission now begin to be spoken of. Here Matthew brings into the discourse sayings found in Mk 13 which deals with events preceding the parousia.

k. [10:17–22] Mk 13:9–13; Lk 21:12–19.

l. [10:17] Acts 5:40.

m. [10:19] Ex 4:11–12; Jer 1:6–10; Lk 12:11–12.

* [10:21] See Mi 7:6 which is cited in Mt 10:35, 36.

n. [10:21–22] 24:9, 13.

* [10:22] To the end: the original meaning was probably "until the parousia." But it is not likely that Matthew expected no missionary disciples to suffer death before then, since he envisages the martyrdom of other Christians (Mt 10:21). For him, the end is probably that of the individual's life (see Mt 10:28).

* [10:23] Before the Son of Man comes: since the coming of the Son of Man at the end of the age had not taken place when this gospel was written, much less during the mission of the Twelve during Jesus' ministry, Matthew cannot have meant the coming to refer to the parousia. It is difficult to know what he understood it to be: perhaps the "proleptic parousia" of Mt 28:16–20, or the destruction of the temple in A.D. 70, viewed as a coming of Jesus in judgment on unbelieving Israel.

o. [10:24–25] Lk 6:40; Jn 13:16; 15:20.

* [10:25] Beelzebul: see Mt 9:34 for the charge linking Jesus with "the prince of demons," who is named Beelzebul in Mt 12:24. The meaning of the name is uncertain; possibly, "lord of the house."

COURAGE UNDER PERSECUTION.

26[p] "Therefore do not be afraid of them. Nothing is concealed that will not be revealed, nor secret that will not be known.*[q] 27 What I say to you in the darkness, speak in the light; what you hear whispered, proclaim on the housetops. 28 And do not be afraid of those who kill the body but cannot kill the soul; rather, be afraid of the one who can destroy both soul and body in Gehenna.[r] 29 Are not two sparrows sold for a small coin? Yet not one of them falls to the ground without your Father's knowledge. 30 Even all the hairs of your head are counted. 31 So do not be afraid; you are worth more than many sparrows. 32* Everyone who acknowledges me before others I will acknowledge before my heavenly Father. 33 But whoever denies me before others, I will deny before my heavenly Father.[s]

p. [10:26–33] Lk 12:2–9.

* [10:26] The concealed and secret coming of the kingdom is to be proclaimed by them, and no fear must be allowed to deter them from that proclamation.

q. [10:26] Mk 4:22; Lk 8:17; 1 Tm 5:25.

r. [10:28] Jas 4:12.

* [10:32–33] In the Q parallel (Lk 12:8–9), the Son of Man will acknowledge those who have acknowledged Jesus, and those who deny him will be denied (by the Son of Man) before the angels of God at the judgment. Here Jesus and the Son of Man are identified, and the acknowledgment or denial will be before his heavenly Father.

s. [10:33] Mk 8:38; Lk 9:26; 2 Tm 2:12; Rev 3:5.

JESUS: A CAUSE OF DIVISION.

34[t] "Do not think that I have come to bring peace upon the earth. I have come to bring not peace but the sword.

35 For I have come to set

a man 'against his father,

a daughter against her mother,

and a daughter-in-law against her mother-in-law;

36 and one's enemies will be those of his household.'

t. [10:34–35] Lk 12:51–53.

THE CONDITIONS OF DISCIPLESHIP.

37[u] "Whoever loves father or mother more than me is not worthy of me, and whoever loves son or daughter more than me is not worthy of me; **38** and whoever does not take up his cross* and follow after me is not worthy of me. **39***[v] Whoever finds his life will lose it, and whoever loses his life for my sake will find it.

u. [10:37–39] 16:24–25; Lk 14:26–27.

* [10:38] The first mention of the cross in Matthew, explicitly that of the disciple, but implicitly that of Jesus (and follow after me). Crucifixion was a form of capital punishment used by the Romans for offenders who were not Roman citizens.

* [10:39] One who denies Jesus in order to save one's earthly life will be condemned to everlasting destruction; loss of earthly life for Jesus' sake will be rewarded by everlasting life in the kingdom.

v. [10:39] Mk 8:35; Lk 9:24; Jn 12:25.

REWARDS.

40 "Whoever receives you receives me,[*] and whoever receives me receives the one who sent me.[w] **41**[*] Whoever receives a prophet because he is a prophet will receive a prophet's reward, and whoever receives a righteous man because he is righteous will receive a righteous man's reward. **42** And whoever gives only a cup of cold water to one of these little ones to drink because he is a disciple—amen, I say to you, he will surely not lose his reward."[x]

[*] [10:40–42] All who receive the disciples of Jesus receive him, and God who sent him, and will be rewarded accordingly.

w. [10:40] Lk 10:16; Jn 12:44; 13:20.

[*] [10:41] A prophet: one who speaks in the name of God; here, the Christian prophets who proclaim the gospel. Righteous man: since righteousness is demanded of all the disciples, it is difficult to take the righteous man of this verse and one of these little ones (Mt 10:42) as indicating different groups within the followers of Jesus. Probably all three designations are used here of Christian missionaries as such.

x. [10:42] 25:40; Mk 9:41.

MATTHEW CHAPTER 11

1 When Jesus finished giving these commands to his twelve disciples,* he went away from that place to teach and to preach in their towns.

IV. OPPOSITION FROM ISRAEL

MESSENGERS FROM JOHN THE BAPTIST.

2 *a When John heard in prison* of the works of the Messiah, he sent his disciples to him **3*** with this question, "Are you the one who is to come, or should we look for another?" **4** Jesus said to them in reply, "Go and tell John what you hear and see: **5*** the blind regain their sight, the lame walk, lepers are cleansed, the deaf hear, the dead are raised, and the poor have the good news proclaimed to them.b **6** And blessed is the one who takes no offense at me."

* [11:1] The closing formula of the discourse refers back to the original addressees, the Twelve.

* [11:2–12:50] The narrative section of the third book deals with the growing opposition to Jesus. It is largely devoted to disputes and attacks relating to faith and discipleship and thus contains much sayings-material, drawn in large part from Q.

a. [11:2–11] Lk 7:18–28.

* [11:2] In prison: see Mt 4:12; 14:1–12. The works of the Messiah: the deeds of Mt 8–9.

* [11:3] The question probably expresses a doubt of the Baptist that Jesus is the one who is to come (cf. Mal 3:1) because his mission has not been one of fiery judgment as John had expected (Mt 3:2).

* [11:5–6] Jesus' response is taken from passages of Isaiah (Is 26:19; 29:18–19; 35:5–6; 61:1) that picture the time of salvation as marked by deeds such as those that Jesus is doing. The beatitude is a warning to the Baptist not to disbelieve because his expectations have not been met.

b. [11:5] Is 26:19; 29:18–19; 35:5–6; 61:1.

7 As they were going off, Jesus began to speak to the crowds about John, "What did you go out to the desert to see? A reed swayed by the wind?[c] **8** Then what did you go out to see? Someone dressed in fine clothing? Those who wear fine clothing are in royal palaces. **9** Then why did you go out? To see a prophet?[*] Yes, I tell you, and more than a prophet. **10** This is the one about whom it is written:

'Behold, I am sending my messenger ahead of you; he will prepare your way before you.'[d]

11 Amen, I say to you, among those born of women there has been none greater than John the Baptist; yet the least in the kingdom of heaven is greater than he.[*] **12** From the days of John the Baptist until now, the kingdom of heaven suffers violence,[*] and the violent are taking it by force.[e] **13** All the prophets and the law[*] prophesied up to the time of John. **14** And if you are willing to accept it, he is Elijah, the one who is to come.[f] **15** Whoever has ears ought to hear.

16[g] "To what shall I compare this generation?[*] It is like children who sit in marketplaces and call to one another, **17** 'We played the flute for you, but you did not dance, we sang a dirge but you did not mourn.' **18** For John came neither eating nor drinking, and they said, 'He is possessed by a demon.'[h] **19** The Son of Man came eating and drinking and they said, 'Look, he is a glutton and a drunkard, a friend of tax collectors and sinners.' But wisdom is vindicated by her works."[i]

* [11:7–19] Jesus' rebuke of John is counterbalanced by a reminder of the greatness of the Baptist's function (Mt 11:7–15) that is followed by a complaint about those who have heeded neither John nor Jesus (Mt 11:16–19).

c. [11:7] 3:3, 5.

* [11:9–10] In common Jewish belief there had been no prophecy in Israel since the last of the Old Testament prophets, Malachi. The coming of a new prophet was eagerly awaited, and Jesus agrees that John was such. Yet he was more than a prophet, for he was the precursor of the one who would bring in the new and final age. The Old Testament quotation is a combination of Mal 3:1; Ex 23:20 with the significant change that the before me of Malachi becomes before you. The messenger now precedes not God, as in the original, but Jesus.

d. [11:10] Ex 23:20; Mal 3:1; Mk 1:2; Lk 1:76.

* [11:11] John's preeminent greatness lies in his function of announcing the imminence of the kingdom (Mt 3:1). But to be in the kingdom is so great a privilege that the least who has it is greater than the Baptist.

* [11:12] The meaning of this difficult saying is probably that the opponents of Jesus are trying to prevent people from accepting the kingdom and to snatch it away from those who have received it.

e. [11:12] Lk 16:16.

* [11:13] All the prophets and the law: Matthew inverts the usual order, "law and prophets," and says that both have prophesied. This emphasis on the prophetic character of the law points to its fulfillment in the teaching of Jesus and to the transitory nature of some of its commandments (see note on Mt 5:17–20).

f. [11:14] 17:10–13; Mal 3:23; Lk 1:17.

g. [11:16–19] Lk 7:31–35.

* [11:16–19] See Lk 7:31–35. The meaning of the parable (Mt 11:16–17) and its explanation (Mt 11:18–19b) is much disputed. A plausible view is that the children of the parable are two groups, one of which proposes different entertainments to the other that will not agree with either proposal. The first represents John, Jesus, and their disciples; the second those who reject John for his asceticism and Jesus for his table association with those despised by the religiously observant. Mt 11:19c (her works) forms an inclusion with Mt 11:2 ("the works of the Messiah"). The original form of the saying is better preserved in Lk 7:35 "…wisdom is vindicated by all her children." There John and Jesus are the children of Wisdom; here the works of Jesus the Messiah are those of divine Wisdom, of which he is the embodiment. Some important textual witnesses, however, have essentially the same reading as in Luke.

h. [11:18] Lk 1:15.

i. [11:19] 9:10–11.

JESUS' TESTIMONY TO JOHN. *

REPROACHES TO UNREPENTANT TOWNS.

20[j] Then he began to reproach the towns where most of his mighty deeds had been done, since they had not repented. **21** "Woe to you, Chorazin! Woe to you, Bethsaida! For if the mighty deeds done in your midst had been done in Tyre and Sidon,[*] they would long ago have repented in sackcloth and ashes.[k] **22** But I tell you, it will be more tolerable for Tyre and Sidon on the day of judgment than for you. **23**[*] And as for you, Capernaum:

'Will you be exalted to heaven?[l]

You will go down to the netherworld.'

For if the mighty deeds done in your midst had been done in Sodom, it would have remained until this day. **24** But I tell you, it will be more tolerable for the land of Sodom on the day of judgment than for you."[m]

j. [11:20–24] Lk 10:12–15.

* [11:21] Tyre and Sidon were pagan cities denounced for their wickedness in the Old Testament; cf. Jl 4:4–7.

k. [11:21] Jl 4:4–7.

* [11:23] Capernaum's pride and punishment are described in language taken from the taunt song against the king of Babylon (Is 14:13–15).

l. [11:23] Is 14:13–15.

m. [11:24] 10:15.

THE PRAISE OF THE FATHER.

25[n] At that time Jesus said in reply,[*] "I give praise to you, Father, Lord of heaven and earth, for although you have hidden these things from the wise and the learned you have revealed them to the childlike. **26** Yes, Father, such has been your gracious will. **27** All things have been handed over to me by my Father. No one knows the Son except the Father, and no one knows the Father except the Son and anyone to whom the Son wishes to reveal him.[o]

n. [11:25–27] Lk 10:21–22.

[*] [11:25–27] This Q saying, identical with Lk 10:21–22 except for minor variations, introduces a joyous note into this section, so dominated by the theme of unbelief. While the wise and the learned, the scribes and Pharisees, have rejected Jesus' preaching and the significance of his mighty deeds, the childlike have accepted them. Acceptance depends upon the Father's revelation, but this is granted to those who are open to receive it and refused to the arrogant. Jesus can speak of all mysteries because he is the Son and there is perfect reciprocity of knowledge between him and the Father; what has been handed over to him is revealed only to those whom he wishes.

o. [11:27] Jn 3:35; 6:46; 7:28; 10:15.

THE GENTLE MASTERY OF CHRIST.

28[*] "Come to me, all you who labor and are burdened,[*] and I will give you rest. **29**[*p] Take my yoke upon you and learn from me, for I am meek and humble of heart; and you will find rest for yourselves. **30** For my yoke is easy, and my burden light."

[*] [11:28–29] These verses are peculiar to Matthew and are similar to Ben Sirach's invitation to learn wisdom and submit to her yoke (Sir 51:23, 26).

[*] [11:28] Who labor and are burdened: burdened by the law as expounded by the scribes and Pharisees (Mt 23:4).

[*] [11:29] In place of the yoke of the law, complicated by scribal interpretation, Jesus invites the burdened to take the yoke of obedience to his word, under which they will find rest; cf. Jer 6:16.

p. [11:29] Sir 51:26; Jer 6:16.

MATTHEW CHAPTER 12

PICKING GRAIN ON THE SABBATH.

1[*] At that time Jesus was going through a field of grain on the sabbath.[a] His disciples were hungry and began to pick the heads[*] of grain and eat them.[b] **2** When the Pharisees saw this, they said to him, "See, your disciples are doing what is unlawful to do on the sabbath." **3** He said to them,[*] "Have you not read what David[c] did when he and his companions were hungry, **4** how he went into the house of God and ate the bread of offering,[d] which neither he nor his companions but only the priests could lawfully eat? **5**[*] Or have you not read in the law that on the sabbath the priests serving in the temple violate the sabbath and are innocent?[e] **6** I say to you, something greater than the temple is here. **7**[*] If you knew what this meant, 'I desire mercy, not sacrifice,'[f] you would not have condemned these innocent men. **8**[*][g] For the Son of Man is Lord of the sabbath."

[*] [12:1–14] Matthew here returns to the Marcan order that he left in Mt 9:18. The two stories depend on Mk 2:23–28; 3:1–6, respectively, and are the only places in either gospel that deal explicitly with Jesus' attitude toward sabbath observance.

a. [12:1–8] Mk 2:23–28; Lk 6:1–5.

[*] [12:1–2] The picking of the heads of grain is here equated with reaping, which was forbidden on the sabbath (Ex 34:21).

b. [12:1] Dt 23:26.

[*] [12:3–4] See 1 Sm 21:2–7. In the Marcan parallel (Mk 2:25–26) the high priest is called Abiathar, although in 1 Samuel this action is attributed to Ahimelech. The Old Testament story is not about a violation of the sabbath rest; its pertinence to this dispute is that a violation of the law was permissible because of David's men being without food.

c. [12:3–4] 1 Sm 21:2–7.

d. [12:4] Lv 24:5–9.

[*] [12:5–6] This and the following argument (Mt 12:7) are peculiar to Matthew. The temple service seems to be the changing of the showbread on the sabbath (Lv 24:8) and the doubling on the sabbath of the usual daily holocausts (Nm 28:9–10). The argument is that the law itself requires work that breaks the sabbath rest, because of the higher duty of temple service. If temple duties outweigh the sabbath law, how much more does the presence of Jesus, with his proclamation of the kingdom (something greater than the temple), justify the conduct of his disciples.

e. [12:5] Lv 24:8; Nm 28:9–10.

[*] [12:7] See note on Mt 9:13.

f. [12:7] Hos 6:6.

[*] [12:8] The ultimate justification for the disciples' violation of the sabbath rest is that Jesus, the Son of Man, has supreme authority over the law.

g. [12:8] Jn 5:16–17.

THE MAN WITH A WITHERED HAND.

9[h] Moving on from there, he went into their synagogue. **10** And behold, there was a man there who had a withered hand. They questioned him, "Is it lawful to cure on the sabbath?"* so that they might accuse him. **11*** He said to them, "Which one of you who has a sheep that falls into a pit on the sabbath will not take hold of it and lift it out? **12** How much more valuable a person is than a sheep. So it is lawful to do good on the sabbath." **13** Then he said to the man, "Stretch out your hand." He stretched it out, and it was restored as sound as the other. **14** But the Pharisees* went out and took counsel against him to put him to death.[i]

h. [12:9–15] Mk 3:1–6; Lk 6:6–11.

* [12:10] Rabbinic tradition later than the gospels allowed relief to be given to a sufferer on the sabbath if life was in danger. This may also have been the view of Jesus' Pharisaic contemporaries. But the case here is not about one in danger of death.

* [12:11] Matthew omits the question posed by Jesus in Mk 3:4 and substitutes one about rescuing a sheep on the sabbath, similar to that in Lk 14:5.

* [12:14] See Mk 3:6. Here the plan to bring about Jesus' death is attributed to the Pharisees only. This is probably due to the situation of Matthew's church, when the sole opponents were the Pharisees.

i. [12:14] Jn 5:18.

THE CHOSEN SERVANT.*

15 When Jesus realized this, he withdrew from that place. Many [people] followed him, and he cured them all,* **16** but he warned them not to make him known. **17** This was to fulfill what had been spoken through Isaiah the prophet:

18 "Behold, my servant whom I have chosen,ʲ

my beloved in whom I delight;

I shall place my spirit upon him,

and he will proclaim justice to the Gentiles.

19 He will not contend* or cry out,

nor will anyone hear his voice in the streets.

20 A bruised reed he will not break,

a smoldering wick he will not quench,

until he brings justice to victory.

21 And in his name the Gentiles will hope."*

---

* [12:15–21] Matthew follows Mk 3:7–12 but summarizes his source in two verses (Mt 12:15, 16) that pick up the withdrawal, the healings, and the command for silence. To this he adds a fulfillment citation from the first Servant Song (Is 42:1–4) that does not correspond exactly to either the Hebrew or the LXX of that passage. It is the longest Old Testament citation in this gospel, emphasizing the meekness of Jesus, the Servant of the Lord, and foretelling the extension of his mission to the Gentiles.

* [12:15] Jesus' knowledge of the Pharisees' plot and his healing all are peculiar to Matthew.

j. [12:18–21] Is 42:1–4.

* [12:19] The servant's not contending is seen as fulfilled in Jesus' withdrawal from the disputes narrated in Mt 12:1–14.

* [12:21] Except for a minor detail, Matthew here follows the LXX, although the meaning of the Hebrew ("the coastlands will wait for his teaching") is similar.

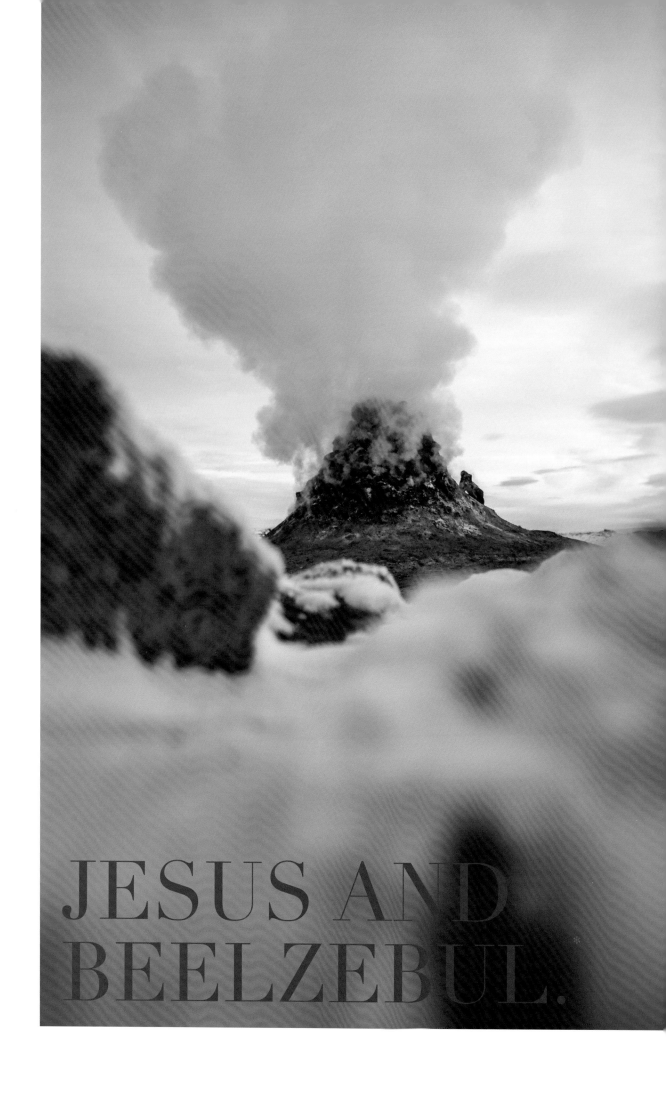

JESUS AND BEELZEBUL.*

22[k] Then they brought to him a demoniac who was blind and mute. He cured the mute person so that he could speak and see. **23**[*][l] All the crowd was astounded, and said, "Could this perhaps be the Son of David?" **24**[*][m] But when the Pharisees heard this, they said, "This man drives out demons only by the power of Beelzebul, the prince of demons." **25**[n] But he knew what they were thinking and said to them,[*] "Every kingdom divided against itself will be laid waste, and no town or house divided against itself will stand. **26** And if Satan drives out Satan, he is divided against himself; how, then, will his kingdom stand? **27** And if I drive out demons by Beelzebul, by whom do your own people[*] drive them out? Therefore they will be your judges. **28**[*][o] But if it is by the Spirit of God that I drive out demons, then the kingdom of God has come upon you. **29**[*] How can anyone enter a strong man's house and steal his property, unless he first ties up the strong man? Then he can plunder his house. **30**[*][p] Whoever is not with me is against me, and whoever does not gather with me scatters. **31**[q] Therefore, I say to you, every sin and blasphemy will be forgiven people, but blasphemy against the Spirit[*] will not be forgiven. **32** And whoever speaks a word against the Son of Man will be forgiven; but whoever speaks against the holy Spirit will not be forgiven, either in this age or in the age to come.

[*] [12:22–32] For the exorcism, see note on Mt 9:32–34. The long discussion combines Marcan and Q material (Mk 3:22–30; Lk 11:19–20, 23; 12:10). Mk 3:20–21 is omitted, with a consequent lessening of the sharpness of Mt 12:48.

k. [12:22–24] 9:32–34; Lk 11:14–15.

[*] [12:23] See note on Mt 9:27.

l. [12:23] 9:27.

[*] [12:24] See note on Mt 10:25.

m. [12:24] 10:25; Mk 3:22.

n. [12:25–29] Mk 3:23–27; Lk 11:17–22.

[*] [12:25–26] Jesus' first response to the Pharisees' charge is that if it were true, Satan would be destroying his own kingdom.

[*] [12:27] Besides pointing out the absurdity of the charge, Jesus asks how the work of Jewish exorcists (your own people) is to be interpreted. Are they, too, to be charged with collusion with Beelzebul? For an example of Jewish exorcism see Josephus, Antiquities 8:42–49.

[*] [12:28] The Q parallel (Lk 11:20) speaks of the "finger" rather than of the "spirit" of God. While the difference is probably due to Matthew's editing, he retains the kingdom of God rather than changing it to his usual "kingdom of heaven." Has come upon you: see Mt 4:17.

o. [12:28] Lk 11:20.

[*] [12:29] A short parable illustrates what Jesus is doing. The strong man is Satan, whom Jesus has tied up and whose house he is plundering. Jewish expectation was that Satan would be chained up in the last days (Rev 20:2); Jesus' exorcisms indicate that those days have begun.

[*] [12:30] This saying, already attached to the preceding verses in Q (see Lk 11:23), warns that there can be no neutrality where Jesus is concerned. Its pertinence in a context where Jesus is addressing not the neutral but the bitterly opposed is not clear. The accusation of scattering, however, does fit the situation. Jesus is the shepherd of God's people (Mt 2:6), his mission is to the lost sheep of Israel (Mt 15:24); the Pharisees, who oppose him, are guilty of scattering the sheep.

p. [12:30] Lk 11:23.

q. [12:31–32] Mk 3:28–30; Lk 12:10.

[*] [12:31] Blasphemy against the Spirit: the sin of attributing to Satan (Mt 12:24) what is the work of the Spirit of God (Mt 12:28).

A TREE AND ITS FRUITS.

33[r] "Either declare[*] the tree good and its fruit is good, or declare the tree rotten and its fruit is rotten, for a tree is known by its fruit. **34**[*][s] You brood of vipers, how can you say good things when you are evil? For from the fullness of the heart the mouth speaks. **35** A good person brings forth good out of a store of goodness, but an evil person brings forth evil out of a store of evil. **36**[*][t] I tell you, on the day of judgment people will render an account for every careless word they speak. **37** By your words you will be acquitted, and by your words you will be condemned."

r. [12:33–35] Lk 6:43–45.

[*] [12:33] Declare: literally, "make." The meaning of this verse is obscure. Possibly it is a challenge to the Pharisees either to declare Jesus and his exorcisms good or both of them bad. A tree is known by its fruit; if the fruit is good, so must the tree be. If the driving out of demons is good, so must its source be.

[*] [12:34] The admission of Jesus' goodness cannot be made by the Pharisees, for they are evil, and the words that proceed from their evil hearts cannot be good.

s. [12:34] 3:7; 23:33; 15:11–12; Lk 3:7.

[*] [12:36–37] If on the day of judgment people will be held accountable for even their careless words, the vicious accusations of the Pharisees will surely lead to their condemnation.

t. [12:36–37] Jas 3:1–2.

THE DEMAND FOR A SIGN.[*]

38 Then some of the scribes and Pharisees said to him, "Teacher,[*] we wish to see a sign from you."^u **39** He said to them in reply, "An evil and unfaithful[*] generation seeks a sign, but no sign will be given it except the sign of Jonah the prophet. **40** Just as Jonah was in the belly of the whale three days and three nights,[*] so will the Son of Man be in the heart of the earth three days and three nights. **41**[*] At the judgment, the men of Nineveh will arise with this generation and condemn it, because they repented at the preaching of Jonah; and there is something greater than Jonah here. **42** At the judgment the queen of the south will arise with this generation and condemn it, because she came from the ends of the earth to hear the wisdom of Solomon; and there is something greater than Solomon here.^v

---

* [12:38–42] This section is mainly from Q (see Lk 11:29–32). Mk 8:11–12, which Matthew has followed in Mt 16:1–4, has a similar demand for a sign. The scribes and Pharisees refuse to accept the exorcisms of Jesus as authentication of his claims and demand a sign that will end all possibility of doubt. Jesus' response is that no such sign will be given. Because his opponents are evil and see him as an agent of Satan, nothing will convince them.

* [12:38] Teacher: see note on Mt 8:19. In Mt 16:1 the request is for a sign "from heaven" (Mk 8:11).

u. [12:38–42] 16:1–4; Jon 2:1; 3:1–10; Mk 8:11–12; Lk 11:29–32.

* [12:39] Unfaithful: literally, "adulterous." The covenant between God and Israel was portrayed as a marriage bond, and unfaithfulness to the covenant as adultery; cf. Hos 2:4–14; Jer 3:6–10.

* [12:40] See Jon 2:1. While in Q the sign was simply Jonah's preaching to the Ninevites (Lk 11:30, 32), Matthew here adds Jonah's sojourn in the belly of the whale for three days and three nights, a prefiguration of Jesus' sojourn in the abode of the dead and, implicitly, of his resurrection.

* [12:41–42] The Ninevites who repented (see Jon 3:1–10) and the queen of the south (i.e., of Sheba; see 1 Kgs 10:1–13) were pagans who responded to lesser opportunities than have been offered to Israel in the ministry of Jesus, something greater than Jonah or Solomon. At the final judgment they will condemn the faithless generation that has rejected him.

v. [12:42] 1 Kgs 10:1–10.

43[w] "When an unclean spirit goes out of a person it roams through arid regions searching for rest but finds none. **44** Then it says, 'I will return to my home from which I came.' But upon returning, it finds it empty, swept clean, and put in order. **45** Then it goes and brings back with itself seven other spirits more evil than itself, and they move in and dwell there; and the last condition of that person is worse than the first. Thus it will be with this evil generation."

* [12:43–45] Another Q passage; cf. Mt 11:24–26. Jesus' ministry has broken Satan's hold over Israel, but the refusal of this evil generation to accept him will lead to a worse situation than what preceded his coming.
w. [12:43–45] Lk 11:24–26.

THE RETURN OF THE UNCLEAN SPIRIT.*

THE TRUE FAMILY OF JESUS.*

46[x] While he was still speaking to the crowds, his mother and his brothers appeared outside, wishing to speak with him. **47** [Someone told him, "Your mother and your brothers are standing outside, asking to speak with you."]* **48** But he said in reply to the one who told him, "Who is my mother? Who are my brothers?" **49** And stretching out his hand toward his disciples, he said, "Here are my mother and my brothers. **50** For whoever does the will of my heavenly Father is my brother, and sister, and mother."

* [12:46–50] See Mk 3:31–35. Matthew has omitted Mk 3:20–21 which is taken up in Mk 3:31 (see note on Mt 12:22–32), yet the point of the story is the same in both gospels: natural kinship with Jesus counts for nothing; only one who does the will of his heavenly Father belongs to his true family.

x. [12:46–50] Mk 3:31–35; Lk 8:19–21.

* [12:47] This verse is omitted in some important textual witnesses, including Codex Sinaiticus (original reading) and Codex Vaticanus.

MATTHEW CHAPTER 13

THE PARABLE OF THE SOWER.

1[*] On that day, Jesus went out of the house and sat down by the sea.^a **2** Such large crowds gathered around him that he got into a boat and sat down, and the whole crowd stood along the shore. **3**[*] And he spoke to them at length in parables,[*] saying: "A sower went out to sow. **4** And as he sowed, some seed fell on the path, and birds came and ate it up. **5** Some fell on rocky ground, where it had little soil. It sprang up at once because the soil was not deep, **6** and when the sun rose it was scorched, and it withered for lack of roots. **7** Some seed fell among thorns, and the thorns grew up and choked it. **8** But some seed fell on rich soil, and produced fruit, a hundred or sixty or thirtyfold. **9** Whoever has ears ought to hear."

* [13:1–53] The discourse in parables is the third great discourse of Jesus in Matthew and constitutes the second part of the third book of the gospel. Matthew follows the Marcan outline (Mk 4:1–35) but has only two of Mark's parables, the five others being from Q and M. In addition to the seven parables, the discourse gives the reason why Jesus uses this type of speech (Mt 13:10–15), declares the blessedness of those who understand his teaching (Mt 13:16–17), explains the parable of the sower (Mt 13:18–23) and of the weeds (Mt 13:36–43), and ends with a concluding statement to the disciples (Mt 13:51–52).

a. [13:1–15] Mk 4:1–12; Lk 8:4–10.

* [13:3–8] Since in Palestine sowing often preceded plowing, much of the seed is scattered on ground that is unsuitable. Yet while much is wasted, the seed that falls on good ground bears fruit in extraordinarily large measure. The point of the parable is that, in spite of some failure because of opposition and indifference, the message of Jesus about the coming of the kingdom will have enormous success.

* [13:3] In parables: the word "parable" (Greek parabolē) is used in the LXX to translate the Hebrew māshāl, a designation covering a wide variety of literary forms such as axioms, proverbs, similitudes, and allegories. In the New Testament the same breadth of meaning of the word is found, but there it primarily designates stories that are illustrative comparisons between Christian truths and events of everyday life. Sometimes the event has a strange element that is quite different from usual experience (e.g., in Mt 13:33 the enormous amount of dough in the parable of the yeast); this is meant to sharpen the curiosity of the hearer. If each detail of such a story is given a figurative meaning, the story is an allegory. Those who maintain a sharp distinction between parable and allegory insist that a parable has only one point of comparison, and that while parables were characteristic of Jesus' teaching, to see allegorical details in them is to introduce meanings that go beyond their original intention and even falsify it. However, to exclude any allegorical elements from a parable is an excessively rigid mode of interpretation, now abandoned by many scholars.

THE
PURPOSE
OF PARABLES.

10 The disciples approached him and said, "Why do you speak to them in parables?" **11**[*] He said to them in reply, "Because knowledge of the mysteries of the kingdom of heaven has been granted to you, but to them it has not been granted. **12**[b] To anyone who has, more will be given[*] and he will grow rich; from anyone who has not, even what he has will be taken away. **13**[*c] This is why I speak to them in parables, because 'they look but do not see and hear but do not listen or understand.'

14[d] Isaiah's prophecy is fulfilled in them, which says:

'You shall indeed hear but not understand,

you shall indeed look but never see.

15 Gross is the heart of this people,

they will hardly hear with their ears, they have closed their eyes,

lest they see with their eyes

and hear with their ears

and understand with their heart and be converted,

and I heal them.'

---

[*] [13:11] Since a parable is figurative speech that demands reflection for understanding, only those who are prepared to explore its meaning can come to know it. To understand is a gift of God, granted to the disciples but not to the crowds. In Semitic fashion, both the disciples' understanding and the crowd's obtuseness are attributed to God. The question of human responsibility for the obtuseness is not dealt with, although it is asserted in Mt 13:13. The mysteries: as in Lk 8:10; Mk 4:11 has "the mystery." The word is used in Dn 2:18, 19, 27 and in the Qumran literature (1QpHab 7:8; 1QS 3:23; 1QM 3:9) to designate a divine plan or decree affecting the course of history that can be known only when revealed. Knowledge of the mysteries of the kingdom of heaven means recognition that the kingdom has become present in the ministry of Jesus.

b. [13:12] 25:29; Mk 4:25; Lk 8:18; 19:26.

[*] [13:12] In the New Testament use of this axiom of practical "wisdom" (see Mt 25:29; Mk 4:25; Lk 8:18; 19:26), the reference transcends the original level. God gives further understanding to one who accepts the revealed mystery; from the one who does not, he will take it away (note the "theological passive," more will be given, what he has will be taken away).

[*] [13:13] Because 'they look...or understand': Matthew softens his Marcan source, which states that Jesus speaks in parables so that the crowds may not understand (Mk 4:12), and makes such speaking a punishment given because they have not accepted his previous clear teaching. However, his citation of Is 6:9–10 in Mt 13:14 supports the harsher Marcan view.

c. [13:13] Jn 9:39.

d. [13:14–15] Is 6:9–10; Jn 12:40; Acts 28:26–27; Rom 11:8.

THE PRIVILEGE OF DISCIPLE-SHIP. *

16[e] "But blessed are your eyes, because they see, and your ears, because they hear. **17** Amen, I say to you, many prophets and righteous people longed to see what you see but did not see it, and to hear what you hear but did not hear it.

---

* [13:16–17] Unlike the unbelieving crowds, the disciples have seen that which the prophets and the righteous of the Old Testament longed to see without having their longing fulfilled.

e. [13:16–17] Lk 10:23–24; 1 Pt 1:10–12.

THE EXPLANATION OF THE PARABLE OF THE SOWER.

* **18**^f "Hear then the parable of the sower. **19** The seed sown on the path is the one who hears the word of the kingdom without understanding it, and the evil one comes and steals away what was sown in his heart. **20** The seed sown on rocky ground is the one who hears the word and receives it at once with joy. **21** But he has no root and lasts only for a time. When some tribulation or persecution comes because of the word, he immediately falls away. **22** The seed sown among thorns is the one who hears the word, but then worldly anxiety and the lure of riches choke the word and it bears no fruit. **23** But the seed sown on rich soil is the one who hears the word and understands it, who indeed bears fruit and yields a hundred or sixty or thirtyfold."

* [13:18–23] See Mk 4:14–20; Lk 8:11–15. In this explanation of the parable the emphasis is on the various types of soil on which the seed falls, i.e., on the dispositions with which the preaching of Jesus is received. The second and third types particularly are explained in such a way as to support the view held by many scholars that the explanation derives not from Jesus but from early Christian reflection upon apostasy from the faith that was the consequence of persecution and worldliness, respectively. Others, however, hold that the explanation may come basically from Jesus even though it was developed in the light of later Christian experience. The four types of persons envisaged are (1) those who never accept the word of the kingdom (Mt 13:19); (2) those who believe for a while but fall away because of persecution (Mt 13:20–21); (3) those who believe, but in whom the word is choked by worldly anxiety and the seduction of riches (Mt 13:22); (4) those who respond to the word and produce fruit abundantly (Mt 13:23).

f. [13:18–23] Mk 4:13–20; Lk 8:11–15.

THE PARABLE OF THE WEEDS AMONG THE WHEAT.

24 He proposed another parable to them.[*] "The kingdom of heaven may be likened to a man who sowed good seed in his field. **25** While everyone was asleep his enemy came and sowed weeds[*] all through the wheat, and then went off. **26** When the crop grew and bore fruit, the weeds appeared as well. **27** The slaves of the householder came to him and said, 'Master, did you not sow good seed in your field? Where have the weeds come from?' **28** He answered, 'An enemy has done this.' His slaves said to him, 'Do you want us to go and pull them up?' **29** He replied, 'No, if you pull up the weeds you might uproot the wheat along with them. **30** Let them grow together until harvest;[*] then at harvest time I will say to the harvesters, "First collect the weeds and tie them in bundles for burning; but gather the wheat into my barn."'"[g]

[*] [13:24–30] This parable is peculiar to Matthew. The comparison in Mt 13:24 does not mean that the kingdom of heaven may be likened simply to the person in question but to the situation narrated in the whole story. The refusal of the householder to allow his slaves to separate the wheat from the weeds while they are still growing is a warning to the disciples not to attempt to anticipate the final judgment of God by a definitive exclusion of sinners from the kingdom. In its present stage it is composed of the good and the bad. The judgment of God alone will eliminate the sinful. Until then there must be patience and the preaching of repentance.

[*] [13:25] Weeds: darnel, a poisonous weed that in its first stage of growth resembles wheat.

[*] [13:30] Harvest: a common biblical metaphor for the time of God's judgment; cf. Jer 51:33; Jl 4:13; Hos 6:11.

g. [13:30] 3:12.

THE PARABLE OF THE MUSTARD SEED.*

31[h] He proposed another parable to them. "The kingdom of heaven is like a mustard seed that a person took and sowed in a field. **32**[*i] It is the smallest of all the seeds, yet when full-grown it is the largest of plants. It becomes a large bush, and the 'birds of the sky come and dwell in its branches.'"

* [13:31–33] See Mk 4:30–32; Lk 13:18–21. The parables of the mustard seed and the yeast illustrate the same point: the amazing contrast between the small beginnings of the kingdom and its marvelous expansion.

h. [13:31–32] Mk 4:30–32; Lk 13:18–19.

*[13:32] See Dn 4:7–9, 17–19 where the birds nesting in the tree represent the people of Nebuchadnezzar's kingdom. See also Ez 17:23; 31:6.

i. [13:32] Ez 17:23; 31:6; Dn 4:7–9, 17–19.

THE PARABLE OF THE YEAST.

33 He spoke to them another parable. "The kingdom of heaven is like yeast* that a woman took and mixed with three measures of wheat flour until the whole batch was leavened."[j]

* [13:33] Except in this Q parable and in Mt 16:12, yeast (or "leaven") is, in New Testament usage, a symbol of corruption (see Mt 16:6, 11–12; Mk 8:15; Lk 12:1; 1 Cor 5:6–8; Gal 5:9). Three measures: an enormous amount, enough to feed a hundred people. The exaggeration of this element of the parable points to the greatness of the kingdom's effect.

j. [13:33] Lk 13:20–21.

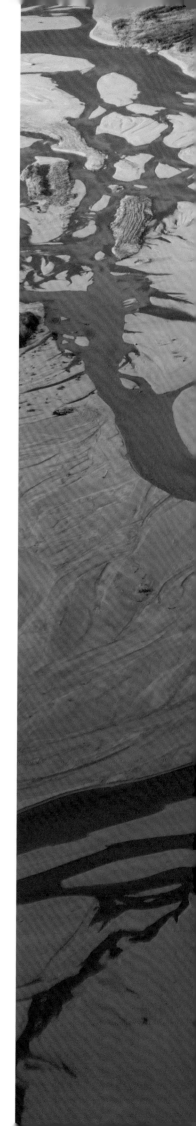

THE USE OF PARABLES.

34 ^{*k} All these things Jesus spoke to the crowds in parables. He spoke to them only in parables,[*]

35 to fulfill what had been said through the prophet:[*]

"I will open my mouth in parables,

I will announce what has lain hidden from the foundation [of the world]."^l

[*] [13:34] Only in parables: see Mt 13:10–15.

k. [13:34–35] Mk 4:33–34.

[*] [13:35] The prophet: some textual witnesses read "Isaiah the prophet." The quotation is actually from Ps 78:2; the first line corresponds to the LXX text of the psalm. The psalm's title ascribes it to Asaph, the founder of one of the guilds of temple musicians. He is called "the prophet" (NAB "the seer") in 2 Chr 29:30, but it is doubtful that Matthew averted to that; for him, any Old Testament text that could be seen as fulfilled in Jesus was prophetic.

l. [13:35] Ps 78:2.

THE EXPLANATION OF THE PARABLE OF THE WEEDS.

36 Then, dismissing the crowds,[*] he went into the house. His disciples approached him and said, "Explain to us the parable of the weeds in the field." **37** [*] He said in reply, "He who sows good seed is the Son of Man, **38** the field is the world,[*] the good seed the children of the kingdom. The weeds are the children of the evil one, **39** and the enemy who sows them is the devil. The harvest is the end of the age,[*] and the harvesters are angels. **40** Just as weeds are collected and burned [up] with fire, so will it be at the end of the age. **41** The Son of Man will send his angels, and they will collect out of his kingdom[*] all who cause others to sin and all evildoers. **42**[m] They will throw them into the fiery furnace, where there will be wailing and grinding of teeth. **43**[*n] Then the righteous will shine like the sun in the kingdom of their Father. Whoever has ears ought to hear.

[*] [13:36] Dismissing the crowds: the return of Jesus to the house marks a break with the crowds, who represent unbelieving Israel. From now on his attention is directed more and more to his disciples and to their instruction. The rest of the discourse is addressed to them alone.

[*] [13:37–43] In the explanation of the parable of the weeds emphasis lies on the fearful end of the wicked, whereas the parable itself concentrates on patience with them until judgment time.

[*] [13:38] The field is the world: this presupposes the resurrection of Jesus and the granting to him of "all power in heaven and on earth" (Mt 28:18).

[*] [13:39] The end of the age: this phrase is found only in Matthew (13:40, 49; 24:3; 28:20).

[*] [13:41] His kingdom: the kingdom of the Son of Man is distinguished from that of the Father (Mt 13:43); see 1 Cor 15:24–25. The church is the place where Jesus' kingdom is manifested, but his royal authority embraces the entire world; see note on Mt 13:38.

m. [13:42] 8:12; Rev 21:8.

[*] [13:43] See Dn 12:3.

n. [13:43] Dn 12:3.

MORE PARABLES.*

44º "The kingdom of heaven is like a treasure buried in a field,* which a person finds and hides again, and out of joy goes and sells all that he has and buys that field. **45** Again, the kingdom of heaven is like a merchant searching for fine pearls. **46** When he finds a pearl of great price, he goes and sells all that he has and buys it. **47** Again, the kingdom of heaven is like a net thrown into the sea, which collects fish of every kind. **48** When it is full they haul it ashore and sit down to put what is good into buckets. What is bad they throw away. **49** Thus it will be at the end of the age. The angels will go out and separate the wicked from the righteous **50** and throw them into the fiery furnace, where there will be wailing and grinding of teeth.

* [13:44–50] The first two of the last three parables of the discourse have the same point. The person who finds a buried treasure and the merchant who finds a pearl of great price sell all that they have to acquire these finds; similarly, the one who understands the supreme value of the kingdom gives up whatever he must to obtain it. The joy with which this is done is made explicit in the first parable, but it may be presumed in the second also. The concluding parable of the fishnet resembles the explanation of the parable of the weeds with its stress upon the final exclusion of evil persons from the kingdom.

o. [13:44–45] Prv 2:4; 4:7.

* [13:44] In the unsettled conditions of Palestine in Jesus' time, it was not unusual to guard valuables by burying them in the ground.

TREASURES NEW AND OLD.

51 "Do you understand* all these things?" They answered, "Yes." **52*** And he replied, "Then every scribe who has been instructed in the kingdom of heaven is like the head of a household who brings from his storeroom both the new and the old." **53** When Jesus finished these parables, he went away from there.

* [13:51] Matthew typically speaks of the understanding of the disciples.

* [13:52] Since Matthew tends to identify the disciples and the Twelve (see note on Mt 10:1), this saying about the Christian scribe cannot be taken as applicable to all who accept the message of Jesus. While the Twelve are in many ways representative of all who believe in him, they are also distinguished from them in certain respects. The church of Matthew has leaders among whom are a group designated as "scribes" (Mt 23:34). Like the scribes of Israel, they are teachers. It is the Twelve and these their later counterparts to whom this verse applies. The scribe…instructed in the kingdom of heaven knows both the teaching of Jesus (the new) and the law and prophets (the old) and provides in his own teaching both the new and the old as interpreted and fulfilled by the new. On the translation head of a household (for the same Greek word translated householder in Mt 13:27), see note on Mt 24:45–51.

V. JESUS, THE KINGDOM, AND THE CHURCH

THE REJECTION AT NAZARETH.

54* He came to his native place and taught the people in their synagogue.^p They were astonished* and said, "Where did this man get such wisdom and mighty deeds?^q **55** Is he not the carpenter's son? Is not his mother named Mary and his brothers James, Joseph, Simon, and Judas?^r **56** Are not his sisters all with us? Where did this man get all this?" **57** And they took offense at him. But Jesus said to them, "A prophet is not without honor except in his native place and in his own house."^s **58** And he did not work many mighty deeds there because of their lack of faith.

* [13:54–17:27] This section is the narrative part of the fourth book of the gospel.

p. [13:54–58] Mk 6:1–6; Lk 4:16–30.

* [13:54–58] After the Sermon on the Mount the crowds are in admiring astonishment at Jesus' teaching (Mt 7:28); here the astonishment is of those who take offense at him. Familiarity with his background and family leads them to regard him as pretentious. Matthew modifies his Marcan source (Mk 6:1–6). Jesus is not the carpenter but the carpenter's son (Mt 13:55), "and among his own kin" is omitted (Mt 13:57), he did not work many mighty deeds in face of such unbelief (Mt 13:58) rather than the Marcan "…he was not able to perform any mighty deed there" (Mt 6:5), and there is no mention of his amazement at his townspeople's lack of faith.

q. [13:54] 2:23; Jn 1:46; 7:15.

r. [13:55] 12:46; 27:56; Jn 6:42.

s. [13:57] Jn 4:44.

MATTHEW CHAPTER 14

HEROD'S OPINION OF JESUS.

1 [*][a] At that time Herod the tetrarch [*][b] heard of the reputation of Jesus[c] **2** and said to his servants, "This man is John the Baptist. He has been raised from the dead; that is why mighty powers are at work in him."

[*] [14:1–12] The murder of the Baptist by Herod Antipas prefigures the death of Jesus (see Mt 17:12). The Marcan source (Mk 6:14–29) is much reduced and in some points changed. In Mark Herod reveres John as a holy man and the desire to kill him is attributed to Herodias (Mk 6:19, 20), whereas here that desire is Herod's from the beginning (Mt 14:5).

a. [14:1–12] Mk 6:14–29.

[*] [14:1] Herod the tetrarch: Herod Antipas, son of Herod the Great. When the latter died, his territory was divided among three of his surviving sons, Archelaus who received half of it (Mt 2:23), Herod Antipas who became ruler of Galilee and Perea, and Philip who became ruler of northern Transjordan. Since he received a quarter of his father's domain, Antipas is accurately designated tetrarch ("ruler of a fourth [part]"), although in Mt 14:9 Matthew repeats the "king" of his Marcan source (Mk 6:26).

b. [14:1–2] Lk 9:7–9.

c. [14:1] Lk 3:1.

THE DEATH OF JOHN THE BAPTIST.

3 Now Herod had arrested John, bound [him], and put him in prison on account of Herodias, the wife of his brother Philip, 4ᵉ for John had said to him, "It is not lawful for you to have her." 5ᶠ Although he wanted to kill him, he feared the people, for they regarded him as a prophet. 6 But at a birthday celebration for Herod, the daughter of Herodias performed a dance before the guests and delighted Herod 7 so much that he swore to give her whatever she might ask for. 8 Prompted by her mother, she said, "Give me here on a platter the head of John the Baptist." 9 The king was distressed, but because of his oaths and the guests who were present, he ordered that it be given, 10 and he had John beheaded in the prison. 11 His head was brought in on a platter and given to the girl, who took it to her mother. 12 His disciples came and took away the corpse and buried him; and they went and told Jesus.

THE RETURN OF THE TWELVE AND THE FEEDING OF THE FIVE THOUSAND*

13^g When Jesus heard of it, he withdrew in a boat to a deserted place by himself. The crowds heard of this and followed him on foot from their towns. **14** When he disembarked and saw the vast crowd, his heart was moved with pity for them, and he cured their sick. **15** When it was evening, the disciples approached him and said, "This is a deserted place and it is already late; dismiss the crowds so that they can go to the villages and buy food for themselves." **16** [Jesus] said to them, "There is no need for them to go away; give them some food yourselves." **17** But they said to him, "Five loaves and two fish are all we have here." **18** Then he said, "Bring them here to me," **19** and he ordered the crowds to sit down on the grass. Taking* the five loaves and the two fish, and looking up to heaven, he said the blessing, broke the loaves, and gave them to the disciples, who in turn gave them to the crowds. **20** They all ate and were satisfied, and they picked up the fragments left over* —twelve wicker baskets full. **21** Those who ate were about five thousand men, not counting women and children.

---

* [14:13–21] The feeding of the five thousand is the only miracle of Jesus that is recounted in all four gospels. The principal reason for that may be that it was seen as anticipating the Eucharist and the final banquet in the kingdom (Mt 8:11; 26:29), but it looks not only forward but backward, to the feeding of Israel with manna in the desert at the time of the Exodus (Ex 16), a miracle that in some contemporary Jewish expectation would be repeated in the messianic age (2 Bar 29:8). It may also be meant to recall Elisha's feeding a hundred men with small provisions (2 Kgs 4:42–44).

g. [14:13–21] 15:32–38; Mk 6:32–44; Lk 9:10–17; Jn 6:1–13.

* [14:19] The taking, saying the blessing, breaking, and giving to the disciples correspond to the actions of Jesus over the bread at the Last Supper (Mt 26:26). Since they were usual at any Jewish meal, that correspondence does not necessarily indicate a eucharistic reference here. Matthew's silence about Jesus' dividing the fish among the people (Mk 6:41) is perhaps more significant in that regard.

* [14:20] The fragments left over: as in Elisha's miracle, food was left over after all had been fed. The word fragments (Greek klasmata) is used, in the singular, of the broken bread of the Eucharist in Didache 9:3–4.

22[h] Then he made the disciples get into the boat and precede him to the other side, while he dismissed the crowds. **23**[i] After doing so, he went up on the mountain by himself to pray. When it was evening he was there alone. **24** Meanwhile the boat, already a few miles offshore, was being tossed about by the waves, for the wind was against it. **25** During the fourth watch of the night,[*] he came toward them, walking on the sea. **26** When the disciples saw him walking on the sea they were terrified. "It is a ghost," they said, and they cried out in fear. **27** At once [Jesus] spoke to them, "Take courage, it is I;[*] do not be afraid." **28** Peter said to him in reply, "Lord, if it is you, command me to come to you on the water." **29** He said, "Come." Peter got out of the boat and began to walk on the water toward Jesus. **30**[j] But when he saw how [strong] the wind was he became frightened; and, beginning to sink, he cried out, "Lord, save me!" **31** Immediately Jesus stretched out his hand and caught him, and said to him, "O you of little faith,[*] why did you doubt?" **32** After they got into the boat, the wind died down. **33**[*k] Those who were in the boat did him homage, saying, "Truly, you are the Son of God."

[*] [14:22–33] The disciples, laboring against the turbulent sea, are saved by Jesus. For his power over the waters, see note on Mt 8:26. Here that power is expressed also by his walking on the sea (Mt 14:25; cf. Ps 77:20; Jb 9:8). Matthew has inserted into the Marcan story (Mk 6:45–52) material that belongs to his special traditions on Peter (Mt 14:28–31).

h. [14:22–33] Mk 6:45–52; Jn 6:16–21.

i. [14:23] Mk 1:35; Lk 5:16; 6:12.

[*] [14:25] The fourth watch of the night: between 3 a.m. and 6 a.m. The Romans divided the twelve hours between 6 p.m. and 6 a.m. into four equal parts called "watches."

[*] [14:27] It is I: see note on Mk 6:50.

j. [14:30–31] 8:25–26.

[*] [14:31] You of little faith: see note on Mt 6:30. Why did you doubt?: the verb is peculiar to Matthew and occurs elsewhere only in Mt 28:17.

[*] [14:33] This confession is in striking contrast to the Marcan parallel (Mk 6:51) where the disciples are "completely astounded."

k. [14:33] 16:16.

THE
WALKING
ON THE WATER.*

THE HEALINGS
AT GENNESARET.

34^l After making the crossing, they came to land at Gennesaret. **35** When the men of that place recognized him, they sent word to all the surrounding country. People brought to him all those who were sick **36**^m and begged him that they might touch only the tassel on his cloak, and as many as touched it were healed.

l. [14:34–36] Mk 6:53–56.

m. [14:36] 9:20–22.

MATTHEW CHAPTER 15

THE TRADITION OF THE ELDERS.*

1[a] Then Pharisees and scribes came to Jesus from Jerusalem and said, 2[b] "Why do your disciples break the tradition of the elders?* They do not wash [their] hands when they eat a meal." 3 He said to them in reply, "And why do you break the commandment of God* for the sake of your tradition? 4[c] For God said, 'Honor your father and your mother,' and 'Whoever curses father or mother shall die.' 5* But you say, 'Whoever says to father or mother, "Any support you might have had from me is dedicated to God," 6 need not honor his father.' You have nullified the word of God for the sake of your tradition. 7 Hypocrites, well did Isaiah prophesy about you when he said:

8[d] 'This people honors me with their lips,*

but their hearts are far from me;

9[e] in vain do they worship me,

teaching as doctrines human precepts.'"

10[f] He summoned the crowd and said to them, "Hear and understand. 11 It is not what enters one's mouth that defiles that person; but what comes out of the mouth is what defiles one." 12 Then his disciples approached and said to him, "Do you know that the Pharisees took offense when they heard what you said?" 13 He said in reply,* "Every plant that my heavenly Father has not planted will be uprooted. 14[g] Let them alone; they are blind guides [of the blind]. If a blind person leads a blind person, both will fall into a pit." 15 Then Peter* said to him in reply, "Explain [this] parable to us." 16 He said to them, "Are even you still without understanding? 17 Do you not realize that everything that enters the mouth passes into the stomach and is expelled into the latrine? 18[h] But the things that come out of the mouth come from the heart, and they defile. 19* For from the heart come evil thoughts, murder, adultery, unchastity, theft, false witness, blasphemy. 20 These are what defile a person, but to eat with unwashed hands does not defile."

* [15:1–20] This dispute begins with the question of the Pharisees and scribes why Jesus' disciples are breaking the tradition of the elders about washing one's hands before eating (Mt 15:2). Jesus' counterquestion accuses his opponents of breaking the commandment of God for the sake of their tradition (Mt 15:3) and illustrates this by their interpretation of the commandment of the Decalogue concerning parents (Mt 15:4–6). Denouncing them as hypocrites, he applies to them a derogatory prophecy of Isaiah (Mt 15:7–8). Then with a wider audience (the crowd, Mt 15:10) he goes beyond the violation of tradition with which the dispute has started. The parable (Mt 15:11) is an attack on the Mosaic law concerning clean and unclean foods, similar to those antitheses that abrogate the law (Mt 5:31–32, 33–34, 38–39). After a warning to his disciples not to follow the moral guidance of the Pharisees (Mt 15:13–14), he explains the parable (Mt 15:15) to them, saying that defilement comes not from what enters the mouth (Mt 15:17) but from the evil thoughts and deeds that rise from within, from the heart (Mt 15:18–20). The last verse returns to the starting point of the dispute (eating with unwashed hands). Because of Matthew's omission of Mk 7:19b, some scholars think that Matthew has weakened the Marcan repudiation of the Mosaic food laws. But that half verse is ambiguous in the Greek, which may be the reason for its omission here.

a. [15:1–20] Mk 7:1–23.

b. [15:2] Lk 11:38.

* [15:2] The tradition of the elders: see note on Mk 7:5. The purpose of the handwashing was to remove defilement caused by contact with what was ritually unclean.

* [15:3–4] For the commandment see Ex 20:12 (//Dt 5:16); 21:17. The honoring of one's parents had to do with supporting them in their needs.

c. [15:4] Ex 20:12; 21:17; Lv 20:9; Dt 5:16; Prv 20:20.

* [15:5] See note on Mk 7:11.

d. [15:8] Is 29:13 LXX.

* [15:8] The text of Is 29:13 is quoted approximately according to the Septuagint.

e. [15:9] Col 2:23.

f. [15:10] Mk 7:14.

* [15:13–14] Jesus leads his disciples away from the teaching authority of the Pharisees.

g. [15:14] 23:16, 19, 24; Lk 6:39; Jn 9:40.

* [15:15] Matthew specifies Peter as the questioner, unlike Mk 7:17. Given his tendency to present the disciples as more understanding than in his Marcan source, it is noteworthy that here he retains the Marcan rebuke, although in a slightly milder form. This may be due to his wish to correct the Jewish Christians within his church who still held to the food laws and thus separated themselves from Gentile Christians who did not observe them.

h. [15:18] 12:34.

* [15:19] The Marcan list of thirteen things that defile (Mk 7:21–22) is here reduced to seven that partially cover the content of the Decalogue.

THE CANAANITE WOMAN'S FAITH.*

21[i] Then Jesus went from that place and withdrew to the region of Tyre and Sidon. 22 And behold, a Canaanite woman of that district came and called out, "Have pity on me, Lord, Son of David! My daughter is tormented by a demon." 23 But he did not say a word in answer to her. His disciples came and asked him, "Send her away, for she keeps calling out after us." 24* He said in reply, "I was sent only to the lost sheep of the house of Israel." 25[j] But the woman came and did him homage, saying, "Lord, help me." 26 He said in reply, "It is not right to take the food of the children* and throw it to the dogs." 27 She said, "Please, Lord, for even the dogs eat the scraps that fall from the table of their masters." 28[k] Then Jesus said to her in reply, "O woman, great is your faith!* Let it be done for you as you wish." And her daughter was healed from that hour.

* [15:21–28] See note on Mt 8:5–13.

i. [15:21–28] Mk 7:24–30.

* [15:24] See note on Mt 10:5–6.

j. [15:25] 10:6.

* [15:26] The children: the people of Israel. Dogs: see note on Mt 7:6.

k. [15:28] 8:10.

* [15:28] As in the case of the cure of the centurion's servant (Mt 8:10), Matthew ascribes Jesus' granting the request to the woman's great faith, a point not made equally explicit in the Marcan parallel (Mk 7:24–30).

THE HEALING OF MANY PEOPLE.

29 Moving on from there Jesus walked by the Sea of Galilee, went up on the mountain, and sat down there. **30**[1] Great crowds came to him, having with them the lame, the blind, the deformed, the mute, and many others. They placed them at his feet, and he cured them. **31** The crowds were amazed when they saw the mute speaking, the deformed made whole, the lame walking, and the blind able to see, and they glorified the God of Israel.

I. [15:30] Is 35:5–6.

THE FEEDING OF THE FOUR THOUSAND.*

32[m] Jesus summoned his disciples and said, "My heart is moved with pity for the crowd, for they have been with me now for three days and have nothing to eat. I do not want to send them away hungry, for fear they may collapse on the way." **33** The disciples said to him, "Where could we ever get enough bread in this deserted place to satisfy such a crowd?" **34** Jesus said to them, "How many loaves do you have?" "Seven," they replied, "and a few fish." **35** He ordered the crowd to sit down on the ground. **36** Then he took the seven loaves and the fish, gave thanks,[*] broke the loaves, and gave them to the disciples, who in turn gave them to the crowds. **37**[n] They all ate and were satisfied. They picked up the fragments left over—seven baskets full. **38** Those who ate were four thousand men, not counting women and children. **39** And when he had dismissed the crowds, he got into the boat and came to the district of Magadan.

[*] [15:32–39] Most probably this story is a doublet of that of the feeding of the five thousand (Mt 14:13–21). It differs from it notably only in that Jesus takes the initiative, not the disciples (Mt 15:32), and in the numbers: the crowd has been with Jesus three days (Mt 15:32), seven loaves are multiplied (Mt 15:36), seven baskets of fragments remain after the feeding (Mt 15:37), and four thousand men are fed (Mt 15:38).

m. [15:32–39] Mk 8:1–10.

[*] [15:36] Gave thanks: see Mt 14:19, "said the blessing." There is no difference in meaning. The thanksgiving was a blessing of God for his benefits.

n. [15:37] 16:10.

MATTHEW CHAPTER 16

THE DEMAND FOR A SIGN.

1 ^{*a} The Pharisees and Sadducees came and, to test him, asked him to show them a sign from heaven. **2**[*] He said to them in reply, "[In the evening you say, 'Tomorrow will be fair, for the sky is red'; **3**^b and, in the morning, 'Today will be stormy, for the sky is red and threatening.' You know how to judge the appearance of the sky, but you cannot judge the signs of the times.] **4**^c An evil and unfaithful generation seeks a sign, but no sign will be given it except the sign of Jonah."[*] Then he left them and went away.

* [16:1] A sign from heaven: see note on Mt 12:38–42.

a. [16:1–10] Mk 8:11–21.

* [16:2–3] The answer of Jesus in these verses is omitted in many important textual witnesses, and it is very uncertain that it is an original part of this gospel. It resembles Lk 12:54–56 and may have been inserted from there. It rebukes the Pharisees and Sadducees who are able to read indications of coming weather but not the indications of the coming kingdom in the signs that Jesus does offer, his mighty deeds and teaching.

b. [16:3] Lk 12:54–56.

c. [16:4] 12:39; Jon 2:1.

* [16:4] See notes on Mt 12:39, 40.

THE LEAVEN OF THE PHARISEES AND SADDUCEES.

5^d In coming to the other side of the sea,[*] the disciples had forgotten to bring bread. **6**^e Jesus said to them, "Look out, and beware of the leaven[*] of the Pharisees and Sadducees." **7**[*] They concluded among themselves, saying, "It is because we have brought no bread." **8** When Jesus became aware of this he said, "You of little faith, why do you conclude among yourselves that it is because you have no bread? **9**^f Do you not yet understand, and do you not remember the five loaves for the five thousand, and how many wicker baskets you took up? **10**^g Or the seven loaves for the four thousand, and how many baskets you took up? **11** How do you not comprehend that I was not speaking to you about bread? Beware of the leaven of the Pharisees and Sadducees." **12** Then they understood[*] that he was not telling them to beware of the leaven of bread, but of the teaching of the Pharisees and Sadducees.

d. [16:5–12] Mk 8:14–21.

[*] [16:5–12] Jesus' warning his disciples against the teaching of the Pharisees and Sadducees comes immediately before his promise to confer on Peter the authority to bind and to loose on earth (Mt 16:19), an authority that will be confirmed in heaven. Such authority most probably has to do, at least in part, with teaching. The rejection of the teaching authority of the Pharisees (see also Mt 12:12–14) prepares for a new one derived from Jesus.

e. [16:6] Lk 12:1.

[*] [16:6] Leaven: see note on Mt 13:33. Sadducees: Matthew's Marcan source speaks rather of "the leaven of Herod" (Mk 8:15).

[*] [16:7–11] The disciples, men of little faith, misunderstand Jesus' metaphorical use of leaven, forgetting that, as the feeding of the crowds shows, he is not at a loss to provide them with bread.

f. [16:9] 14:17–21; Jn 6:9.

g. [16:10] 15:34–38.

[*] [16:12] After his rebuke, the disciples understand that by leaven he meant the corrupting influence of the teaching of the Pharisees and Sadducees. The evangelist probably understands this teaching as common to both groups. Since at the time of Jesus' ministry the two differed widely on points of teaching, e.g., the resurrection of the dead, and at the time of the evangelist the Sadducee party was no longer a force in Judaism, the supposed common teaching fits neither period. The disciples' eventual understanding of Jesus' warning contrasts with their continuing obtuseness in the Marcan parallel (Mk 8:14–21).

PETER'S CONFESSION ABOUT JESUS.[*]

13[h] When Jesus went into the region of Caesarea Philippi[*] he asked his disciples, "Who do people say that the Son of Man is?" **14**[i] They replied, "Some say John the Baptist,[*] others Elijah, still others Jeremiah or one of the prophets." **15** He said to them, "But who do you say that I am?" **16**[*j] Simon Peter said in reply, "You are the Messiah, the Son of the living God." **17** Jesus said to him in reply, "Blessed are you, Simon son of Jonah. For flesh and blood[*] has not revealed this to you, but my heavenly Father. **18**[k] And so I say to you, you are Peter, and upon this rock I will build my church,[*] and the gates of the netherworld shall not prevail against it. **19**[l] I will give you the keys to the kingdom of heaven.[*] Whatever you bind on earth shall be bound in heaven; and whatever you loose on earth shall be loosed in heaven." **20**[*m] Then he strictly ordered his disciples to tell no one that he was the Messiah.

* [16:13–20] The Marcan confession of Jesus as Messiah, made by Peter as spokesman for the other disciples (Mk 8:27–29; cf. also Lk 9:18–20), is modified significantly here. The confession is of Jesus both as Messiah and as Son of the living God (Mt 16:16). Jesus' response, drawn principally from material peculiar to Matthew, attributes the confession to a divine revelation granted to Peter alone (Mt 16:17) and makes him the rock on which Jesus will build his church (Mt 16:18) and the disciple whose authority in the church on earth will be confirmed in heaven, i.e., by God (Mt 16:19).

h. [16:13–16] Mk 8:27–29; Lk 9:18–20.

* [16:13] Caesarea Philippi: situated about twenty miles north of the Sea of Galilee in the territory ruled by Philip, a son of Herod the Great, tetrarch from 4 B.C. until his death in A.D. 34 (see note on Mt 14:1). He rebuilt the town of Paneas, naming it Caesarea in honor of the emperor, and Philippi ("of Philip") to distinguish it from the seaport in Samaria that was also called Caesarea. Who do people say that the Son of Man is?: although the question differs from the Marcan parallel (Mk 8:27: "Who…that I am?"), the meaning is the same, for Jesus here refers to himself as the Son of Man (cf. Mt 16:15).

i. [16:14] 14:2.

* [16:14] John the Baptist: see Mt 14:2. Elijah: cf. Mal 3:23–24; Sir 48:10; and see note on Mt 3:4. Jeremiah: an addition of Matthew to the Marcan source.

* [16:16] The Son of the living God: see Mt 2:15; 3:17. The addition of this exalted title to the Marcan confession eliminates whatever ambiguity was attached to the title Messiah. This, among other things, supports the view proposed by many scholars that Matthew has here combined his source's confession with a post-resurrectional confession of faith in Jesus as Son of the living God that belonged to the appearance of the risen Jesus to Peter; cf. 1 Cor 15:5; Lk 24:34.

j. [16:16] Jn 6:69.

* [16:17] Flesh and blood: a Semitic expression for human beings, especially in their weakness. Has not revealed this…but my heavenly Father: that Peter's faith is spoken of as coming not through human means but through a revelation from God is similar to Paul's description of his recognition of who Jesus was; see Gal 1:15–16, "…when he [God]…was pleased to reveal his Son to me…."

k. [16:18] Jn 1:42.

* [16:18] You are Peter, and upon this rock I will build my church: the Aramaic word kēpā' meaning rock and transliterated into Greek as Kēphas is the name by which Peter is called in the Pauline letters (1 Cor 1:12; 3:22; 9:5;

15:4; Gal 1:18; 2:9, 11, 14) except in Gal 2:7–8 ("Peter"). It is translated as Petros ("Peter") in Jn 1:42. The presumed original Aramaic of Jesus' statement would have been, in English, "You are the Rock (Kēpā') and upon this rock (kēpā') I will build my church." The Greek text probably means the same, for the difference in gender between the masculine noun petros, the disciple's new name, and the feminine noun petra (rock) may be due simply to the unsuitability of using a feminine noun as the proper name of a male. Although the two words were generally used with slightly different nuances, they were also used interchangeably with the same meaning, "rock." Church: this word (Greek ekklēsia) occurs in the gospels only here and in Mt 18:17 (twice). There are several possibilities for an Aramaic original. Jesus' church means the community that he will gather and that, like a building, will have Peter as its solid foundation. That function of Peter consists in his being witness to Jesus as the Messiah, the Son of the living God. The gates of the netherworld shall not prevail against it: the netherworld (Greek Hadēs, the abode of the dead) is conceived of as a walled city whose gates will not close in upon the church of Jesus, i.e., it will not be overcome by the power of death.

l. [16:19] Is 22:22; Rev 3:7.

* [16:19] The keys to the kingdom of heaven: the image of the keys is probably drawn from Is 22:15–25 where Eliakim, who succeeds Shebna as master of the palace, is given "the key of the House of David," which he authoritatively "opens" and "shuts" (Is 22:22). Whatever you bind…loosed in heaven: there are many instances in rabbinic literature of the binding-loosing imagery. Of the several meanings given there to the metaphor, two are of special importance here: the giving of authoritative teaching, and the lifting or imposing of the ban of excommunication. It is disputed whether the image of the keys and that of binding and loosing are different metaphors meaning the same thing. In any case, the promise of the keys is given to Peter alone. In Mt 18:18 all the disciples are given the power of binding and loosing, but the context of that verse suggests that there the power of excommunication alone is intended. That the keys are those to the kingdom of heaven and that Peter's exercise of authority in the church on earth will be confirmed in heaven show an intimate connection between, but not an identification of, the church and the kingdom of heaven.

* [16:20] Cf. Mk 8:30. Matthew makes explicit that the prohibition has to do with speaking of Jesus as the Messiah; see note on Mk 8:27–30.

m. [16:20] Mk 8:30; Lk 9:21.

THE FIRST PREDICTION OF THE PASSION.*

21[n] From that time on, Jesus began to show his disciples that he* must go to Jerusalem and suffer greatly from the elders, the chief priests, and the scribes, and be killed and on the third day be raised.[o] **22*** Then Peter took him aside and began to rebuke him, "God forbid, Lord! No such thing shall ever happen to you." **23**[p] He turned and said to Peter, "Get behind me, Satan! You are an obstacle to me. You are thinking not as God does, but as human beings do."

* [16:21–23] This first prediction of the passion follows Mk 8:31–33 in the main and serves as a corrective to an understanding of Jesus' messiahship as solely one of glory and triumph. By his addition of from that time on (Mt 16:21) Matthew has emphasized that Jesus' revelation of his coming suffering and death marks a new phase of the gospel. Neither this nor the two later passion predictions (Mt 17:22–23; 20:17–19) can be taken as sayings that, as they stand, go back to Jesus himself. However, it is probable that he foresaw that his mission would entail suffering and perhaps death, but was confident that he would ultimately be vindicated by God (see Mt 26:29).

n. [16:21–28] Mk 8:31–9:1; Lk 9:22–27.

* [16:21] He: the Marcan parallel (Mk 8:31) has "the Son of Man." Since Matthew has already designated Jesus by that title (Mt 15:13), its omission here is not significant. The Matthean prediction is equally about the sufferings of the Son of Man. Must: this necessity is part of the tradition of all the synoptics; cf. Mk 8:31; Lk 9:21. The elders, the chief priests, and the scribes: see note on Mk 8:31. On the third day: so also Lk 9:22, against the Marcan "after three days" (Mk 8:31). Matthew's formulation is, in the Greek, almost identical with the pre-Pauline fragment of the kerygma in 1 Cor 15:4 and also with Hos 6:2, which many take to be the Old Testament background to the confession that Jesus was raised on the third day. Josephus uses "after three days" and "on the third day" interchangeably (Antiquities 7:280–81; 8:214, 218) and there is probably no difference in meaning between the two phrases.

o. [16:21] 17:22–23; 20:17–19.

* [16:22–23] Peter's refusal to accept Jesus' predicted suffering and death is seen as a satanic attempt to deflect Jesus from his God-appointed course, and the disciple is addressed in terms that recall Jesus' dismissal of the devil in the temptation account (Mt 4:10: "Get away, Satan!"). Peter's satanic purpose is emphasized by Matthew's addition to the Marcan source of the words You are an obstacle to me.

p. [16:23] 4:10.

THE CONDITIONS OF DISCIPLESHIP.*

24[q] Then Jesus said to his disciples, "Whoever wishes to come after me must deny himself,* take up his cross, and follow me. 25[r] For whoever wishes to save his life will lose it, but whoever loses his life for my sake will find it.* 26 What profit would there be for one to gain the whole world and forfeit his life? Or what can one give in exchange for his life? 27*[s] For the Son of Man will come with his angels in his Father's glory, and then he will repay everyone according to his conduct. 28* Amen, I say to you, there are some standing here who will not taste death until they see the Son of Man coming in his kingdom."

* [16:24–28] A readiness to follow Jesus even to giving up one's life for him is the condition for true discipleship; this will be repaid by him at the final judgment.

q. [16:24] Lk 14:27.

* [16:24] Deny himself: to deny someone is to disown him (see Mt 10:33; 26:34–35) and to deny oneself is to disown oneself as the center of one's existence.

r. [16:25] Lk 17:33; Jn 12:25.

* [16:25] See notes on Mt 10:38, 39.

* [16:27] The parousia and final judgment are described in Mt 25:31 in terms almost identical with these.

s. [16:27] 25:31–33; Jb 34:11; Ps 62:13; Jer 17:10; 2 Thes 1:7–8.

* [16:28] Coming in his kingdom: since the kingdom of the Son of Man has been described as "the world" and Jesus' sovereignty precedes his final coming in glory (Mt 13:38, 41), the coming in this verse is not the parousia as in the preceding but the manifestation of Jesus' rule after his resurrection; see notes on Mt 13:38, 41.

MATTHEW CHAPTER 17

THE TRANSFIG-RATION OF JESUS.*

1[a] After six days Jesus took Peter, James, and John his brother, and led them up a high mountain by themselves.[*] 2[*][b] And he was transfigured before them; his face shone like the sun and his clothes became white as light. 3[*] And behold, Moses and Elijah appeared to them, conversing with him. 4 Then Peter said to Jesus in reply, "Lord, it is good that we are here. If you wish, I will make three tents[*] here, one for you, one for Moses, and one for Elijah." 5[c] While he was still speaking, behold, a bright cloud cast a shadow over them,[*] then from the cloud came a voice that said, "This is my beloved Son, with whom I am well pleased; listen to him." 6[*] When the disciples heard this, they fell prostrate and were very much afraid. 7 But Jesus came and touched them, saying, "Rise, and do not be afraid." 8 And when the disciples raised their eyes, they saw no one else but Jesus alone.

[*] [17:1–8] The account of the transfiguration confirms that Jesus is the Son of God (Mt 17:5) and points to fulfillment of the prediction that he will come in his Father's glory at the end of the age (Mt 16:27). It has been explained by some as a resurrection appearance retrojected into the time of Jesus' ministry, but that is not probable since the account lacks many of the usual elements of the resurrection-appearance narratives. It draws upon motifs from the Old Testament and noncanonical Jewish apocalyptic literature that express the presence of the heavenly and the divine, e.g., brilliant light, white garments, and the overshadowing cloud.

a. [17:1–8] Mk 9:2–8; Lk 9:28–36.

[*] [17:1] These three disciples are also taken apart from the others by Jesus in Gethsemane (Mt 26:37). A high mountain: this has been identified with Tabor or Hermon, but probably no specific mountain was intended by the evangelist or by his Marcan source (Mk 9:2). Its meaning is theological rather than geographical, possibly recalling the revelation to Moses on Mount Sinai (Ex 24:12–18) and to Elijah at the same place (1 Kgs 19:8–18; Horeb = Sinai).

[*] [17:2] His face shone like the sun: this is a Matthean addition; cf. Dn 10:6. His clothes became white as light: cf. Dn 7:9, where the clothing of God appears "snow bright." For the white garments of other heavenly beings, see Rev 4:4; 7:9; 19:14.

b. [17:2] 28:3; Dn 7:9; 10:6; Rev 4:4; 7:9; 19:14.

[*] [17:3] See note on Mk 9:5.

[*] [17:4] Three tents: the booths in which the Israelites lived during the feast of Tabernacles (cf. Jn 7:2) were meant to recall their ancestors' dwelling in booths during the journey from Egypt to the promised land (Lv 23:39–42). The same Greek word, skēnē, here translated tents, is used in the LXX for the booths of that feast, and some scholars have suggested that there is an allusion here to that liturgical custom.

c. [17:5] 3:17; Dt 18:15; 2 Pt 1:17.

[*] [17:5] Cloud cast a shadow over them: see note on Mk 9:7. This is my beloved Son…listen to him: cf. Mt 3:17. The voice repeats the baptismal proclamation about Jesus, with the addition of the command listen to him. The latter is a reference to Dt 18:15 in which the Israelites are commanded to listen to the prophet like Moses whom God will raise up for them. The command to listen to Jesus is general, but in this context it probably applies particularly to the preceding predictions of his passion and resurrection (Mt 16:21) and of his coming (Mt 16:27, 28).

[*] [17:6–7] A Matthean addition; cf. Dn 10:9–10, 18–19.

THE COMING OF ELIJAH. *

9^d As they were coming down from the mountain, Jesus charged them, "Do not tell the vision[*] to anyone until the Son of Man has been raised from the dead." **10**^{*e} Then the disciples asked him, "Why do the scribes say that Elijah must come first?" **11**^f He said in reply,[*] "Elijah will indeed come and restore all things; **12**^g but I tell you that Elijah has already come, and they did not recognize him but did to him whatever they pleased. So also will the Son of Man suffer at their hands." **13**[*] Then the disciples understood that he was speaking to them of John the Baptist.

THE HEALING OF A BOY WITH A DEMON.*

14[h] When they came to the crowd a man approached, knelt down before him, **15** and said, "Lord, have pity on my son, for he is a lunatic* and suffers severely; often he falls into fire, and often into water. **16** I brought him to your disciples, but they could not cure him." **17**[i] Jesus said in reply, "O faithless and perverse* generation, how long will I be with you? How long will I endure you? Bring him here to me." **18** Jesus rebuked him and the demon came out of him,* and from that hour the boy was cured. **19** Then the disciples approached Jesus in private and said, "Why could we not drive it out?" **20**[*j] He said to them, "Because of your little faith. Amen, I say to you, if you have faith the size of a mustard seed, you will say to this mountain, 'Move from here to there,' and it will move. Nothing will be impossible for you." [**21**]*

* [17:14–20] Matthew has greatly shortened the Marcan story (Mk 9:14–29). Leaving aside several details of the boy's illness, he concentrates on the need for faith, not so much on the part of the boy's father (as does Mark, for Matthew omits Mk 9:22b–24) but on that of his own disciples whose inability to drive out the demon is ascribed to their little faith (Mt 17:20).

h. [17:14–21] Mk 9:14–29; Lk 9:37–43.

* [17:15] A lunatic: this description of the boy is peculiar to Matthew. The word occurs in the New Testament only here and in Mt 4:24 and means one affected or struck by the moon. The symptoms of the boy's illness point to epilepsy, and attacks of this were thought to be caused by phases of the moon.

i. [17:17] Dt 32:5 LXX.

* [17:17] Faithless and perverse: so Matthew and Luke (Lk 9:41) against Mark's faithless (Mk 9:19). The Greek word here translated perverse is the same as that in Dt 32:5 LXX, where Moses speaks to his people. There is a problem in knowing to whom the reproach is addressed. Since the Matthean Jesus normally chides his disciples for their little faith (as in Mt 17:20), it would appear that the charge of lack of faith could not be made against them and that the reproach is addressed to unbelievers among the Jews. However in Mt 17:20b (if you have faith the size of a mustard seed), which is certainly addressed to the disciples, they appear to have not even the smallest faith; if they had, they would have been able to cure the boy. In the light of Mt 17:20b the reproach of Mt 17:17 could have applied to the disciples. There seems to be an inconsistency between the charge of little faith in Mt 17:20a and that of not even a little in Mt 17:20b.

* [17:18] The demon came out of him: not until this verse does Matthew indicate that the boy's illness is a case of demoniacal possession.

* [17:20] The entire verse is an addition of Matthew who (according to the better attested text) omits the reason given for the disciples' inability in Mk 9:29. Little faith: see note on Mt 6:30. Faith the size of a mustard seed…and it will move: a combination of a Q saying (cf. Lk 17:6) with a Marcan saying (cf. Mk 11:23).

j. [17:20] 21:21; Lk 17:6; 1 Cor 13:2.

* [17:21] Some manuscripts add, "But this kind does not come out except by prayer and fasting"; this is a variant of the better reading of Mk 9:29.

22[k] As they were gathering in Galilee, Jesus said to them, "The Son of Man is to be handed over to men, **23** and they will kill him, and he will be raised on the third day." And they were overwhelmed with grief.

* [17:22–23] The second passion prediction (cf. Mt 16:21–23) is the least detailed of the three and may be the earliest. In the Marcan parallel the disciples do not understand (Mk 9:32); here they understand and are overwhelmed with grief at the prospect of Jesus' death (Mt 17:23).

k. [17:22–23] 16:21; 20:18–19.

THE SECOND PREDICTION OF THE PASSION.*

PAYMENT
OF THE
TEMPLE TAX.*

24[1] When they came to Capernaum, the collectors of the temple tax[*] approached Peter and said, "Doesn't your teacher pay the temple tax?" **25** "Yes," he said.[*] When he came into the house, before he had time to speak, Jesus asked him, "What is your opinion, Simon? From whom do the kings of the earth take tolls or census tax? From their subjects or from foreigners?" **26**[*] When he said, "From foreigners," Jesus said to him, "Then the subjects are exempt. **27** But that we may not offend them,[*] go to the sea, drop in a hook, and take the first fish that comes up. Open its mouth and you will find a coin worth twice the temple tax. Give that to them for me and for you."

[*] [17:24–27] Like Mt 14:28–31 and Mt 16:16b–19, this episode comes from Matthew's special material on Peter. Although the question of the collectors concerns Jesus' payment of the temple tax, it is put to Peter. It is he who receives instruction from Jesus about freedom from the obligation of payment and yet why it should be made. The means of doing so is provided miraculously. The pericope deals with a problem of Matthew's church, whether its members should pay the temple tax, and the answer is given through a word of Jesus conveyed to Peter. Some scholars see here an example of the teaching authority of Peter exercised in the name of Jesus (see Mt 16:19). The specific problem was a Jewish Christian one and may have arisen when the Matthean church was composed largely of that group.

l. [17:24] Ex 30:11–16; Neh 10:33.

[*] [17:24] The temple tax: before the destruction of the Jerusalem temple in A.D. 70 every male Jew above nineteen years of age was obliged to make an annual contribution to its upkeep (cf. Ex 30:11–16; Neh 10:33). After the destruction the Romans imposed upon Jews the obligation of paying that tax for the temple of Jupiter Capitolinus. There is disagreement about which period the story deals with.

[*] [17:25] From their subjects or from foreigners?: the Greek word here translated subjects literally means "sons."

[*] [17:26] Then the subjects are exempt: just as subjects are not bound by laws applying to foreigners, neither are Jesus and his disciples, who belong to the kingdom of heaven, bound by the duty of paying the temple tax imposed on those who are not of the kingdom. If the Greek is translated "sons," the freedom of Jesus, the Son of God, and of his disciples, children ("sons") of the kingdom (cf. Mt 13:38), is even more clear.

[*] [17:27] That we may not offend them: though they are exempt (Mt 17:26), Jesus and his disciples are to avoid giving offense; therefore the tax is to be paid. A coin worth twice the temple tax: literally, "a stater," a Greek coin worth two double drachmas. Two double drachmas were equal to the Jewish shekel and the tax was a half-shekel. For me and for you: not only Jesus but Peter pays the tax, and this example serves as a standard for the conduct of all the disciples.

MATTHEW CHAPTER 18 *

* [18:1–35] This discourse of the fourth book of the gospel is often called the "church order" discourse, but it lacks most of the considerations usually connected with church order, such as various offices in the church and the duties of each, and deals principally with the relations that must obtain among the members of the church. Beginning with the warning that greatness in the kingdom of heaven is measured not by rank or power but by childlikeness (Mt 18:1–5), it deals with the care that the disciples must take not to cause the little ones to sin or to neglect them if they stray from the community (Mt 18:6–14), the correction of members who sin (Mt 18:15–18), the efficacy of the prayer of the disciples because of the presence of Jesus (Mt 18:19–20), and the forgiveness that must be repeatedly extended to sinful members who repent (Mt 18:21–35).

THE GREATEST IN THE KINGDOM.

1[a] At that time the disciples[*] approached Jesus and said, "Who is the greatest in the kingdom of heaven?" 2 He called a child over, placed it in their midst, 3[b] and said, "Amen, I say to you, unless you turn and become like children,[*] you will not enter the kingdom of heaven. 4[c] Whoever humbles himself like this child is the greatest in the kingdom of heaven. 5[*] And whoever receives one child such as this in my name receives me.

a. [18:1–5] Mk 9:36–37; Lk 9:46–48.

* [18:1] The initiative is taken not by Jesus as in the Marcan parallel (Mk 9:33–34) but by the disciples. Kingdom of heaven: this may mean the kingdom in its fullness, i.e., after the parousia and the final judgment. But what follows about causes of sin, church discipline, and forgiveness, all dealing with the present age, suggests that the question has to do with rank also in the church, where the kingdom is manifested here and now, although only partially and by anticipation; see notes on Mt 3:2; 4:17.

b. [18:3] 19:14; Mk 10:15; Lk 18:17.

* [18:3] Become like children: the child is held up as a model for the disciples not because of any supposed innocence of children but because of their complete dependence on, and trust in, their parents. So must the disciples be, in respect to God.

c. [18:4] 23:12.

* [18:5] Cf. Mt 10:40.

TEMPTATIONS TO SIN.

6[d] "Whoever causes one of these little ones[*] who believe in me to sin, it would be better for him to have a great millstone hung around his neck and to be drowned in the depths of the sea. **7**[*] Woe to the world because of things that cause sin! Such things must come, but woe to the one through whom they come! **8**[e] If your hand or foot causes you to sin,[*] cut it off and throw it away. It is better for you to enter into life maimed or crippled than with two hands or two feet to be thrown into eternal fire. **9** And if your eye causes you to sin, tear it out and throw it away. It is better for you to enter into life with one eye than with two eyes to be thrown into fiery Gehenna.

d. [18:6–7] Mk 9:42; Lk 17:1–2.

[*] [18:6] One of these little ones: the thought passes from the child of Mt 18:2–4 to the disciples, little ones because of their becoming like children. It is difficult to know whether this is a designation of all who are disciples or of those who are insignificant in contrast to others, e.g., the leaders of the community. Since apart from this chapter the designation little ones occurs in Matthew only in Mt 10:42 where it means disciples as such, that is its more likely meaning here. Who believe in me: since discipleship is impossible without at least some degree of faith, this further specification seems superfluous. However, it serves to indicate that the warning against causing a little one to sin is principally directed against whatever would lead such a one to a weakening or loss of faith. The Greek verb skandalizein, here translated causes…to sin, means literally "causes to stumble"; what the stumbling is depends on the context. It is used of falling away from faith in Mt 13:21. According to the better reading of Mk 9:42, in me is a Matthean addition to the Marcan source. It would be better…depths of the sea: cf. Mk 9:42.

[*][18:7] This is a Q saying; cf. Lk 17:1. The inevitability of things that cause sin (literally, "scandals") does not take away the responsibility of the one through whom they come.

e. [18:8–9] 5:29–30; Mk 9:43–47.

[*] [18:8-9] These verses are a doublet of Mt 5:29–30. In that context they have to do with causes of sexual sin. As in the Marcan source from which they have been drawn (Mk 9:42–48), they differ from the first warning about scandal, which deals with causing another person to sin, for they concern what causes oneself to sin and they do not seem to be related to another's loss of faith, as the first warning is. It is difficult to know how Matthew understood the logical connection between these verses and Mt 18:6–7.

THE PARABLE
OF THE LOST
SHEEP.*

10[f] "See that you do not despise one of these little ones,[*] for I say to you that their angels in heaven always look upon the face of my heavenly Father. [**11**][g][*] **12** What is your opinion? If a man has a hundred sheep and one of them goes astray, will he not leave the ninety-nine in the hills and go in search of the stray? **13** And if he finds it, amen, I say to you, he rejoices more over it than over the ninety-nine that did not stray. **14** In just the same way, it is not the will of your heavenly Father that one of these little ones be lost.

* [18:10–14] The first and last verses are peculiar to Matthew. The parable itself comes from Q; see Lk 15:3–7. In Luke it serves as justification for Jesus' table-companionship with sinners; here, it is an exhortation for the disciples to seek out fellow disciples who have gone astray. Not only must no one cause a fellow disciple to sin, but those who have strayed must be sought out and, if possible, brought back to the community. The joy of the shepherd on finding the sheep, though not absent in Mt 18:13 is more emphasized in Luke. By his addition of Mt 18:10, 14 Matthew has drawn out explicitly the application of the parable to the care of the little ones.

f. [18:10–14] Ez 34:1–3, 16; Lk 15:3–7.

* [18:10] Their angels in heaven…my heavenly Father: for the Jewish belief in angels as guardians of nations and individuals, see Dn 10:13, 20–21; Tb 5:4–7; 1QH 5:20–22; as intercessors who present the prayers of human beings to God, see Tb 13:12, 15. The high worth of the little ones is indicated by their being represented before God by these heavenly beings.

g. [18:11] Lk 19:10.

* [18:11] Some manuscripts add, "For the Son of Man has come to save what was lost"; cf. Mt 9:13. This is practically identical with Lk 19:10 and is probably a copyist's addition from that source.

A BROTHER WHO SINS.*

15[h] "If your brother* sins [against you], go and tell him his fault between you and him alone. If he listens to you, you have won over your brother. **16**[*i] If he does not listen, take one or two others along with you, so that 'every fact may be established on the testimony of two or three witnesses.' **17**[j] If he refuses to listen to them, tell the church.* If he refuses to listen even to the church, then treat him as you would a Gentile or a tax collector. **18**[*k] Amen, I say to you, whatever you bind on earth shall be bound in heaven, and whatever you loose on earth shall be loosed in heaven. **19**[*l] Again, [amen,] I say to you, if two of you agree on earth about anything for which they are to pray, it shall be granted to them by my heavenly Father. **20**[*m] For where two or three are gathered together in my name, there am I in the midst of them."

* [18:15–20] Passing from the duty of Christian disciples toward those who have strayed from their number, the discourse now turns to how they are to deal with one who sins and yet remains within the community. First there is to be private correction (Mt 18:15); if this is unsuccessful, further correction before two or three witnesses (Mt 18:16); if this fails, the matter is to be brought before the assembled community (the church), and if the sinner refuses to attend to the correction of the church, he is to be expelled (Mt 18:17). The church's judgment will be ratified in heaven, i.e., by God (Mt 18:18). This three-step process of correction corresponds, though not exactly, to the procedure of the Qumran community; see 1QS 5:25–6:1; 6:24–7:25; CD 9:2–8. The section ends with a saying about the favorable response of God to prayer, even to that of a very small number, for Jesus is in the midst of any gathering of his disciples, however small (Mt 18:19–20). Whether this prayer has anything to do with the preceding judgment is uncertain.

h. [18:15] Lv 19:17; Sir 19:13; Gal 6:1.

* [18:15] Your brother: a fellow disciple; see Mt 23:8. The bracketed words, against you, are widely attested but they are not in the important codices Sinaiticus and Vaticanus or in some other textual witnesses. Their omission broadens the type of sin in question. Won over: literally, "gained."

* [18:16] Cf. Dt 19:15.

i. [18:16] Dt 19:15; Jn 8:17; 1 Tm 5:19.

j. [18:17] 1 Cor 5:1–13.

* [18:17] The church: the second of the only two instances of this word in the gospels; see note on Mt 16:18. Here it refers not to the entire church of Jesus, as in Mt 16:18, but to the local congregation. Treat him…a Gentile or a tax collector: just as the observant Jew avoided the company of Gentiles and tax collectors, so must the congregation of Christian disciples separate itself from the arrogantly sinful member who refuses to repent even when convicted of his sin by the whole church. Such a one is to be set outside the fellowship of the community. The harsh language about Gentile and tax collector probably reflects a stage of the Matthean church when it was principally composed of Jewish Christians. That time had long since passed, but the principle of exclusion for such a sinner remained. Paul makes a similar demand for excommunication in 1 Cor 5:1–13.

* [18:18] Except for the plural of the verbs bind and loose, this verse is practically identical with Mt 16:19b and many scholars understand it as granting to all the disciples what was previously given to Peter alone. For a different view, based on the different contexts of the two verses, see note on Mt 16:19.

k. [18:18] 16:19; Jn 20:23.

* [18:19–20] Some take these verses as applying to prayer on the occasion of the church's gathering to deal with the sinner of Mt 18:17. Unless an a fortiori argument is supposed, this seems unlikely. God's answer to the prayer of two or three envisages a different situation from one that involves the entire congregation. In addition, the object of this prayer is expressed in most general terms as anything for which they are to pray.

l. [18:19] 7:7–8; Jn 15:7.

* [18:20] For where two or three…midst of them: the presence of Jesus guarantees the efficacy of the prayer. This saying is similar to one attributed to a rabbi executed in A.D. 135 at the time of the second Jewish revolt: "…When two sit and there are between them the words of the Torah, the divine presence (Shekinah) rests upon them" (Pirqê ʾAbôt 3, 3).

m. [18:20] 1 Cor 5:4.

THE PARABLE OF THE UNFORGIVING SERVANT.*

21[n] Then Peter approaching asked him, "Lord, if my brother sins against me, how often must I forgive him? As many as seven times?" **22**[*] Jesus answered, "I say to you, not seven times but seventy-seven times. **23**[o] That is why the kingdom of heaven may be likened to a king who decided to settle accounts with his servants. **24**[*] When he began the accounting, a debtor was brought before him who owed him a huge amount. **25** Since he had no way of paying it back, his master ordered him to be sold, along with his wife, his children, and all his property, in payment of the debt. **26**[*] At that, the servant fell down, did him homage, and said, 'Be patient with me, and I will pay you back in full.' **27** Moved with compassion the master of that servant let him go and forgave him the loan. **28** When that servant had left, he found one of his fellow servants who owed him a much smaller amount.[*] He seized him and started to choke him, demanding, 'Pay back what you owe.' **29** Falling to his knees, his fellow servant begged him, 'Be patient with me, and I will pay you back.' **30** But he refused. Instead, he had him put in prison until he paid back the debt. **31** Now when his fellow servants saw what had happened, they were deeply disturbed, and went to their master and reported the whole affair. **32** His master summoned him and said to him, 'You wicked servant! I forgave you your entire debt because you begged me to. **33**[p] Should you not have had pity on your fellow servant, as I had pity on you?' **34** Then in anger his master handed him over to the torturers until he should pay back the whole debt.[*] **35**[*q] So will my heavenly Father do to you, unless each of you forgives his brother from his heart."

* [18:21–35] The final section of the discourse deals with the forgiveness that the disciples are to give to their fellow disciples who sin against them. To the question of Peter how often forgiveness is to be granted (Mt 18:21), Jesus answers that it is to be given without limit (Mt 18:22) and illustrates this with the parable of the unmerciful servant (Mt 18:23–34), warning that his heavenly Father will give those who do not forgive the same treatment as that given to the unmerciful servant (Mt 18:35). Mt 18:21–22 correspond to Lk 17:4; the parable and the final warning are peculiar to Matthew. That the parable did not originally belong to this context is suggested by the fact that it really does not deal with repeated forgiveness, which is the point of Peter's question and Jesus' reply.

n. [18:21–22] 6:12; Lk 17:4.

* [18:22] Seventy-seven times: the Greek corresponds exactly to the LXX of Gn 4:24. There is probably an allusion, by contrast, to the limitless vengeance of Lamech in the Genesis text. In any case, what is demanded of the disciples is limitless forgiveness.

o. [18:23] 25:19.

* [18:24] A huge amount: literally, "ten thousand talents." The talent was a unit of coinage of high but varying value depending on its metal (gold, silver, copper) and its place of origin. It is mentioned in the New Testament only here and in Mt 25:14–30.

* [18:26] Pay you back in full: an empty promise, given the size of the debt.

* [18:28] A much smaller amount: literally, "a hundred denarii." A denarius was the normal daily wage of a laborer. The difference between the two debts is enormous and brings out the absurdity of the conduct of the Christian who has received the great forgiveness of God and yet refuses to forgive the relatively minor offenses done to him.

p. [18:33] Sir 28:4.

* [18:34] Since the debt is so great as to be unpayable, the punishment will be endless.

* [18:35] The Father's forgiveness, already given, will be withdrawn at the final judgment for those who have not imitated his forgiveness by their own.

q. [18:35] 6:15; Jas 2:13.

MATTHEW CHAPTER 19

MARRIAGE AND DIVORCE.

1* When Jesus* finished these words,* he left Galilee and went to the district of Judea across the Jordan. 2 Great crowds followed him, and he cured them there. 3ᵃ Some Pharisees approached him, and tested him,* saying, "Is it lawful for a man to divorce his wife for any cause whatever?" 4*ᵇ He said in reply, "Have you not read that from the beginning the Creator 'made them male and female' 5ᶜ and said, 'For this reason a man shall leave his father and mother and be joined to his wife, and the two shall become one flesh'? 6 So they are no longer two, but one flesh. Therefore, what God has joined together, no human being must separate." 7*ᵈ They said to him, "Then why did Moses command that the man give the woman a bill of divorce and dismiss [her]?" 8 He said to them, "Because of the hardness of your hearts Moses allowed you to divorce your wives, but from the beginning it was not so. 9ᵉ I say to you,* whoever divorces his wife (unless the marriage is unlawful) and marries another commits adultery." 10 [His] disciples said to him, "If that is the case of a man with his wife, it is better not to marry." 11 He answered, "Not all can accept [this] word,* but only those to whom that is granted. 12 Some are incapable of marriage because they were born so; some, because they were made so by others; some, because they have renounced marriage* for the sake of the kingdom of heaven. Whoever can accept this ought to accept it."

* [19:1–23:39] The narrative section of the fifth book of the gospel. The first part (Mt 19:1–20:34) has for its setting the journey of Jesus from Galilee to Jerusalem; the second (Mt 21:1–23:39) deals with Jesus' ministry in Jerusalem up to the final great discourse of the gospel (Mt 24–25). Matthew follows the Marcan sequence of events, though adding material both special to this gospel and drawn from Q. The second part ends with the denunciation of the scribes and Pharisees (Mt 23:1–36) followed by Jesus' lament over Jerusalem (Mt 23:37–39). This long and important speech raises a problem for the view that Matthew is structured around five other discourses of Jesus (see Introduction) and that this one has no such function in the gospel. However, it is to be noted that this speech lacks the customary concluding formula that follows the five discourses (see note on Mt 7:28), and that those discourses are all addressed either exclusively (Mt 10; 18; 24; 25) or primarily (Mt 5–7; 13) to the disciples, whereas this is addressed primarily to the scribes and Pharisees (Mt 23:13–36). Consequently, it seems plausible to maintain that the evangelist did not intend to give it the structural importance of the five other discourses, and that, in spite of its being composed of sayings-material, it belongs to the narrative section of this book. In that regard, it is similar to the sayings-material of Mt 11:7–30. Some have proposed that Matthew wished to regard it as part of the final discourse of Mt 24–25, but the intervening material (Mt 24:1–4) and the change in matter and style of those chapters do not support that view.

* [19:1] In giving Jesus' teaching on divorce (Mt 19:3–9), Matthew here follows his Marcan source (Mk 10:2–12) as he does Q in Mt 5:31–32 (cf. Lk 16:18). Mt 19:10–12 are peculiar to Matthew.

*[19:1] When Jesus finished these words: see note on Mt 7:28–29. The district of Judea across the Jordan: an inexact designation of the territory. Judea did not extend across the Jordan; the territory east of the river was Perea. The route to Jerusalem by way of Perea avoided passage through Samaria.

a. [19:3–9] Mk 10:2–12.

* [19:3] Tested him: the verb is used of attempts of Jesus' opponents to embarrass him by challenging him to do something they think impossible (Mt 16:1; Mk 8:11; Lk 11:16) or by having him say something that they can use against him (Mt 22:18, 35; Mk 10:2; 12:15). For any cause whatever: this is peculiar to Matthew and has been interpreted by some as meaning that Jesus was being asked to take sides in the dispute between the schools of Hillel and Shammai on the reasons for divorce, the latter holding a stricter position than the former. It is unlikely, however, that to ask Jesus' opinion about the differing views of two Jewish schools, both highly respected, could be described as "testing" him, for the reason indicated above.

* [19:4–6] Matthew recasts his Marcan source, omitting Jesus' question about Moses' command (Mk 10:3) and having him recall at once two Genesis texts that show the will and purpose of the Creator in making human beings male and female (Gn 1:27), namely, that a man may be joined to his wife in marriage in the intimacy of one flesh (Gn 2:24). What God has thus joined must not be separated by any human being. (The NAB translation of the Hebrew bāśār of Gn 2:24 as "body" rather than "flesh" obscures the reference of Matthew to that text.)

b. [19:4] Gn 1:27.

c. [19:5] Gn 2:24; 1 Cor 6:16; Eph 5:31.

* [19:7] See Dt 24:1–4.

d. [19:7] Dt 24:1–4.

e. [19:9] 5:32; Lk 16:18; 1 Cor 7:10–11.

* [19:9] Moses' concession to human sinfulness (the hardness of your hearts, Mt 19:8) is repudiated by Jesus, and the original will of the Creator is reaffirmed against that concession. (Unless the marriage is unlawful): see note on Mt 5:31–32. There is some evidence suggesting that Jesus' absolute prohibition of divorce was paralleled in the Qumran community (see 11QTemple 57:17–19; CD 4:12b–5:14). Matthew removes Mark's setting of this verse as spoken to the disciples alone "in the house" (Mk 10:10) and also his extension of the divorce prohibition to the case of a woman's divorcing her husband (Mk 10:12), probably because in Palestine, unlike the places where Roman and Greek law prevailed, the woman was not allowed to initiate the divorce.

* [19:11] [This] word: probably the disciples' "it is better not to marry" (Mt 19:10). Jesus agrees but says that celibacy is not for all but only for those to whom that is granted by God.

* [19:12] Incapable of marriage: literally, "eunuchs." Three classes are mentioned, eunuchs from birth, eunuchs by castration, and those who have voluntarily renounced marriage (literally, "have made themselves eunuchs") for the sake of the kingdom, i.e., to devote themselves entirely to its service. Some scholars take the last class to be those who have been divorced by their spouses and have refused to enter another marriage. But it is more likely that it is rather those who have chosen never to marry, since that suits better the optional nature of the decision: whoever can…ought to accept it.

BLESSING OF THE CHILDREN.*

13[f] Then children were brought to him that he might lay his hands on them and pray. The disciples rebuked them, 14[g] but Jesus said, "Let the children come to me, and do not prevent them; for the kingdom of heaven belongs to such as these." 15 After he placed his hands on them, he went away.

* [19:13–15] This account is understood by some as intended to justify the practice of infant baptism. That interpretation is based principally on the command not to prevent the children from coming, since that word sometimes has a baptismal connotation in the New Testament; see Acts 8:36.

f. [19:13–15] Mk 10:13–16; Lk 18:15–17.

g. [19:14] 18:3; Acts 8:36.

THE RICH YOUNG MAN.[*]

16[h] Now someone approached him and said, "Teacher, what good must I do to gain eternal life?"[*] **17** He answered him, "Why do you ask me about the good? There is only One who is good.[*] If you wish to enter into life, keep the commandments." **18**[*][i] He asked him, "Which ones?" And Jesus replied, " 'You shall not kill; you shall not commit adultery; you shall not steal; you shall not bear false witness; **19** honor your father and your mother'; and 'you shall love your neighbor as yourself.'" **20**[*] The young man said to him, "All of these I have observed. What do I still lack?" **21**[j] Jesus said to him, "If you wish to be perfect,[*] go, sell what you have and give to [the] poor, and you will have treasure in heaven. Then come, follow me." **22** When the young man heard this statement, he went away sad, for he had many possessions. **23**[*] Then Jesus said to his disciples, "Amen, I say to you, it will be hard for one who is rich to enter the kingdom of heaven. **24**[k] Again I say to you, it is easier for a camel to pass through the eye of a needle than for one who is rich to enter the kingdom of God." **25**[*] When the disciples heard this, they were greatly astonished and said, "Who then can be saved?" **26**[l] Jesus looked at them and said, "For human beings this is impossible, but for God all things are possible." **27**[m] Then Peter said to him in reply, "We have given up everything and followed you. What will there be for us?" **28**[*][n] Jesus said to them, "Amen, I say to you that you who have followed me, in the new age, when the Son of Man is seated on his throne of glory, will yourselves sit on twelve thrones, judging the twelve tribes of Israel. **29** And everyone who has given up houses or brothers or sisters or father or mother or children or lands for the sake of my name will receive a hundred times more, and will inherit eternal life. **30**[*][o] But many who are first will be last, and the last will be first.

* [19:16–30] Cf. Mk 10:17–31. This story does not set up a "two-tier" morality, that of those who seek (only) eternal life (Mt 19:16) and that of those who wish to be perfect (Mt 19:21). It speaks rather of the obstacle that riches constitute for the following of Jesus and of the impossibility, humanly speaking, for one who has many possessions (Mt 19:22) to enter the kingdom (Mt 19:24). Actual renunciation of riches is not demanded of all; Matthew counts the rich Joseph of Arimathea as a disciple of Jesus (Mt 27:57). But only the poor in spirit (Mt 5:3) can enter the kingdom and, as here, such poverty may entail the sacrifice of one's possessions. The Twelve, who have given up everything (Mt 19:27) to follow Jesus, will have as their reward a share in Jesus' (the Son of Man's) judging the twelve tribes of Israel (Mt 19:28), and all who have similarly sacrificed family or property for his sake will inherit eternal life (Mt 19:29).

h. [19:16–30] Mk 10:17–31; Lk 18:18–30.

* [19:16] Gain eternal life: this is equivalent to "entering into life" (Mt 19:17) and "being saved" (Mt 19:25); the life is that of the new age after the final judgment (see Mt 25:46). It probably is also equivalent here to "entering the kingdom of heaven" (Mt 19:23) or "the kingdom of God" (Mt 19:24), but see notes on Mt 3:2; 4:17; 18:1 for the wider reference of the kingdom in Matthew.

* [19:17] By Matthew's reformulation of the Marcan question and reply (Mk 10:17–18) Jesus' repudiation of the term "good" for himself has been softened. Yet the Marcan assertion that "no one is good but God alone" stands, with only unimportant verbal modification.

* [19:18–19] The first five commandments cited are from the Decalogue (see Ex 20:12–16; Dt 5:16–20). Matthew omits Mark's "you shall not defraud" (Mk 10:19; see Dt 24:14) and adds Lv 19:18. This combination of commandments of the Decalogue with Lv 19:18 is partially the same as Paul's enumeration of the demands of Christian morality in Rom 13:9.

i. [19:18–19] Ex 20:12–16; Dt 5:16–20 / Lv 19:18; Rom 13:9.

* [19:20] Young man: in Matthew alone of the synoptics the questioner is said to be a young man; thus the Marcan "from my youth" (Mk 10:20) is omitted.

j. [19:21] 5:48; 6:20.

* [19:21] If you wish to be perfect: to be perfect is demanded of all Christians; see Mt 5:48. In the case of this man, it involves selling his possessions and giving to the poor; only so can he follow Jesus.

* [19:23–24] Riches are an obstacle to entering the kingdom that cannot be overcome by human power. The comparison with the impossibility of a camel's passing through the eye of a needle should not be mitigated by such suppositions as that the eye of a needle means a low or narrow gate. The kingdom of God: as in Mt 12:28; 21:31, 43 instead of Matthew's usual kingdom of heaven.

k. [19:24] 7:14.

* [19:25–26] See note on Mk 10:23–27.

l. [19:26] Gn 18:14; Jb 42:2; Lk 1:37.

m. [19:27] 4:20, 22.

* [19:28] This saying, directed to the Twelve, is from Q; see Lk 22:29–30. The new age: the Greek word here translated "new age" occurs in the New Testament only here and in Ti 3:5. Literally, it means "rebirth" or "regeneration," and is used in Titus of spiritual rebirth through baptism. Here it means the "rebirth" effected by the coming of the kingdom. Since that coming has various stages (see notes on Mt 3:2; 4:17), the new age could be taken as referring to the time after the resurrection when the Twelve will govern the true Israel, i.e., the church of Jesus. (For "judge" in the sense of "govern," cf. Jgs 12:8, 9, 11; 15:20; 16:31; Ps 2:10). But since it is connected here with the time when the Son of Man will be seated on his throne of glory, language that Matthew uses in Mt 25:31 for the time of final judgment, it is more likely that what the Twelve are promised is that they will be joined with Jesus then in judging the people of Israel.

n. [19:28] 25:31; Dn 7:9, 22; Lk 22:30; Rev 3:21; 20:4.

* [19:30] Different interpretations have been given to this saying, which comes from Mk 10:31. In view of Matthew's associating it with the following parable (Mt 20:1–15) and substantially repeating it (in reverse order) at the end of that parable (Mt 20:16), it may be that his meaning is that all who respond to the call of Jesus, at whatever time (first or last), will be the same in respect to inheriting the benefits of the kingdom, which is the gift of God.

o. [19:30] 20:16.

MATTHEW CHAPTER 20

THE WORKERS IN THE VINEYARD.*

1 "The kingdom of heaven is like a landowner who went out at dawn to hire laborers for his vineyard. **2** After agreeing with them for the usual daily wage, he sent them into his vineyard. **3** Going out about nine o'clock, he saw others standing idle in the marketplace, **4*** and he said to them, 'You too go into my vineyard, and I will give you what is just.' **5** So they went off. [And] he went out again around noon, and around three o'clock, and did likewise. **6** Going out about five o'clock, he found others standing around, and said to them, 'Why do you stand here idle all day?' **7** They answered, 'Because no one has hired us.' He said to them, 'You too go into my vineyard.' **8***a When it was evening the owner of the vineyard said to his foreman, 'Summon the laborers and give them their pay, beginning with the last and ending with the first.' **9** When those who had started about five o'clock came, each received the usual daily wage. **10** So when the first came, they thought that they would receive more, but each of them also got the usual wage. **11** And on receiving it they grumbled against the landowner, **12** saying, 'These last ones worked only one hour, and you have made them equal to us, who bore the day's burden and the heat.' **13** He said to one of them in reply, 'My friend, I am not cheating you.* Did you not agree with me for the usual daily wage? **14*** Take what is yours and go. What if I wish to give this last one the same as you? **15** [Or] am I not free to do as I wish with my own money? Are you envious because I am generous?' **16*** Thus, the last will be first, and the first will be last."

---

* [20:1–16] This parable is peculiar to Matthew. It is difficult to know whether the evangelist composed it or received it as part of his traditional material and, if the latter is the case, what its original reference was. In its present context its close association with Mt 19:30 suggests that its teaching is the equality of all the disciples in the reward of inheriting eternal life.

* [20:4] What is just: although the wage is not stipulated as in the case of those first hired, it will be fair.

* [20:8] Beginning with the last...the first: this element of the parable has no other purpose than to show how the first knew what the last were given (Mt 20:12).

a. [20:8] Lv 19:13; Dt 24:15.

* [20:13] I am not cheating you: literally, "I am not treating you unjustly."

* [20:14–15] The owner's conduct involves no violation of justice (Mt 20:4, 13), and that all the workers receive the same wage is due only to his generosity to the latest arrivals; the resentment of the first comes from envy.

* [20:16] See note on Mt 19:30.

THE THIRD PREDICTION OF THE PASSION.*

17[b] As Jesus was going up to Jerusalem, he took the twelve [disciples] aside by themselves, and said to them on the way, **18** "Behold, we are going up to Jerusalem, and the Son of Man will be handed over to the chief priests and the scribes, and they will condemn him to death, **19** and hand him over to the Gentiles to be mocked and scourged and crucified, and he will be raised on the third day."

* [20:17–19] Cf. Mk 10:32–34. This is the third and the most detailed of the passion predictions (Mt 16:21–23; 17:22–23). It speaks of Jesus' being handed over to the Gentiles (Mt 27:2), his being mocked (Mt 27:27–30), scourged (Mt 27:26), and crucified (Mt 27:31, 35). In all but the last of these points Matthew agrees with his Marcan source, but whereas Mark speaks of Jesus' being killed (Mk 10:34), Matthew has the specific to be…crucified.

b. [20:17–19] 16:21; 17:22–23; Mk 10:32–34; Lk 18:31–33.

THE REQUEST OF JAMES AND JOHN.*

20[c] Then the mother* of the sons of Zebedee approached him with her sons and did him homage, wishing to ask him for something. **21** He said to her, "What do you wish?" She answered him, "Command that these two sons of mine sit, one at your right and the other at your left, in your kingdom." **22** Jesus said in reply, "You do not know what you are asking.* Can you drink the cup that I am going to drink?" They said to him, "We can." **23** He replied, "My cup you will indeed drink, but to sit at my right and at my left [, this] is not mine to give but is for those for whom it has been prepared by my Father." **24**[d] When the ten heard this, they became indignant at the two brothers. **25** But Jesus summoned them and said, "You know that the rulers of the Gentiles lord it over them, and the great ones make their authority over them felt. **26** But it shall not be so among you. Rather, whoever wishes to be great among you shall be your servant; **27**[e] whoever wishes to be first among you shall be your slave. **28**[f] Just so, the Son of Man did not come to be served but to serve and to give his life as a ransom* for many."

* [20:20–28] Cf. Mk 10:35–45. The request of the sons of Zebedee, made through their mother, for the highest places of honor in the kingdom, and the indignation of the other ten disciples at this request, show that neither the two brothers nor the others have understood that what makes for greatness in the kingdom is not lordly power but humble service. Jesus gives the example, and his ministry of service will reach its highest point when he gives his life for the deliverance of the human race from sin.

c. [20:20–28] Mk 10:35–45.

* [20:20–21] The reason for Matthew's making the mother the petitioner (cf. Mk 10:35) is not clear. Possibly he intends an allusion to Bathsheba's seeking the kingdom for Solomon; see 1 Kgs 1:11–21. Your kingdom: see note on Mt 16:28.

* [20:22] You do not know what you are asking: the Greek verbs are plural and, with the rest of the verse, indicate that the answer is addressed not to the woman but to her sons. Drink the cup: see note on Mk 10:38–40. Matthew omits the Marcan "or be baptized with the baptism with which I am baptized" (Mk 10:38).

d. [20:24–27] Lk 22:25–27.

e. [20:27] Mk 9:35.

f. [20:28] 26:28; Is 53:12; Rom 5:6; 1 Tm 2:6.

* [20:28] Ransom: this noun, which occurs in the New Testament only here and in the Marcan parallel (Mk 10:45), does not necessarily express the idea of liberation by payment of some price. The cognate verb is used frequently in the LXX of God's liberating Israel from Egypt or from Babylonia after the Exile; see Ex 6:6; 15:13; Ps 77:16 (76 LXX); Is 43:1; 44:22. The liberation brought by Jesus' death will be for many; cf. Is 53:12. Many does not mean that some are excluded, but is a Semitism designating the collectivity who benefit from the service of the one, and is equivalent to "all." While there are few verbal contacts between this saying and the fourth Servant Song (Is 52:13–53:12), the ideas of that passage are reflected here.

THE HEALING OF TWO BLIND MEN.*

29ᵍ As they left Jericho, a great crowd followed him. **30**ʰ Two blind men were sitting by the roadside, and when they heard that Jesus was passing by, they cried out, "[Lord,]* Son of David, have pity on us!" **31** The crowd warned them to be silent, but they called out all the more, "Lord, Son of David, have pity on us!" **32** Jesus stopped and called them and said, "What do you want me to do for you?" **33** They answered him, "Lord, let our eyes be opened." **34** Moved with pity, Jesus touched their eyes. Immediately they received their sight, and followed him.

---

* [20:29–34] The cure of the blind men is probably symbolic of what will happen to the disciples, now blind to the meaning of Jesus' passion and to the necessity of their sharing his suffering. As the men are given sight, so, after the resurrection, will the disciples come to see that to which they are now blind. Matthew has abbreviated his Marcan source (Mk 10:46–52) and has made Mark's one man two. Such doubling is characteristic of this gospel; see Mt 8:28–34 (//Mk 5:1–20) and the note on Mt 9:27–31.

g. [20:29–34] Mk 10:46–52; Lk 18:35–43.

h. [20:30] 9:27.

* [20:30] [Lord,]: some important textual witnesses omit this, but that may be because copyists assimilated this verse to Mt 9:27. Son of David: see note on Mt 9:27.

MATTHEW CHAPTER 21

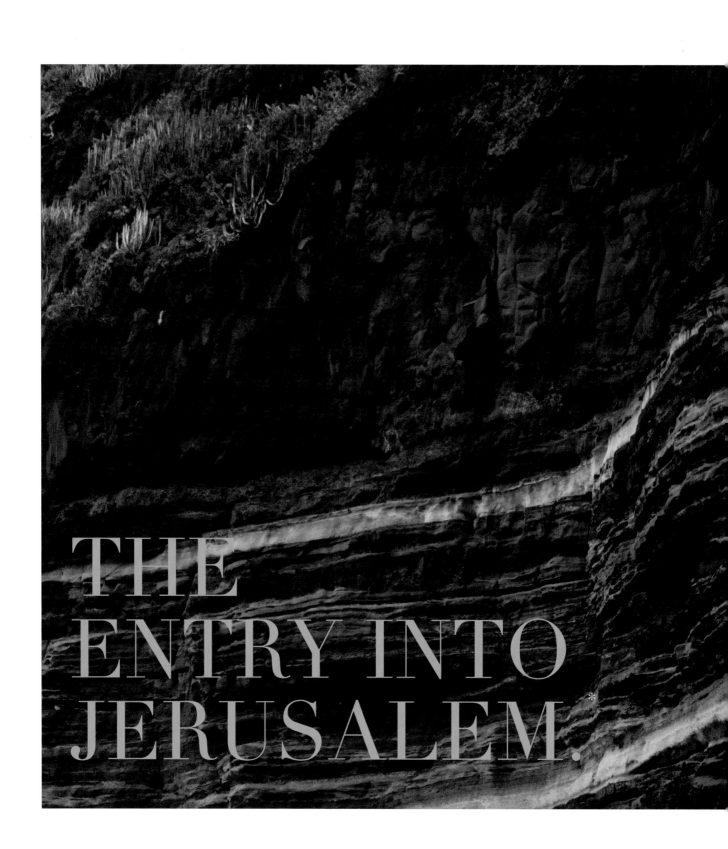

THE ENTRY INTO JERUSALEM.*

1[a] When they drew near Jerusalem and came to Bethphage* on the Mount of Olives, Jesus sent two disciples, **2** saying to them, "Go into the village opposite you, and immediately you will find an ass tethered, and a colt with her.* Untie them and bring them here to me. **3** And if anyone should say anything to you, reply, 'The master has need of them.' Then he will send them at once." **4*** This happened so that what had been spoken through the prophet might be fulfilled:

5[b] "Say to daughter Zion,

'Behold, your king comes to you,

meek and riding on an ass,

and on a colt, the foal of a beast of burden.'"

6 The disciples went and did as Jesus had ordered them. **7*** They brought the ass and the colt and laid their cloaks over them, and he sat upon them. **8***[c] The very large crowd spread their cloaks on the road, while others cut branches from the trees and strewed them on the road.

9[d] The crowds preceding him and those following kept crying out and saying:

"Hosanna* to the Son of David;

blessed is he who comes in the name of the Lord;

hosanna in the highest."

10 And when he entered Jerusalem the whole city was shaken* and asked, "Who is this?" **11** And the crowds replied, "This is Jesus the prophet,* from Nazareth in Galilee."

* [21:1–11] Jesus' coming to Jerusalem is in accordance with the divine will that he must go there (cf. Mt 16:21) to suffer, die, and be raised. He prepares for his entry into the city in such a way as to make it a fulfillment of the prophecy of Zec 9:9 (Mt 21:2) that emphasizes the humility of the king who comes (Mt 21:5). That prophecy, absent from the Marcan parallel account (Mk 11:1–11) although found also in the Johannine account of the entry (Jn 12:15), is the center of the Matthean story. During the procession from Bethphage to Jerusalem, Jesus is acclaimed as the Davidic messianic king by the crowds who accompany him (Mt 21:9). On his arrival the whole city was shaken, and to the inquiry of the amazed populace about Jesus' identity the crowds with him reply that he is the prophet, from Nazareth in Galilee (Mt 21:10, 11).

a. [21:1–11] Mk 11:1–11; Lk 19:28–38; Jn 12:12–15.

* [21:1] Bethphage: a village that can no longer be certainly identified. Mark mentions it before Bethany (Mk 11:1), which suggests that it lay to the east of the latter. The Mount of Olives: the hill east of Jerusalem that is spoken of in Zec 14:4 as the place where the Lord will come to rescue Jerusalem from the enemy nations.

* [21:2] An ass tethered, and a colt with her: instead of the one animal of Mk 11:2, Matthew has two, as demanded by his understanding of Zec 9:9.

* [21:4–5] The prophet: this fulfillment citation is actually composed of two distinct Old Testament texts, Is 62:11 (Say to daughter Zion) and Zec 9:9. The ass and the colt are the same animal in the prophecy, mentioned twice in different ways, the common Hebrew literary device of poetic parallelism. That Matthew takes them as two is one of the reasons why some scholars think that he was a Gentile rather than a Jewish Christian who would presumably not make that mistake (see Introduction).

b. [21:5] Is 62:11; Zec 9:9.

* [21:7] Upon them: upon the two animals; an awkward picture resulting from Matthew's misunderstanding of the prophecy.

* [21:8] Spread…on the road: cf. 2 Kgs 9:13. There is a similarity between the cutting and strewing of the branches and the festivities of Tabernacles (Lv 23:39–40); see also 2 Mc 10:5–8 where the celebration of the rededication of the temple is compared to that of Tabernacles.

c. [21:8] 2 Kgs 9:13.

d. [21:9] Ps 118:25–26.

* [21:9] Hosanna: the Hebrew means "(O Lord) grant salvation"; see Ps 118:25, but that invocation had become an acclamation of jubilation and welcome. Blessed is he…in the name of the Lord: see Ps 118:26 and the note on Jn 12:13. In the highest: probably only an intensification of the acclamation, although Hosanna in the highest could be taken as a prayer, "May God save (him)."

* [21:10] Was shaken: in the gospels this verb is peculiar to Matthew where it is used also of the earthquake at the time of the crucifixion (Mt 27:51) and of the terror of the guards of Jesus' tomb at the appearance of the angel (Mt 28:4). For Matthew's use of the cognate noun, see note on Mt 8:24.

* [21:11] The prophet: see Mt 16:14 ("one of the prophets") and 21:46.

THE CLEANSING OF THE TEMPLE.[*]

12^e Jesus entered the temple area and drove out all those engaged in selling and buying there. He overturned the tables of the money changers and the seats of those who were selling doves.^{*f} **13**^g And he said to them, "It is written:

'My house shall be a house of prayer,'[*]

but you are making it a den of thieves."

14^h The blind and the lame[*] approached him in the temple area, and he cured them. **15** When the chief priests and the scribes saw the wondrous things[*] he was doing, and the children crying out in the temple area, "Hosanna to the Son of David," they were indignant **16**^{*i} and said to him, "Do you hear what they are saying?" Jesus said to them, "Yes; and have you never read the text, 'Out of the mouths of infants and nurslings you have brought forth praise'?" **17** And leaving them, he went out of the city to Bethany, and there he spent the night.

* [21:12–17] Matthew changes the order of (Mk 11:11, 12, 15) and places the cleansing of the temple on the same day as the entry into Jerusalem, immediately after it. The activities going on in the temple area were not secular but connected with the temple worship. Thus Jesus' attack on those so engaged and his charge that they were making God's house of prayer a den of thieves (Mt 21:12–13) constituted a claim to authority over the religious practices of Israel and were a challenge to the priestly authorities. Mt 21:14–17 are peculiar to Matthew. Jesus' healings and his countenancing the children's cries of praise rouse the indignation of the chief priests and the scribes (Mt 21:15). These two groups appear in the infancy narrative (Mt 2:4) and have been mentioned in the first and third passion predictions (Mt 16:21; 20:18). Now, as the passion approaches, they come on the scene again, exhibiting their hostility to Jesus.

e. [21:12–17] Mk 11:15–19; Lk 19:45–48; Jn 2:14–22.

* [21:12] These activities were carried on in the court of the Gentiles, the outermost court of the temple area. Animals for sacrifice were sold; the doves were for those who could not afford a more expensive offering; see Lv 5:7. Tables of the money changers: only the coinage of Tyre could be used for the purchases; other money had to be exchanged for that.

f. [21:12] Lv 5:7.

g. [21:13] Is 56:7; Jer 7:11.

* [21:13] 'My house…prayer': cf. Is 56:7. Matthew omits the final words of the quotation, "for all peoples" ("all nations"), possibly because for him the worship of the God of Israel by all nations belongs to the time after the resurrection; see Mt 28:19. A den of thieves: the phrase is taken from Jer 7:11.

h. [21:14] 2 Sm 5:8 LXX.

* [21:14] The blind and the lame: according to 2 Sm 5:8 LXX the blind and the lame were forbidden to enter "the house of the Lord," the temple. These are the last of Jesus' healings in Matthew.

* [21:15] The wondrous things: the healings.

* [21:16] 'Out of the mouths…praise': cf. Ps 8:3 LXX.

i. [21:16] Ps 8:2 LXX; Wis 10:21.

THE CURSING OF THE FIG TREE.*

18[j] When he was going back to the city in the morning, he was hungry. **19**[k] Seeing a fig tree by the road, he went over to it, but found nothing on it except leaves. And he said to it, "May no fruit ever come from you again." And immediately the fig tree withered. **20** When the disciples saw this, they were amazed and said, "How was it that the fig tree withered immediately?" **21**[*l] Jesus said to them in reply, "Amen, I say to you, if you have faith and do not waver, not only will you do what has been done to the fig tree, but even if you say to this mountain, 'Be lifted up and thrown into the sea,' it will be done. **22**[m] Whatever you ask for in prayer with faith, you will receive."

* [21:18–22] In Mark the effect of Jesus' cursing the fig tree is not immediate; see Mk 11:14, 20. By making it so, Matthew has heightened the miracle. Jesus' act seems arbitrary and ill-tempered, but it is a prophetic action similar to those of Old Testament prophets that vividly symbolize some part of their preaching; see, e.g., Ez 12:1–20. It is a sign of the judgment that is to come upon the Israel that with all its apparent piety lacks the fruit of good deeds (Mt 3:10) and will soon bear the punishment of its fruitlessness (Mt 21:43). Some scholars propose that this story is the development in tradition of a parable of Jesus about the destiny of a fruitless tree, such as Lk 13:6–9. Jesus' answer to the question of the amazed disciples (Mt 21:20) makes the miracle an example of the power of prayer made with unwavering faith (Mt 21:21–22).

j. [21:18–22] Mk 11:12–14, 20–24.

k. [21:19] Jer 8:13; Lk 13:6–9.

* [21:21] See Mt 17:20.

l. [21:21] 17:20; Lk 17:6.

m. [21:22] 7:7; 1 Jn 3:22.

23[n] When he had come into the temple area, the chief priests and the elders of the people approached him as he was teaching and said, "By what authority are you doing these things?[*] And who gave you this authority?"[o] **24** Jesus said to them in reply, "I shall ask you one question,[*] and if you answer it for me, then I shall tell you by what authority I do these things. **25** Where was John's baptism from? Was it of heavenly or of human origin?" They discussed this among themselves and said, "If we say 'Of heavenly origin,' he will say to us, 'Then why did you not believe him?' **26**[*p] But if we say, 'Of human origin,' we fear the crowd, for they all regard John as a prophet." **27** So they said to Jesus in reply, "We do not know." He himself said to them, "Neither shall I tell you by what authority I do these things.[*]

[*] [21:23–27] Cf. Mk 11:27–33. This is the first of five controversies between Jesus and the religious authorities of Judaism in Mt 21:23–22:46, presented in the form of questions and answers.

n. [21:23–27] Mk 11:27–33; Lk 20:1–8.

[*] [21:23] These things: probably his entry into the city, his cleansing of the temple, and his healings there.

o. [21:23] Jn 2:18.

[*] [21:24] To reply by counterquestion was common in rabbinical debate.

[*] [21:26] We fear…as a prophet: cf. Mt 14:5.

p. [21:26] 14:5.

[*] [21:27] Since through embarrassment on the one hand and fear on the other the religious authorities claim ignorance of the origin of John's baptism, they show themselves incapable of speaking with authority; hence Jesus refuses to discuss with them the grounds of his authority.

THE AUTHORITY OF JESUS QUESTIONED.*

THE PARABLE OF THE TWO SONS *

28 "What is your opinion? A man had two sons. He came to the first and said, 'Son, go out and work in the vineyard today.' **29** He said in reply, 'I will not,' but afterwards he changed his mind and went. **30** The man came to the other son and gave the same order. He said in reply, 'Yes, sir,' but did not go. **31*** Which of the two did his father's will?" They answered, "The first." Jesus said to them, "Amen, I say to you, tax collectors and prostitutes are entering the kingdom of God before you. **32***q When John came to you in the way of righteousness, you did not believe him; but tax collectors and prostitutes did. Yet even when you saw that, you did not later change your minds and believe him.

* [21:28–32] The series of controversies is interrupted by three parables on the judgment of Israel (Mt 21:28–22:14) of which this, peculiar to Matthew, is the first. The second (Mt 21:33–46) comes from Mark (12:1–12), and the third (Mt 22:1–14) from Q; see Lk 14:15–24. This interruption of the controversies is similar to that in Mark, although Mark has only one parable between the first and second controversy. As regards Matthew's first parable, Mt 21:28–30 if taken by themselves could point simply to the difference between saying and doing, a theme of much importance in this gospel (cf. Mt 7:21; 12:50); that may have been the parable's original reference. However, it is given a more specific application by the addition of Mt 21:31–32. The two sons represent, respectively, the religious leaders and the religious outcasts who followed John's call to repentance. By the answer they give to Jesus' question (Mt 21:31) the leaders condemn themselves. There is much confusion in the textual tradition of the parable. Of the three different forms of the text given by important textual witnesses, one has the leaders answer that the son who agreed to go but did not was the one who did the father's will. Although some scholars accept that as the original reading, their arguments in favor of it seem unconvincing. The choice probably lies only between a reading that puts the son who agrees and then disobeys before the son who at first refuses and then obeys, and the reading followed in the present translation. The witnesses to the latter reading are slightly better than those that support the other.

* [21:31] Entering...before you: this probably means "they enter; you do not."

* [21:32] Cf. Lk 7:29–30. Although the thought is similar to that of the Lucan text, the formulation is so different that it is improbable that the saying comes from Q. Came to you...way of righteousness: several meanings are possible: that John himself was righteous, that he taught righteousness to others, or that he had an important place in God's plan of salvation. For the last, see note on Mt 3:14–15.

q. [21:32] Lk 7:29–30.

THE PARABLE OF THE TENANTS.*

33ʳ "Hear another parable. There was a landowner who planted a vineyard,* put a hedge around it, dug a wine press in it, and built a tower. Then he leased it to tenants and went on a journey.ˢ 34 When vintage time drew near, he sent his servants* to the tenants to obtain his produce. 35 But the tenants seized the servants and one they beat, another they killed, and a third they stoned. 36 Again he sent other servants, more numerous than the first ones, but they treated them in the same way. 37 Finally, he sent his son to them, thinking, 'They will respect my son.' 38* But when the tenants saw the son, they said to one another, 'This is the heir. Come, let us kill him and acquire his inheritance.' 39*ᵗ They seized him, threw him out of the vineyard, and killed him. 40 What will the owner of the vineyard do to those tenants when he comes?" 41 They answered* him, "He will put those wretched men to a wretched death and lease his vineyard to other tenants who will give him the produce at the proper times." 42*ᵘ Jesus said to them, "Did you never read in the scriptures:

'The stone that the builders rejected
has become the cornerstone;
by the Lord has this been done,
and it is wonderful in our eyes'?

43* Therefore, I say to you, the kingdom of God will be taken away from you and given to a people that will produce its fruit. 44 [* The one who falls on this stone will be dashed to pieces; and it will crush anyone on whom it falls.]" 45 When the chief priests and the Pharisees* heard his parables, they knew that he was speaking about them. 46 And although they were attempting to arrest him, they feared the crowds, for they regarded him as a prophet.

* [21:33–46] Cf. Mk 12:1–12. In this parable there is a close correspondence between most of the details of the story and the situation that it illustrates, the dealings of God with his people. Because of that heavy allegorizing, some scholars think that it does not in any way go back to Jesus, but represents the theology of the later church. That judgment applies to the Marcan parallel as well, although the allegorizing has gone farther in Matthew. There are others who believe that while many of the allegorical elements are due to church sources, they have been added to a basic parable spoken by Jesus. This view is now supported by the Gospel of Thomas 65, where a less allegorized and probably more primitive form of the parable is found.

r. [21:33–46] Mk 12:1–12; Lk 20:9–19.

* [21:33] Planted a vineyard…a tower: cf. Is 5:1–2. The vineyard is defined in Is 5:7 as "the house of Israel."

s. [21:33] Is 5:1–2, 7.

* [21:34–35] His servants: Matthew has two sendings of servants as against Mark's three sendings of a single servant (Mk 12:2–5a) followed by a statement about the sending of "many others" (Mk 12:2, 5b). That these servants stand for the prophets sent by God to Israel is clearly implied but not made explicit here, but see Mt 23:37. His produce: cf. Mk 12:2 "some of the produce." The produce is the good works demanded by God, and his claim to them is total.

* [21:38] Acquire his inheritance: if a Jewish proselyte died without heir, the tenants of his land would have final claim on it.

* [21:39] Threw him out…and killed him: the change in the Marcan order where the son is killed and his corpse then thrown out (Mk 12:8) was probably made because of the tradition that Jesus died outside the city of Jerusalem; see Jn 19:17; Heb 13:12.

t. [21:39] Heb 13:12.

* [21:41] They answered: in Mk 12:9 the question is answered by Jesus himself; here the leaders answer and so condemn themselves; cf. Mt 21:31. Matthew adds that the new tenants to whom the vineyard will be transferred will give the owner the produce at the proper times.

* [21:42] Cf. Ps 118:22–23. The psalm was used in the early church as a prophecy of Jesus' resurrection; see Acts 4:11; 1 Pt 2:7. If, as some think, the original parable ended at Mt 21:39 it was thought necessary to complete it by a reference to Jesus' vindication by God.

u. [21:42] Ps 118:22–23; Is 28:16; Acts 4:11; 1 Pt 2:7.

* [21:43] Peculiar to Matthew. Kingdom of God: see note on Mt 19:23–24. Its presence here instead of Matthew's usual "kingdom of heaven" may indicate that the saying came from Matthew's own traditional material. A people that will produce its fruit: believing Israelites and Gentiles, the church of Jesus.

* [21:44] The majority of textual witnesses omit this verse. It is probably an early addition to Matthew from Lk 20:18 with which it is practically identical.

* [21:45] The Pharisees: Matthew inserts into the group of Jewish leaders (Mt 21:23) those who represented the Judaism of his own time.

MATTHEW CHAPTER 22

THE PARABLE OF THE WEDDING FEAST.[*]

1[a] Jesus again in reply spoke to them in parables, saying, 2 "The kingdom of heaven may be likened to a king who gave a wedding feast[*] for his son. 3[*] He dispatched his servants to summon the invited guests to the feast, but they refused to come. 4 A second time he sent other servants, saying, 'Tell those invited: "Behold, I have prepared my banquet, my calves and fattened cattle are killed, and everything is ready; come to the feast."' 5 Some ignored the invitation and went away, one to his farm, another to his business. 6[b] The rest laid hold of his servants, mistreated them, and killed them. 7[*] The king was enraged and sent his troops, destroyed those murderers, and burned their city. 8 Then he said to his servants, 'The feast is ready, but those who were invited were not worthy to come. 9 Go out, therefore, into the main roads and invite to the feast whomever you find.' 10 The servants went out into the streets and gathered all they found, bad and good alike,[*] and the hall was filled with guests. 11[*] But when the king came in to meet the guests he saw a man there not dressed in a wedding garment. 12 He said to him, 'My friend, how is it that you came in here without a wedding garment?' But he was reduced to silence. 13[*c] Then the king said to his attendants, 'Bind his hands and feet, and cast him into the darkness outside, where there will be wailing and grinding of teeth.' 14 Many are invited, but few are chosen."

* [22:1–14] This parable is from Q; see Lk 14:15–24. It has been given many allegorical traits by Matthew, e.g., the burning of the city of the guests who refused the invitation (Mt 22:7), which corresponds to the destruction of Jerusalem by the Romans in A.D. 70. It has similarities with the preceding parable of the tenants: the sending of two groups of servants (Mt 22:3, 4), the murder of the servants (Mt 22:6), the punishment of the murderers (Mt 22:7), and the entrance of a new group into a privileged situation of which the others had proved themselves unworthy (Mt 22:8–10). The parable ends with a section that is peculiar to Matthew (Mt 22:11–14), which some take as a distinct parable. Matthew presents the kingdom in its double aspect, already present and something that can be entered here and now (Mt 22:1–10), and something that will be possessed only by those present members who can stand the scrutiny of the final judgment (Mt 22:11–14). The parable is not only a statement of God's judgment on Israel but a warning to Matthew's church.

a. [22:1–14] Lk 14:15–24.

* [22:2] Wedding feast: the Old Testament's portrayal of final salvation under the image of a banquet (Is 25:6) is taken up also in Mt 8:11; cf. Lk 13:15.

* [22:3–4] Servants…other servants: probably Christian missionaries in both instances; cf. Mt 23:34.

b. [22:6] 21:35.

* [22:7] See note on Mt 22:1–14.

* [22:10] Bad and good alike: cf. Mt 13:47.

* [22:11] A wedding garment: the repentance, change of heart and mind, that is the condition for entrance into the kingdom (Mt 3:2; 4:17) must be continued in a life of good deeds (Mt 7:21–23).

* [22:13] Wailing and grinding of teeth: the Christian who lacks the wedding garment of good deeds will suffer the same fate as those Jews who have rejected Jesus; see note on Mt 8:11–12.

c. [22:13] 8:12; 25:30.

PAYING TAXES TO THE EMPEROR.*

15[d] Then the Pharisees* went off and plotted how they might entrap him in speech. 16 They sent their disciples to him, with the Herodians,* saying, "Teacher, we know that you are a truthful man and that you teach the way of God in accordance with the truth. And you are not concerned with anyone's opinion, for you do not regard a person's status. 17* Tell us, then, what is your opinion: Is it lawful to pay the census tax to Caesar or not?" 18 Knowing their malice, Jesus said, "Why are you testing me, you hypocrites? 19* Show me the coin that pays the census tax." Then they handed him the Roman coin. 20 He said to them, "Whose image is this and whose inscription?" 21[e] They replied, "Caesar's."* At that he said to them, "Then repay to Caesar what belongs to Caesar and to God what belongs to God." 22 When they heard this they were amazed, and leaving him they went away.

* [22:15–22] The series of controversies between Jesus and the representatives of Judaism (see note on Mt 21:23–27) is resumed. As in the first (Mt 21:23–27), here and in the following disputes Matthew follows his Marcan source with few modifications.

d. [22:15–22] Mk 12:13–17; Lk 20:20–26.

* [22:15] The Pharisees: while Matthew retains the Marcan union of Pharisees and Herodians in this account, he clearly emphasizes the Pharisees' part. They alone are mentioned here, and the Herodians are joined with them only in a prepositional phrase of Mt 22:16. Entrap him in speech: the question that they will pose is intended to force Jesus to take either a position contrary to that held by the majority of the people or one that will bring him into conflict with the Roman authorities.

* [22:16] Herodians: see note on Mk 3:6. They would favor payment of the tax; the Pharisees did not.

* [22:17] Is it lawful: the law to which they refer is the law of God.

* [22:19] They handed him the Roman coin: their readiness in producing the money implies their use of it and their acceptance of the financial advantages of the Roman administration in Palestine.

e. [22:21] Rom 13:7.

* [22:21] Caesar's: the emperor Tiberius (A.D. 14–37). Repay to Caesar what belongs to Caesar: those who willingly use the coin that is Caesar's should repay him in kind. The answer avoids taking sides in the question of the lawfulness of the tax. To God what belongs to God: Jesus raises the debate to a new level. Those who have hypocritically asked about tax in respect to its relation to the law of God should be concerned rather with repaying God with the good deeds that are his due; cf. Mt 21:41, 43.

THE QUESTION ABOUT THE RESURRECTION.[*]

23[f] On that day Sadducees approached him, saying that there is no resurrection.[*] They put this question to him, **24**[g] saying, "Teacher, Moses said, 'If a man dies[*] without children, his brother shall marry his wife and raise up descendants for his brother.' **25** Now there were seven brothers among us. The first married and died and, having no descendants, left his wife to his brother. **26** The same happened with the second and the third, through all seven. **27** Finally the woman died. **28** Now at the resurrection, of the seven, whose wife will she be? For they all had been married to her." **29**[*] Jesus said to them in reply, "You are misled because you do not know the scriptures or the power of God. **30** At the resurrection they neither marry nor are given in marriage but are like the angels in heaven. **31** And concerning the resurrection of the dead, have you not read what was said to you[*] by God, **32**[h] 'I am the God of Abraham, the God of Isaac, and the God of Jacob'? He is not the God of the dead but of the living." **33** When the crowds heard this, they were astonished at his teaching.

* [22:23–33] Here Jesus' opponents are the Sadducees, members of the powerful priestly party of his time; see note on Mt 3:7. Denying the resurrection of the dead, a teaching of relatively late origin in Judaism (cf. Dn 12:2), they appeal to a law of the Pentateuch (Dt 25:5–10) and present a case based on it that would make resurrection from the dead ridiculous (Mt 22:24–28). Jesus chides them for knowing neither the scriptures nor the power of God (Mt 22:29). His argument in respect to God's power contradicts the notion, held even by many proponents as well as by opponents of the teaching, that the life of those raised from the dead would be essentially a continuation of the type of life they had had before death (Mt 22:30). His argument based on the scriptures (Mt 22:31–32) is of a sort that was accepted as valid among Jews of the time.

f. [22:23–33] Mk 12:18–27; Lk 20:27–40.

* [22:23] Saying that there is no resurrection: in the Marcan parallel (Mk 22:18) the Sadducees are correctly defined as those "who say there is no resurrection"; see also Lk 20:27. Matthew's rewording of Mark can mean that these particular Sadducees deny the resurrection, which would imply that he was not aware that the denial was characteristic of the party. For some scholars this is an indication of his being a Gentile Christian; see note on Mt 21:4–5.

g. [22:24] Gn 38:8; Dt 25:5–6.

* [22:24] 'If a man dies…his brother': this is known as the "law of the levirate," from the Latin levir, "brother-in-law." Its purpose was to continue the family line of the deceased brother (Dt 25:6).

* [22:29] The sexual relationships of this world will be transcended; the risen body will be the work of the creative power of God.

* [22:31–32] Cf. Ex 3:6. In the Pentateuch, which the Sadducees accepted as normative for Jewish belief and practice, God speaks even now (to you) of himself as the God of the patriarchs who died centuries ago. He identifies himself in relation to them, and because of their relation to him, the living God, they too are alive. This might appear no argument for the resurrection, but simply for life after death as conceived in Wis 3:1–3. But the general thought of early first-century Judaism was not influenced by that conception; for it human immortality was connected with the existence of the body.

h. [22:32] Ex 3:6.

THE GREATEST COMMAND-MENT.*

34[i] When the Pharisees heard that he had silenced the Sadducees, they gathered together, **35** and one of them [a scholar of the law]* tested him by asking, **36** "Teacher,* which commandment in the law is the greatest?" **37**[j] He said to him,* "You shall love the Lord, your God, with all your heart, with all your soul, and with all your mind. **38** This is the greatest and the first commandment. **39**[k] The second is like it:* You shall love your neighbor as yourself. **40**[*1] The whole law and the prophets depend on these two commandments."

* [22:34–40] The Marcan parallel (Mk 12:28–34) is an exchange between Jesus and a scribe who is impressed by the way in which Jesus has conducted himself in the previous controversy (Mk 12:28), who compliments him for the answer he gives him (Mk 12:32), and who is said by Jesus to be "not far from the kingdom of God" (Mk 12:34). Matthew has sharpened that scene. The questioner, as the representative of other Pharisees, tests Jesus by his question (Mt 22:34–35), and both his reaction to Jesus' reply and Jesus' commendation of him are lacking.

i. [22:34–40] Mk 12:28–34; Lk 10:25–28.

* [22:35] [A scholar of the law]: meaning "scribe." Although this reading is supported by the vast majority of textual witnesses, it is the only time that the Greek word so translated occurs in Matthew. It is relatively frequent in Luke, and there is reason to think that it may have been added here by a copyist since it occurs in the Lucan parallel (Lk 10:25–28). Tested: see note on Mt 19:3.

* [22:36] For the devout Jew all the commandments were to be kept with equal care, but there is evidence of preoccupation in Jewish sources with the question put to Jesus.

j. [22:37] Dt 6:5.

* [22:37–38] Cf. Dt 6:5. Matthew omits the first part of Mark's fuller quotation (Mk 12:29; Dt 6:4–5), probably because he considered its monotheistic emphasis needless for his church. The love of God must engage the total person (heart, soul, mind).

k. [22:39] Lv 19:18; Jas 2:8.

* [22:39] Jesus goes beyond the extent of the question put to him and joins to the greatest and the first commandment a second, that of love of neighbor, Lv 19:18; see note on Mt 19:18–19. This combination of the two commandments may already have been made in Judaism.

* [22:40] The double commandment is the source from which the whole law and the prophets are derived.

l. [22:40] Rom 13:8–10; Gal 5:14.

THE QUESTION ABOUT DAVID'S SON.[*]

41^m While the Pharisees were gathered together, Jesus questioned them,[*] **42**[*] saying, "What is your opinion about the Messiah? Whose son is he?" They replied, "David's." **43** He said to them, "How, then, does David, inspired by the Spirit, call him 'lord,' saying:

44ⁿ 'The Lord said to my lord,

"Sit at my right hand

until I place your enemies under your feet"'?

45[*] If David calls him 'lord,' how can he be his son?" **46**^o No one was able to answer him a word, nor from that day on did anyone dare to ask him any more questions.

* [22:41–46] Having answered the questions of his opponents in the preceding three controversies, Jesus now puts a question to them about the sonship of the Messiah. Their easy response (Mt 22:43a) is countered by his quoting a verse of Ps 110 that raises a problem for their response (43b–45). They are unable to solve it and from that day on their questioning of him is ended.

m. [22:41–46] Mk 12:35–37; Lk 20:41–44.

* [22:41] The Pharisees…questioned them: Mark is not specific about who are questioned (Mk 12:35).

* [22:42–44] David's: this view of the Pharisees was based on such Old Testament texts as Is 11:1–9; Jer 23:5; and Ez 34:23; see also the extrabiblical Psalms of Solomon 17:21. How, then…saying: Jesus cites Ps 110:1 accepting the Davidic authorship of the psalm, a common view of his time. The psalm was probably composed for the enthronement of a Davidic king of Judah. Matthew assumes that the Pharisees interpret it as referring to the Messiah, although there is no clear evidence that it was so interpreted in the Judaism of Jesus' time. It was widely used in the early church as referring to the exaltation of the risen Jesus. My lord: understood as the Messiah.

n. [22:44] Ps 110:1; Acts 2:35; Heb 1:13.

* [22:45] Since Matthew presents Jesus both as Messiah (Mt 16:16) and as Son of David (Mt 1:1; see also note on Mt 9:27), the question is not meant to imply Jesus' denial of Davidic sonship. It probably means that although he is the Son of David, he is someone greater, Son of Man and Son of God, and recognized as greater by David who calls him my 'lord.'

o. [22:46] Lk 20:40.

MATTHEW CHAPTER 23 *

* [23:1–39] The final section of the narrative part of the fifth book of the gospel is a denunciation by Jesus of the scribes and the Pharisees (see note on Mt 3:7). It depends in part on Mark and Q (cf. Mk 12:38–39; Lk 11:37–52; 13:34–35), but in the main it is peculiar to Matthew. (For the reasons against considering this extensive body of sayings-material either as one of the structural discourses of this gospel or as part of the one that follows in Mt 24–25, see note on Mt 19:1–23:39.) While the tradition of a deep opposition between Jesus and the Pharisees is well founded, this speech reflects an opposition that goes beyond that of Jesus' ministry and must be seen as expressing the bitter conflict between Pharisaic Judaism and the church of Matthew at the time when the gospel was composed. The complaint often made that the speech ignores the positive qualities of Pharisaism and of its better representatives is true, but the complaint overlooks the circumstances that gave rise to the invective. Nor is the speech purely anti-Pharisaic. The evangelist discerns in his church many of the same faults that he finds in its opponents and warns his fellow Christians to look to their own conduct and attitudes.

DENUNCIATION OF THE SCRIBES AND PHARISEES.

1[a] Then Jesus spoke to the crowds and to his disciples, 2[*] saying, "The scribes and the Pharisees have taken their seat on the chair of Moses. 3 Therefore, do and observe all things whatsoever they tell you, but do not follow their example. For they preach but they do not practice. 4[b] They tie up heavy burdens[*] [hard to carry] and lay them on people's shoulders, but they will not lift a finger to move them. 5[*c] All their works are performed to be seen. They widen their phylacteries and lengthen their tassels. 6[*d] They love places of honor at banquets, seats of honor in synagogues, 7 greetings in marketplaces, and the salutation 'Rabbi.' 8[*] As for you, do not be called 'Rabbi.' You have but one teacher, and you are all brothers. 9 Call no one on earth your father; you have but one Father in heaven. 10 Do not be called 'Master'; you have but one master, the Messiah. 11[e] The greatest among you must be your servant. 12[f] Whoever exalts himself will be humbled; but whoever humbles himself will be exalted.

13[*g] "Woe to you, scribes and Pharisees, you hypocrites. You lock the kingdom of heaven[*] before human beings. You do not enter yourselves, nor do you allow entrance to those trying to enter. [14][*]

15[*] "Woe to you, scribes and Pharisees, you hypocrites. You traverse sea and land to make one convert, and when that happens you make him a child of Gehenna twice as much as yourselves.

16[*h] "Woe to you, blind guides, who say, 'If one swears by the temple, it means nothing, but if one swears by the gold of the temple, one is obligated.' 17 Blind fools, which is greater, the gold, or the temple that made the gold sacred? 18 And you say, 'If one swears by the altar, it means nothing, but if one swears by the gift on the altar, one is obligated.' 19 You blind ones, which is greater, the gift, or the altar that makes the gift sacred? 20[i] One who swears by the altar swears by it and all that is upon it; 21 one who swears by the temple swears by it and by him who dwells in it; 22 one who swears by heaven swears by the throne of God and by him who is seated on it.

23[j] "Woe to you, scribes and Pharisees, you hypocrites. You pay tithes[*] of mint and dill and cummin, and have neglected the weightier things of the law: judgment and mercy and fidelity. [But] these you should have done, without neglecting the others. **24**[*k] Blind guides, who strain out the gnat and swallow the camel!

25[*l] "Woe to you, scribes and Pharisees, you hypocrites. You cleanse the outside of cup and dish, but inside they are full of plunder and self-indulgence. **26** Blind Pharisee, cleanse first the inside of the cup, so that the outside also may be clean.

27[*] "Woe to you, scribes and Pharisees, you hypocrites. You are like whitewashed tombs, which appear beautiful on the outside, but inside are full of dead men's bones and every kind of filth. **28**[m] Even so, on the outside you appear righteous, but inside you are filled with hypocrisy and evildoing.

29[*] "Woe to you, scribes and Pharisees,[*] you hypocrites. You build the tombs of the prophets and adorn the memorials of the righteous, **30**[n] and you say, 'If we had lived in the days of our ancestors, we would not have joined them in shedding the prophets' blood.' **31**[o] Thus you bear witness against yourselves that you are the children of those who murdered the prophets; **32** now fill up what your ancestors measured out! **33**[p] You serpents, you brood of vipers, how can you flee from the judgment of Gehenna? **34**[*q] Therefore, behold, I send to you prophets and wise men and scribes; some of them you will kill and crucify, some of them you will scourge in your synagogues and pursue from town to town, **35** so that there may come upon you all the righteous blood shed upon earth, from the righteous blood of Abel to the blood of Zechariah, the son of Barachiah, whom you murdered between the sanctuary and the altar. **36** Amen, I say to you, all these things will come upon this generation.

speech, denounces the Pharisees as blind guides in respect to their teaching on oaths (Mt 23:16–22), this commandment to observe all things whatsoever they (the scribes and Pharisees) tell you cannot be taken as the evangelist's understanding of the proper standard of conduct for his church. The saying may reflect a period when the Matthean community was largely Jewish Christian and was still seeking to avoid a complete break with the synagogue. Matthew has incorporated this traditional material into the speech in accordance with his view of the course of salvation history, in which he portrays the time of Jesus' ministry as marked by the fidelity to the law, although with significant pointers to the new situation that would exist after his death and resurrection (see note on Mt 5:17–20). The crowds and the disciples (Mt 23:1) are exhorted not to follow the example of the Jewish leaders, whose deeds do not conform to their teaching (Mt 23:3).

b. [23:4] Lk 11:46.

* [23:4] Tie up heavy burdens: see note on Mt 11:28.

* [23:5] To the charge of preaching but not practicing (Mt 23:3), Jesus adds that of acting in order to earn praise. The disciples have already been warned against this same fault (see note on Mt 6:1–18). Phylacteries: the Mosaic law required that during prayer small boxes containing parchments on which verses of scripture were written be worn on the left forearm and the forehead (see Ex 13:9, 16; Dt 6:8; 11:18). Tassels: see note on Mt 9:20. The widening of phylacteries and the lengthening of tassels were for the purpose of making these evidences of piety more noticeable.

c. [23:5] 6:1–6; Ex 13:9, 16; Nm 15:38–39; Dt 6:8; 11:18.

* [23:6–7] Cf. Mk 12:38–39. 'Rabbi': literally, "my great one," a title of respect for teachers and leaders.

d. [23:6–7] Mk 12:38–39; Lk 11:43; 20:46.

* [23:8–12] These verses, warning against the use of various titles, are addressed to the disciples alone. While only the title 'Rabbi' has been said to be used in addressing the scribes and Pharisees (Mt 23:7), the implication is that Father and 'Master' also were. The prohibition of these titles to the disciples suggests that their use was present in Matthew's church. The Matthean Jesus forbids not only the titles but the spirit of superiority and pride that is shown by their acceptance. Whoever exalts…will be exalted: cf. Lk 14:11.

e. [23:11] 20:26.

f. [23:12] Lk 14:11; 18:14.

* [23:13–36] This series of seven "woes," directed against the scribes and Pharisees and addressed to them, is the heart of the speech. The phrase woe to occurs often in the prophetic and apocalyptic literature, expressing horror of a sin and punishment for those who commit it. Hypocrites: see note on Mt 6:2. The hypocrisy of the scribes and Pharisees consists in the difference between their speech and action (Mt 23:3) and in demonstrations of piety that have no other purpose than to enhance their reputation as religious persons (Mt 23:5).

g. [23:13] Lk 11:52.

* [23:13] You lock the kingdom of heaven: cf. Mt 16:19 where Jesus tells Peter that he will give him the keys to the kingdom of heaven. The purpose of the authority expressed by that metaphor is to give entrance into the kingdom (the kingdom is closed only to those who reject the authority); here the charge is made that the authority of the scribes and Pharisees is exercised in such a way as to be an obstacle to entrance. Cf. Lk 11:52 where the accusation against the "scholars of the law" (Matthew's scribes) is that they "have taken away the key of knowledge."

* [23:14] Some manuscripts add a verse here or after Mt 23:12, "Woe to you, scribes and Pharisees, you hypocrites. You devour the houses of widows and, as a pretext, recite lengthy prayers. Because of this, you will receive a very severe condemnation." Cf. Mk 12:40; Lk 20:47. This "woe" is almost identical with Mk 12:40 and seems to be an interpolation derived from that text.

a. [23:1–39] Mk 12:38–39; Lk 11:37–52; 13:34–35.

*[23:2–3] Have taken their seat…Moses: it is uncertain whether this is simply a metaphor for Mosaic teaching authority or refers to an actual chair on which the teacher sat. It has been proved that there was a seat so designated in synagogues of a later period than that of this gospel. Do and observe…they tell you: since the Matthean Jesus abrogates Mosaic law (Mt 5:31–42), warns his disciples against the teaching of the Pharisees (Mt 14:1–12), and, in this

continued on next page

* [23:15] In the first century A.D. until the First Jewish Revolt against Rome (A.D. 66–70), many Pharisees conducted a vigorous missionary campaign among Gentiles. Convert: literally, "proselyte," a Gentile who accepted Judaism fully by submitting to circumcision and all other requirements of Mosaic law. Child of Gehenna: worthy of everlasting punishment; for Gehenna, see note on Mt 5:22. Twice as much as yourselves: possibly this refers simply to the zeal of the convert, surpassing that of the one who converted him.

* [23:16–22] An attack on the casuistry that declared some oaths binding (one is obligated) and others not (it means nothing) and held the binding oath to be the one made by something of lesser value (the gold; the gift on the altar). Such teaching, which inverts the order of values, reveals the teachers to be blind guides; cf. Mt 15:14. Since the Matthean Jesus forbids all oaths to his disciples (Mt 5:33–37), this woe does not set up a standard for Christian moral conduct, but ridicules the Pharisees on their own terms.

h. [23:16] 15:14.

i. [23:20–22] 5:34–35.

j. [23:23] Lv 27:30; Dt 14:22; Lk 11:42.

* [23:23] The Mosaic law ordered tithing of the produce of the land (Lv 27:30; Dt 14:22–23), and the scribal tradition is said here to have extended this law to even the smallest herbs. The practice is criticized not in itself but because it shows the Pharisees' preoccupation with matters of less importance while they neglect the weightier things of the law.

* [23:24] Cf. Lv 11:41–45 that forbids the eating of any "swarming creature." The Pharisees' scrupulosity about minor matters and neglect of greater ones (Mt 23:23) is further brought out by this contrast between straining liquids that might contain a tiny "swarming creature" and yet swallowing the camel. The latter was one of the unclean animals forbidden by the law (Lv 11:4), but it is hardly possible that the scribes and Pharisees are being denounced as guilty of so gross a violation of the food laws. To swallow the camel is only a hyperbolic way of speaking of their neglect of what is important.

k. [23:24] Lv 11:41–45.

* [23:25–26] The ritual washing of utensils for dining (cf. Mk 7:4) is turned into a metaphor illustrating a concern for appearances while inner purity is ignored. The scribes and Pharisees are compared to cups carefully washed on the outside but filthy within. Self-indulgence: the Greek word here translated means lack of self-control, whether in drinking or in sexual conduct.

l. [23:25–26] Mk 7:4; Lk 11:39.

* [23:27–28] The sixth woe, like the preceding one, deals with concern for externals and neglect of what is inside. Since contact with dead bodies, even when one was unaware of it, caused ritual impurity (Nm 19:11–22), tombs were whitewashed so that no one would contract such impurity inadvertently.

m. [23:28] Lk 16:15; 18:9.

* [23:29–36] The final woe is the most serious indictment of all. It portrays the scribes and Pharisees as standing in the same line as their ancestors who murdered the prophets and the righteous.

* [23:29–32] In spite of honoring the slain dead by building their tombs and adorning their memorials, and claiming that they would not have joined in their ancestors' crimes if they had lived in their days, the scribes and Pharisees are true children of their ancestors and are defiantly ordered by Jesus to fill up what those ancestors measured out. This order reflects the Jewish

notion that there was an allotted measure of suffering that had to be completed before God's final judgment would take place.

n. [23:30] Lk 11:47.

o. [23:31] Acts 7:52.

p. [23:33] 3:7; 12:34.

* [23:34–36] There are important differences between the Matthean and the Lucan form of this Q material; cf. Lk 11:49–51. In Luke the one who sends the emissaries is the "wisdom of God." If, as many scholars think, that is the original wording of Q, Matthew, by making Jesus the sender, has presented him as the personified divine wisdom. In Luke, wisdom's emissaries are the Old Testament "prophets" and the Christian "apostles." Matthew's prophets and wise men and scribes are probably Christian disciples alone; cf. Mt 10:41 and see note on Mt 13:52. You will kill: see Mt 24:9. Scourge in your synagogues…town to town: see Mt 10:17, 23 and the note on Mt 10:17. All the righteous blood shed upon the earth: the slaying of the disciples is in continuity with all the shedding of righteous blood beginning with that of Abel. The persecution of Jesus' disciples by this generation involves the persecutors in the guilt of their murderous ancestors. The blood of Zechariah: see note on Lk 11:51. By identifying him as the son of Barachiah Matthew understands him to be Zechariah the Old Testament minor prophet; see Zec 1:1.

q. [23:34–36] 5:12; Gn 4:8; 2 Chr 24:20–22; Zec 1:1; Lk 11:49–51; Rev 18:24.

THE LAMENT OVER JERUSALEM.[*]

37[r] "Jerusalem, Jerusalem, you who kill the prophets and stone those sent to you, how many times I yearned to gather your children together, as a hen gathers her young under her wings, but you were unwilling![s] **38**[t] Behold, your house will be abandoned, desolate. **39**[u] I tell you, you will not see me again until you say, 'Blessed is he who comes in the name of the Lord.'"

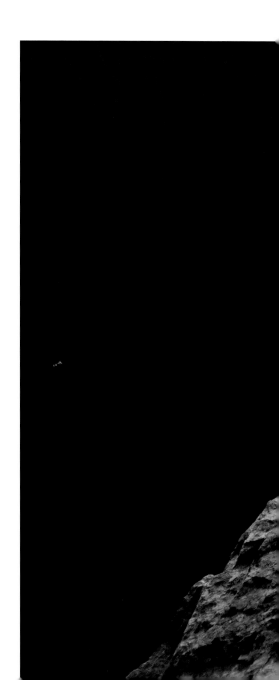

[*] [23:37–39] Cf. Lk 13:34–35. The denunciation of Pharisaic Judaism ends with this lament over Jerusalem, which has repeatedly rejected and murdered those whom God has sent to her. How many times: this may refer to various visits of Jesus to the city, an aspect of his ministry found in John but otherwise not in the synoptics. As a hen…under her wings: for imagery similar to this, see Ps 17:8; 91:4. Your house…desolate: probably an allusion to the destruction of the temple in A.D. 70. You will not see me…in the name of the Lord: Israel will not see Jesus again until he comes in glory for the final judgment. The acclamation has been interpreted in contrasting ways, as an indication that Israel will at last accept Jesus at that time, and as its troubled recognition of him as its dreaded judge who will pronounce its condemnation; in support of the latter view see Mt 24:30.

r. [23:37–39] Lk 13:34–35; 19:41–44.

s. [23:37] 21:35.

t. [23:38] Jer 12:7.

u. [23:39] Ps 118:26.

MATTHEW CHAPTER 24

THE DESTRUCTION OF THE TEMPLE FORETOLD.

1 [*][a] Jesus left the temple area and was going away, when his disciples approached him to point out the temple buildings. **2** [*] He said to them in reply, "You see all these things, do you not? Amen, I say to you, there will not be left here a stone upon another stone that will not be thrown down."

---

[*] [24:1–25:46] The discourse of the fifth book, the last of the five around which the gospel is structured. It is called the "eschatological" discourse since it deals with the coming of the new age (the eschaton) in its fullness, with events that will precede it, and with how the disciples are to conduct themselves while awaiting an event that is as certain as its exact time is unknown to all but the Father (Mt 24:36). The discourse may be divided into two parts, Mt 24:1–44 and Mt 24:45–25:46. In the first, Matthew follows his Marcan source (Mk 13:1–37) closely. The second is drawn from Q and from the evangelist's own traditional material. Both parts show Matthew's editing of his sources by deletions, additions, and modifications. The vigilant waiting that is emphasized in the second part does not mean a cessation of ordinary activity and concentration only on what is to come, but a faithful accomplishment of duties at hand, with awareness that the end, for which the disciples must always be ready, will entail the great judgment by which the everlasting destiny of all will be determined.

a. [24:1–44] Mk 13:1–37; Lk 21:5–36.

[*] [24:2] As in Mark, Jesus predicts the destruction of the temple. By omitting the Marcan story of the widow's contribution (Mk 12:41–44) that immediately precedes the prediction in that gospel, Matthew has established a close connection between it and Mt 23:38, "…your house will be abandoned desolate."

THE BEGINNING OF CALAMITIES.

3 As he was sitting on the Mount of Olives,[*] the disciples approached him privately and said, "Tell us, when will this happen, and what sign will there be of your coming, and of the end of the age?" **4**[*] Jesus said to them in reply, "See that no one deceives you. **5** For many will come in my name, saying, 'I am the Messiah,' and they will deceive many. **6**[b] You will hear of wars[*] and reports of wars; see that you are not alarmed, for these things must happen, but it will not yet be the end. **7**[c] Nation will rise against nation, and kingdom against kingdom; there will be famines and earthquakes from place to place. **8**[*] All these are the beginning of the labor pains. **9**[*d] Then they will hand you over to persecution, and they will kill you. You will be hated by all nations because of my name. **10** And then many will be led into sin; they will betray and hate one another. **11** Many false prophets will arise and deceive many; **12** and because of the increase of evildoing, the love of many will grow cold. **13**[e] But the one who perseveres to the end will be saved. **14**[f] And this gospel of the kingdom will be preached throughout the world as a witness to all nations,[*] and then the end will come.

* [24:3] The Mount of Olives: see note on Mt 21:1. The disciples: cf. Mk 13:3–4 where only Peter, James, John, and Andrew put the question that is answered by the discourse. In both gospels, however, the question is put privately: the ensuing discourse is only for those who are disciples of Jesus. When will this happen…end of the age?: Matthew distinguishes carefully between the destruction of the temple (this) and the coming of Jesus that will bring the end of the age. In Mark the two events are more closely connected, a fact that may be explained by Mark's believing that the one would immediately succeed the other. Coming: this translates the Greek word parousia, which is used in the gospels only here and in Mt 24:27, 37, 39. It designated the official visit of a ruler to a city or the manifestation of a saving deity, and it was used by Christians to refer to the final coming of Jesus in glory, a term first found in the New Testament with that meaning in 1 Thes 2:19. The end of the age: see note on Mt 13:39.

* [24:4–14] This section of the discourse deals with calamities in the world (Mt 24:6–7) and in the church (Mt 24:9–12). The former must happen before the end comes (Mt 24:6), but they are only the beginning of the labor pains (Mt 24:8). (It may be noted that the Greek word translated the end in Mt 24:6 and in Mt 24:13–14 is not the same as the phrase "the end of the age" in Mt 24:3, although the meaning is the same.) The latter are sufferings of the church, both from within and without, that will last until the gospel is preached…to all nations. Then the end will come and those who have endured the sufferings with fidelity will be saved (Mt 24:13–14).

b. [24:6] Dn 2:28 LXX.

* [24:6–7] The disturbances mentioned here are a commonplace of apocalyptic language, as is the assurance that they must happen (see Dn 2:28 LXX), for that is the plan of God. Kingdom against kingdom: see Is 19:2.

c. [24:7] Is 19:2.

* [24:8] The labor pains: the tribulations leading up to the end of the age are compared to the pains of a woman about to give birth. There is much attestation for rabbinic use of the phrase "the woes (or birth pains) of the Messiah"

after the New Testament period, but in at least one instance it is attributed to a rabbi who lived in the late first century A.D. In this Jewish usage it meant the distress of the time preceding the coming of the Messiah; here, the labor pains precede the coming of the Son of Man in glory.

* [24:9–12] Matthew has used Mk 13:9–12 in his missionary discourse (Mt 10:17–21) and omits it here. Besides the sufferings, including death, and the hatred of all nations that the disciples will have to endure, there will be worse affliction within the church itself. This is described in Mt 24:10–12, which are peculiar to Matthew. Will be led into sin: literally, "will be scandalized," probably meaning that they will become apostates; see Mt 13:21 where "fall away" translates the same Greek word as here. Betray: in the Greek this is the same word as the hand over of Mt 24:9. The handing over to persecution and hatred from outside will have their counterpart within the church. False prophets: these are Christians; see note on Mt 7:15–20. Evildoing: see Mt 7:23. Because of the apocalyptic nature of much of this discourse, the literal meaning of this description of the church should not be pressed too hard. However, there is reason to think that Matthew's addition of these verses reflects in some measure the condition of his community.

d. [24:9] 10:17.

e. [24:13] 10:22.

f. [24:14] 28:19; Rom 10:18.

* [24:14] Except for the last part (and then the end will come), this verse substantially repeats Mk 13:10. The Matthean addition raises a problem since what follows in Mt 24:15–23 refers to the horrors of the First Jewish Revolt including the destruction of the temple, and Matthew, writing after that time, knew that the parousia of Jesus was still in the future. A solution may be that the evangelist saw the events of those verses as foreshadowing the cosmic disturbances that he associates with the parousia (Mt 24:29) so that the period in which the former took place could be understood as belonging to the end.

THE GREAT TRIBULATION.*

15[g] "When you see the desolating abomination* spoken of through Daniel the prophet standing in the holy place (let the reader understand), **16** then those in Judea must flee* to the mountains, **17**[*h] a person on the housetop must not go down to get things out of his house, **18** a person in the field must not return to get his cloak. **19** Woe to pregnant women and nursing mothers in those days. **20*** Pray that your flight not be in winter or on the sabbath, **21**[*i] for at that time there will be great tribulation, such as has not been since the beginning of the world until now, nor ever will be. **22** And if those days had not been shortened, no one would be saved; but for the sake of the elect they will be shortened. **23**[j] If anyone says to you then, 'Look, here is the Messiah!' or, 'There he is!' do not believe it. **24** False messiahs and false prophets will arise, and they will perform signs and wonders so great as to deceive, if that were possible, even the elect. **25** Behold, I have told it to you beforehand. **26** So if they say to you, 'He is in the desert,' do not go out there; if they say, 'He is in the inner rooms,' do not believe it.* **27**[k] For just as lightning comes from the east and is seen as far as the west, so will the coming of the Son of Man be. **28** Wherever the corpse is, there the vultures will gather.

* [24:15–28] Cf. Mk 13:14–23; Lk 17:23–24, 37. A further stage in the tribulations that will precede the coming of the Son of Man, and an answer to the question of Mt 24:3a, "when will this (the destruction of the temple) happen?"
g. [24:15] Dn 9:27; 11:31; 12:11; Mk 13:14.
* [24:15] The desolating abomination: in 167 B.C. the Syrian king Antiochus IV Epiphanes desecrated the temple by setting up in it a statue of Zeus Olympios (see 1 Mc 1:54). That event is referred to in Dn 12:11 LXX as the "desolating abomination" (NAB "horrible abomination") and the same Greek term is used here; cf. also Dn 9:27; 11:31. Although the desecration had taken place before Daniel was written, it is presented there as a future event, and Matthew sees that "prophecy" fulfilled in the desecration of the temple by the Romans. In the holy place: the temple; more precise than Mark's where he should not (Mk 13:14). Let the reader understand: this parenthetical remark, taken from Mk 13:14 invites the reader to realize the meaning of Daniel's "prophecy."
* [24:16] The tradition that the Christians of Jerusalem fled from that city to Pella, a city of Transjordan, at the time of the First Jewish Revolt is found in Eusebius (Ecclesiastical History, 3.5.3), who attributes the flight to "a certain oracle given by revelation before the war." The tradition is not improbable but the Matthean command, derived from its Marcan source, is vague in respect to the place of flight (to the mountains), although some scholars see it as applicable to the flight to Pella.
* [24:17–19] Haste is essential, and the journey will be particularly difficult for women who are burdened with unborn or infant children.
h. [24:17] Lk 17:31.
* [24:20] On the sabbath: this addition to in winter (cf. Mk 13:18) has been understood as an indication that Matthew was addressed to a church still observing the Mosaic law of sabbath rest and the scribal limitations upon the length of journeys that might lawfully be made on that day. That interpretation conflicts with Matthew's view on sabbath observance (cf. Mt 12:1–14). The meaning of the addition may be that those undertaking on the sabbath a journey such as the one here ordered would be offending the sensibilities of law-observant Jews and would incur their hostility.
* [24:21] For the unparalleled distress of that time, see Dn 12:1.
i. [24:21] Dn 12:1.
j. [24:23] Lk 17:23.
* [24:26–28] Claims that the Messiah is to be found in some distant or secret place must be ignored. The coming of the Son of Man will be as clear as lightning is to all and as the corpse of an animal is to vultures; cf. Lk 17:24, 37. Here there is clear identification of the Son of Man and the Messiah; cf. Mt 24:23.
k. [24:27–28] Lk 17:24, 37.

THE COMING OF THE SON OF MAN.

29[*][l] "Immediately after the tribulation of those days,

the sun will be darkened,

and the moon will not give its light,

and the stars will fall from the sky,

and the powers of the heavens will be shaken.

30[m] And then the sign of the Son of Man[*] will appear in heaven, and all the tribes of the earth will mourn, and they will see the Son of Man coming upon the clouds of heaven with power and great glory. **31**[n] And he will send out his angels[*] with a trumpet blast, and they will gather his elect from the four winds, from one end of the heavens to the other.

[*] [24:29] The answer to the question of Mt 24:3b, "What sign will there be of your coming?" Immediately after…those days: the shortening of time between the preceding tribulation and the parousia has been explained as Matthew's use of a supposed device of Old Testament prophecy whereby certainty that a predicted event will occur is expressed by depicting it as imminent. While it is questionable that that is an acceptable understanding of the Old Testament predictions, it may be applicable here, for Matthew knew that the parousia had not come immediately after the fall of Jerusalem, and it is unlikely that he is attributing a mistaken calculation of time to Jesus. The sun…be shaken: cf. Is 13:10, 13.

l. [24:29] Is 13:10, 13; Ez 32:7; Am 8:9.

m. [24:30] Dn 7:13; Zec 12:12–14; Rev 1:7.

[*] [24:30] The sign of the Son of Man: perhaps this means the sign that is the glorious appearance of the Son of Man; cf. Mt 12:39–40 where "the sign of Jonah" is Jonah's being in the "belly of the whale." Tribes of the earth will mourn: peculiar to Matthew; cf. Zec 12:12–14. Coming upon the clouds…glory: cf. Dn 7:13, although there the "one like a son of man" comes to God to receive kingship; here the Son of Man comes from heaven for judgment.

n. [24:31] Is 27:13; 1 Cor 15:52; 1 Thes 4:16.

[*] [24:31] Send out his angels: cf. Mt 13:41 where they are sent out to collect the wicked for punishment. Trumpet blast: cf. Is 27:13; 1 Thes 4:16.

THE LESSON OF THE FIG TREE.*

32 "Learn a lesson from the fig tree. When its branch becomes tender and sprouts leaves, you know that summer is near. **33** In the same way, when you see all these things, know that he is near, at the gates. **34** Amen, I say to you, this generation* will not pass away until all these things have taken place. **35**º Heaven and earth will pass away, but my words will not pass away.

* [24:32–35] Cf. Mk 13:28–31.

* [24:34] The difficulty raised by this verse cannot be satisfactorily removed by the supposition that this generation means the Jewish people throughout the course of their history, much less the entire human race. Perhaps for Matthew it means the generation to which he and his community belonged.

o. [24:35] Is 40:8.

36[p] "But of that day and hour no one knows, neither the angels of heaven, nor the Son,[*] but the Father alone. **37**[*q] For as it was in the days of Noah, so it will be at the coming of the Son of Man. **38** In [those] days before the flood, they were eating and drinking, marrying and giving in marriage, up to the day that Noah entered the ark. **39** They did not know until the flood came and carried them all away. So will it be [also] at the coming of the Son of Man. **40**[*r] Two men will be out in the field; one will be taken, and one will be left. **41** Two women will be grinding at the mill; one will be taken, and one will be left. **42**[*s] Therefore, stay awake! For you do not know on which day your Lord will come. **43**[t] Be sure of this: if the master of the house had known the hour of night when the thief was coming, he would have stayed awake and not let his house be broken into. **44** So too, you also must be prepared, for at an hour you do not expect, the Son of Man will come.

[*] [24:36–44] The statement of Mt 24:34 is now counterbalanced by one that declares that the exact time of the parousia is known only to the Father (Mt 24:36), and the disciples are warned to be always ready for it. This section is drawn from Mark and Q (cf. Lk 17:26–27, 34–35; 12:39–40).

p. [24:36] Acts 1:7.

[*] [24:36] Many textual witnesses omit nor the Son, which follows Mk 13:32. Since its omission can be explained by reluctance to attribute this ignorance to the Son, the reading that includes it is probably original.

[*] [24:37–39] Cf. Lk 17:26–27. In the days of Noah: the Old Testament account of the flood lays no emphasis upon what is central for Matthew, i.e., the unexpected coming of the flood upon those who were unprepared for it.

q. [24:37–39] Gn 6:5–7:23; Lk 17:26–27; 2 Pt 3:6.

[*] [24:40–41] Cf. Lk 17:34–35. Taken…left: the former probably means taken into the kingdom; the latter, left for destruction. People in the same situation will be dealt with in opposite ways. In this context, the discrimination between them will be based on their readiness for the coming of the Son of Man.

r. [24:40–41] Lk 17:34–35.

[*] [24:42–44] Cf. Lk 12:39–40. The theme of vigilance and readiness is continued with the bold comparison of the Son of Man to a thief who comes to break into a house.

s. [24:42–44] 25:13; Lk 12:39–40.

t. [24:43] 1 Thes 5:2.

THE UNKNOWN DAY AND HOUR.*

THE FAITHFUL OR THE UNFAITHFUL SERVANT.*

45[u] "Who, then, is the faithful and prudent servant, whom the master has put in charge of his household to distribute to them their food at the proper time?* **46** Blessed is that servant whom his master on his arrival finds doing so. **47** Amen, I say to you, he will put him in charge of all his property. **48*** But if that wicked servant says to himself, 'My master is long delayed,' **49** and begins to beat his fellow servants, and eat and drink with drunkards, **50** the servant's master will come on an unexpected day and at an unknown hour **51**[v] and will punish him severely* and assign him a place with the hypocrites, where there will be wailing and grinding of teeth.

* [24:45–51] The second part of the discourse (see note on Mt 24:1–25:46) begins with this parable of the faithful or unfaithful servant; cf. Lk 12:41–46. It is addressed to the leaders of Matthew's church; the servant has been put in charge of his master's household (Mt 24:45) even though that household is composed of those who are his fellow servants (Mt 24:49).

u. [24:45–51] Lk 12:41–46.

* [24:45] To distribute…proper time: readiness for the master's return means a vigilance that is accompanied by faithful performance of the duty assigned.

* [24:48] My master…delayed: the note of delay is found also in the other parables of this section; cf. Mt 25:5, 19.

v. [24:51] 13:42; 25:30.

* [24:51] Punish him severely: the Greek verb, found in the New Testament only here and in the Lucan parallel (Lk 12:46), means, literally, "cut in two." With the hypocrites: see note on Mt 6:2. Matthew classes the unfaithful Christian leader with the unbelieving leaders of Judaism. Wailing and grinding of teeth: see note on Mt 8:11–12.

MATTHEW CHAPTER 25

THE PARABLE OF THE TEN VIRGINS.*

1 "Then* the kingdom of heaven will be like ten virgins who took their lamps and went out to meet the bridegroom. **2*** Five of them were foolish and five were wise. **3** The foolish ones, when taking their lamps, brought no oil with them, **4** but the wise brought flasks of oil with their lamps. **5** Since the bridegroom was long delayed, they all became drowsy and fell asleep. **6** At midnight, there was a cry, 'Behold, the bridegroom! Come out to meet him!' **7** Then all those virgins got up and trimmed their lamps. **8** The foolish ones said to the wise, 'Give us some of your oil, for our lamps are going out.' **9** But the wise ones replied, 'No, for there may not be enough for us and you. Go instead to the merchants and buy some for yourselves.' **10** While they went off to buy it, the bridegroom came and those who were ready went into the wedding feast with him. Then the door was locked. **11***ᵃ Afterwards the other virgins came and said, 'Lord, Lord, open the door for us!' **12** But he said in reply, 'Amen, I say to you, I do not know you.' **13**ᵇ Therefore, stay awake,* for you know neither the day nor the hour.

* [25:1–13] Peculiar to Matthew.

* [25:1] Then: at the time of the parousia. Kingdom…will be like: see note on Mt 13:24–30.

* [25:2–4] Foolish…wise: cf. the contrasted "wise man" and "fool" of Mt 7:24, 26 where the two are distinguished by good deeds and lack of them, and such deeds may be signified by the oil of this parable.

* [25:11–12] Lord, Lord: cf. Mt 7:21. I do not know you: cf. Mt 7:23 where the Greek verb is different but synonymous.

a. [25:11–12] 7:21, 23; Lk 13:25–27.

b. [25:13] 24:42; Mk 13:33.

* [25:13] Stay awake: some scholars see this command as an addition to the original parable of Matthew's traditional material, since in Mt 25:5 all the virgins, wise and foolish, fall asleep. But the wise virgins are adequately equipped for their task, and stay awake may mean no more than to be prepared; cf. Mt 24:42, 44.

THE PARABLE OF THE TALENTS.*

14^c "It will be as when a man who was going on a journey* called in his servants and entrusted his possessions to them. 15 To one he gave five talents;* to another, two; to a third, one—to each according to his ability. Then he went away. Immediately 16 the one who received five talents went and traded with them, and made another five. 17 Likewise, the one who received two made another two. 18* But the man who received one went off and dug a hole in the ground and buried his master's money. 19 After a long time the master of those servants came back and settled accounts with them. 20 The one who had received five talents came forward bringing the additional five.* He said, 'Master, you gave me five talents. See, I have made five more.' 21^d His master said to him, 'Well done, my good and faithful servant. Since you were faithful in small matters, I will give you great responsibilities. Come, share your master's joy.' 22 [Then] the one who had received two talents also came forward and said, 'Master, you gave me two talents. See, I have made two more.' 23 His master said

to him, 'Well done, my good and faithful servant. Since you were faithful in small matters, I will give you great responsibilities. Come, share your master's joy.' 24 Then the one who had received the one talent came forward and said, 'Master, I knew you were a demanding person, harvesting where you did not plant and gathering where you did not scatter; 25 so out of fear I went off and buried your talent in the ground. Here it is back.' 26 His master said to him in reply, 'You wicked, lazy servant!* So you knew that I harvest where I did not plant and gather where I did not scatter? 27 Should you not then have put my money in the bank so that I could have got it back with interest on my return? 28 Now then! Take the talent from him and give it to the one with ten. 29*e For to everyone who has, more will be given and he will grow rich; but from the one who has not, even what he has will be taken away. 30* And throw this useless servant into the darkness outside, where there will be wailing and grinding of teeth.'

* [25:14–30] Cf. Lk 19:12–27.

c. [25:14–30] Lk 19:12–27.

* [25:14] It will be as when…journey: literally, "For just as a man who was going on a journey." Although the comparison is not completed, the sense is clear; the kingdom of heaven is like the situation here described. Faithful use of one's gifts will lead to participation in the fullness of the kingdom, lazy inactivity to exclusion from it.

* [25:15] Talents: see note on Mt 18:24.

* [25:18] Buried his master's money: see note on Mt 13:44.

* [25:20–23] Although the first two servants have received and doubled large sums, their faithful trading is regarded by the master as fidelity in small matters only, compared with the great responsibilities now to be given to them. The latter are unspecified. Share your master's joy: probably the joy of the banquet of the kingdom; cf. Mt 8:11.

d. [25:21] Lk 16:10.

* [25:26–28] Wicked, lazy servant: this man's inactivity is not negligible but seriously culpable. As punishment, he loses the gift he had received, that is now given to the first servant, whose possessions are already great.

* [25:29] See note on Mt 13:12 where there is a similar application of this maxim.

e. [25:29] 13:12; Mk 4:25; Lk 8:18; 19:26.

* [25:30] See note on Mt 8:11–12.

THE JUDGMENT OF THE NATIONS.*

31[f] "When the Son of Man comes in his glory, and all the angels with him, he will sit upon his glorious throne, **32**[g] and all the nations[*] will be assembled before him. And he will separate them one from another, as a shepherd separates the sheep from the goats. **33** He will place the sheep on his right and the goats on his left. **34** Then the king will say to those on his right, 'Come, you who are blessed by my Father. Inherit the kingdom prepared for you from the foundation of the world. **35**[h] For I was hungry and you gave me food, I was thirsty and you gave me drink, a stranger and you welcomed me, **36** naked and you clothed me, ill and you cared for me, in prison and you visited me.' **37** Then the righteous[*] will answer him and say, 'Lord, when did we see you hungry and feed you, or thirsty and give you drink? **38** When did we see you a stranger and welcome you, or naked and clothe you? **39** When did we see you ill or in prison, and visit you?' **40**[i] And the king will say to them in reply, 'Amen, I say to you, whatever you did for one of these least brothers of mine, you did for me.' **41**[*][j] Then he will say to those on his left, 'Depart from me, you accursed, into the eternal fire prepared for the devil and his angels. **42**[k] For I was hungry and you gave me no food, I was thirsty and you gave me no drink, **43** a stranger and you gave me no welcome, naked and you gave me no clothing, ill and in prison, and you did not care for me.' **44**[*] Then they will answer and say, 'Lord, when did we see you hungry or thirsty or a stranger or naked or ill or in prison, and not minister to your needs?' **45** He will answer them, 'Amen, I say to you, what you did not do for one of these least ones, you did not do for me.' **46**[l] And these will go off to eternal punishment, but the righteous to eternal life."

[*] [25:31–46] The conclusion of the discourse, which is peculiar to Matthew, portrays the final judgment that will accompany the parousia. Although often called a "parable," it is not really such, for the only parabolic elements are the depiction of the Son of Man as a shepherd and of the righteous and the wicked as sheep and goats respectively (Mt 25:32–33). The criterion of judgment will be the deeds of mercy that have been done for the least of Jesus' brothers (Mt 25:40). A difficult and important question is the identification of these least brothers. Are they all people who have suffered hunger, thirst, etc. (Mt 25:35, 36) or a particular group of such sufferers? Scholars are divided in their response and arguments can be made for either side. But leaving aside the problem of what the traditional material that Matthew edited may have meant, it seems that a stronger case can be made for the view that in the evangelist's sense the sufferers are Christians, probably Christian missionaries whose sufferings were brought upon them by their preaching of the gospel. The criterion of judgment for all the nations is their treatment of those who have borne to the world the message of Jesus, and this means ultimately their acceptance or rejection of Jesus himself; cf. Mt 10:40, "Whoever receives you, receives me." See note on Mt 16:27.

f. [25:31] 16:27; Dt 33:2 LXX.

g. [25:32] Ez 34:17.

[*] [25:32] All the nations: before the end the gospel will have been preached throughout the world (Mt 24:14); thus the Gentiles will be judged on their response to it. But the phrase all the nations includes the Jews also, for at the judgment "the Son of Man...will repay everyone according to his conduct" (Mt 16:27).

h. [25:35–36] Is 58:7; Ez 18:7.

[*] [25:37–40] The righteous will be astonished that in caring for the needs of the sufferers they were ministering to the Lord himself. One of these least brothers of mine: cf. Mt 10:42.

i. [25:40] 10:40, 42.

[*] [25:41] Fire prepared...his angels: cf. 1 Enoch 10:13 where it is said of the evil angels and Semyaza, their leader, "In those days they will lead them into the bottom of the fire—and in torment—in the prison (where) they will be locked up forever."

j. [25:41] 7:23; Lk 13:27.

k. [25:42–43] Jb 22:7; Jas 2:15–16.

[*] [25:44–45] The accursed (Mt 25:41) will be likewise astonished that their neglect of the sufferers was neglect of the Lord and will receive from him a similar answer.

l. [25:46] Dn 12:2.

MATTHEW CHAPTER 26

VII. THE PASSION AND RESURRECTION

THE CONSPIRACY AGAINST JESUS.

1[*] When Jesus finished all these words,[*] he said to his disciples, **2**^a "You know that in two days' time it will be Passover, and the Son of Man will be handed over to be crucified." **3**[*] Then the chief priests and the elders of the people assembled in the palace of the high priest, who was called Caiaphas, **4**^b and they consulted together to arrest Jesus by treachery and put him to death. **5** But they said, "Not during the festival,* that there may not be a riot among the people."

* [26:1–28:20] The five books with alternating narrative and discourse (Mt 3:1–25:46) that give this gospel its distinctive structure lead up to the climactic events that are the center of Christian belief and the origin of the Christian church, the passion and resurrection of Jesus. In his passion narrative (Mt 26 and 27) Matthew follows his Marcan source closely but with omissions (e.g., Mk 14:51–52) and additions (e.g., Mt 27:3–10, 19). Some of the additions indicate that he utilized traditions that he had received from elsewhere; others are due to his own theological insight (e.g., Mt 26:28 "…for the forgiveness of sins"; Mt 27:52). In his editing Matthew also altered Mark in some minor details. But there is no need to suppose that he knew any passion narrative other than Mark's.

* [26:1–2] When Jesus finished all these words: see note on Mt 7:28–29. "You know…crucified": Matthew turns Mark's statement of the time (Mk 14:1) into Jesus' final prediction of his passion. Passover: see note on Mk 14:1.

a. [26:2–5] Mk 14:1–2; Lk 22:1–2.

* [26:3] Caiaphas was high priest from A.D. 18 to 36.

b. [26:4] Jn 11:47–53.

THE ANOINTING AT BETHANY.*

6^c Now when Jesus was in Bethany in the house of Simon the leper, **7** a woman came up to him with an alabaster jar of costly perfumed oil, and poured it on his head while he was reclining at table. **8** When the disciples saw this, they were indignant and said, "Why this waste? **9** It could have been sold for much, and the money given to the poor." **10** Since Jesus knew this, he said to them, "Why do you make trouble for the woman? She has done a good thing for me. **11**^d The poor you will always have with you; but you will not always have me. **12*** In pouring this perfumed oil upon my body, she did it to prepare me for burial. **13** Amen, I say to you, wherever this gospel is proclaimed in the whole world, what she has done will be spoken of, in memory of her."

* [26:6–13] See notes on Mk 14:3–9 and Jn 12:1–8.

c. [26:6–13] Mk 14:3–9; Jn 12:1–8.

d. [26:11] Dt 15:11.

* [26:12] To prepare me for burial: cf. Mk 14:8. In accordance with the interpretation of this act as Jesus' burial anointing, Matthew, more consistent than Mark, changes the purpose of the visit of the women to Jesus' tomb; they do not go to anoint him (Mk 16:1) but "to see the tomb" (Mt 28:1).

THE BETRAYAL BY JUDAS.

14^e Then one of the Twelve, who was called Judas Iscariot,[*] went to the chief priests **15**^{*f} and said, "What are you willing to give me if I hand him over to you?" They paid him thirty pieces of silver, **16** and from that time on he looked for an opportunity to hand him over.

e. [26:14–16] Mk 14:10–11; Lk 22:3–6.

* [26:14] Iscariot: see note on Lk 6:16.

* [26:15] The motive of avarice is introduced by Judas's question about the price for betrayal, which is absent in the Marcan source (Mk 14:10–11). Hand him over: the same Greek verb is used to express the saving purpose of God by which Jesus is handed over to death (cf. Mt 17:22; 20:18; 26:2) and the human malice that hands him over. Thirty pieces of silver: the price of the betrayal is found only in Matthew. It is derived from Zec 11:12 where it is the wages paid to the rejected shepherd, a cheap price (Zec 11:13). That amount is also the compensation paid to one whose slave has been gored by an ox (Ex 21:32).

f. [26:15] Zec 11:12.

PREPARATIONS FOR THE PASSOVER.

17^g On the first day of the Feast of Unleavened Bread,[*] the disciples approached Jesus and said, "Where do you want us to prepare for you to eat the Passover?"^h **18**[*] He said, "Go into the city to a certain man and tell him, 'The teacher says, "My appointed time draws near; in your house I shall celebrate the Passover with my disciples."'" **19** The disciples then did as Jesus had ordered, and prepared the Passover.

g. [26:17–25] Mk 14:12–21; Lk 22:7–23.

* [26:17] The first day of the Feast of Unleavened Bread: see note on Mk 14:1. Matthew omits Mark's "when they sacrificed the Passover lamb."

h. [26:17] Ex 12:14–20.

* [26:18] By omitting much of Mk 14:13–15, adding My appointed time draws near, and turning the question into a statement, in your house I shall celebrate the Passover, Matthew has given this passage a solemnity and majesty greater than that of his source.

THE BETRAYER.

20 When it was evening, he reclined at table with the Twelve. **21** And while they were eating, he said, "Amen, I say to you, one of you will betray me."* **22** Deeply distressed at this, they began to say to him one after another, "Surely it is not I, Lord?" **23** He said in reply, "He who has dipped his hand into the dish with me is the one who will betray me. **24***i The Son of Man indeed goes, as it is written of him, but woe to that man by whom the Son of Man is betrayed. It would be better for that man if he had never been born." **25*** Then Judas, his betrayer, said in reply, "Surely it is not I, Rabbi?" He answered, "You have said so."

* [26:21] Given Matthew's interest in the fulfillment of the Old Testament, it is curious that he omits the Marcan designation of Jesus' betrayer as "one who is eating with me" (Mk 14:18), since that is probably an allusion to Ps 41:10. However, the shocking fact that the betrayer is one who shares table fellowship with Jesus is emphasized in Mt 26:23.

* [26:24] It would be better...born: the enormity of the deed is such that it would be better not to exist than to do it.

i. [26:24] Is 53:8–10.

* [26:25] Peculiar to Matthew. You have said so: cf. Mt 26:64; 27:11. This is a half-affirmative. Emphasis is laid on the pronoun and the answer implies that the statement would not have been made if the question had not been asked.

THE LORD'S SUPPER.

26 [*][j] While they were eating, Jesus took bread, said the blessing, broke it, and giving it to his disciples said, "Take and eat; this is my body."[*][k] **27** Then he took a cup, gave thanks,[*] and gave it to them, saying, "Drink from it, all of you, **28**[l] for this is my blood of the covenant, which will be shed on behalf of many for the forgiveness of sins. **29**[*] I tell you, from now on I shall not drink this fruit of the vine until the day when I drink it with you new in the kingdom of my Father." **30**[*] Then, after singing a hymn, they went out to the Mount of Olives.

[*] [26:26–29] See note on Mk 14:22–24. The Marcan-Matthean is one of the two major New Testament traditions of the words of Jesus when instituting the Eucharist. The other (and earlier) is the Pauline-Lucan (1 Cor 11:23–25; Lk 22:19–20). Each shows the influence of Christian liturgical usage, but the Marcan-Matthean is more developed in that regard than the Pauline-Lucan. The words over the bread and cup succeed each other without the intervening meal mentioned in 1 Cor 11:25; Lk 22:20; and there is parallelism between the consecratory words (this is my body…this is my blood). Matthew follows Mark closely but with some changes.

j. [26:26–30] Mk 14:22–26; Lk 22:14–23; 1 Cor 11:23–25.

[*] [26:26] See note on Mt 14:19. Said the blessing: a prayer blessing God. Take and eat: literally, Take, eat. Eat is an addition to Mark's "take it" (literally, "take"; Mk 14:22). This is my body: the bread is identified with Jesus himself.

k. [26:26–27] 1 Cor 10:16.

[*] [26:27–28] Gave thanks: see note on Mt 15:36. Gave it to them…all of you: cf. Mk 14:23–24. In the Marcan sequence the disciples drink and then Jesus says the interpretative words. Matthew has changed this into a command to drink followed by those words. My blood: see Lv 17:11 for the concept that the blood is "the seat of life" and that when placed on the altar it "makes atonement." Which will be shed: the present participle, "being shed" or "going to be shed," is future in relation to the Last Supper. On behalf of: Greek peri; see note on Mk 14:24. Many: see note on Mt 20:28. For the forgiveness of sins: a Matthean addition. The same phrase occurs in Mk 1:4 in connection with John's baptism but Matthew avoids it there (Mt 3:11). He places it here probably because he wishes to emphasize that it is the sacrificial death of Jesus that brings forgiveness of sins.

l. [26:28] Ex 24:8; Is 53:12.

[*] [26:29] Although his death will interrupt the table fellowship he has had with the disciples, Jesus confidently predicts his vindication by God and a new table fellowship with them at the banquet of the kingdom.

[*] [26:30] See note on Mk 14:26.

PETER'S DENIAL FORETOLD.

31[m] Then Jesus said to them, "This night all of you will have your faith in me shaken,[*] for it is written:[n]

'I will strike the shepherd,

and the sheep of the flock will be dispersed';

32 but after I have been raised up, I shall go before you to Galilee."

33 Peter said to him in reply, "Though all may have their faith in you shaken, mine will never be." **34**[*][o] Jesus said to him, "Amen, I say to you, this very night before the cock crows, you will deny me three times."[p] **35** Peter said to him, "Even though I should have to die with you, I will not deny you." And all the disciples spoke likewise.

m. [26:31–35] Mk 14:7–31.

[*] [26:31] Will have…shaken: literally, "will be scandalized in me"; see note on Mt 24:9–12. I will strike… dispersed: cf. Zec 13:7.

n. [26:31] Zec 13:7; Jn 16:32.

[*] [26:34] Before the cock crows: see note on Mt 14:25. The third watch of the night was called "cock-crow." Deny me: see note on Mt 16:24.

o. [26:34–35] Lk 22:33–34; Jn 13:37–38.

p. [26:34] 26:69–75.

THE AGONY IN THE GARDEN.

36 *q Then Jesus came with them to a place called Gethsemane,* and he said to his disciples, "Sit here while I go over there and pray." **37** r He took along Peter and the two sons of Zebedee,* and began to feel sorrow and distress. **38** t Then he said to them, "My soul is sorrowful even to death.* Remain here and keep watch with me." **39** u He advanced a little and fell prostrate in prayer, saying, "My Father,* if it is possible, let this cup pass from me; yet, not as I will, but as you will." **40** When he returned to his disciples he found them asleep. He said to Peter, "So you could not keep watch with me for one hour? **41** Watch and pray that you may not un-dergo the test.* The spirit is willing, but the flesh is weak." **42** *v Withdrawing a second time, he prayed again, "My Father, if it is not possible that this cup pass without my drinking it, your will be done!" **43** Then he returned once more and found them asleep, for they could not keep their eyes open. **44** He left them and withdrew again and prayed a third time, saying the same thing again. **45** w Then he returned to his disciples and said to them, "Are you still sleeping and taking your rest? Behold, the hour is at hand when the Son of Man is to be hand-ed over to sinners. **46** Get up, let us go. Look, my betrayer is at hand."

* [26:36–56] Cf. Mk 14:32–52. The account of Jesus in Gethsemane is divided between that of his agony (Mt 26:36–46) and that of his betrayal and arrest (Mt 26:47–56). Jesus' sorrow and distress (Mt 26:37) in face of death is unrelieved by the presence of his three disciples who, though urged to watch with him (Mt 26:38, 41), fall asleep (Mt 26:40, 43). He prays that if…possible his death may be avoided (Mt 26:39) but that his Father's will be done (Mt 26:39, 42, 44). Knowing then that his death must take place, he announces to his companions that the hour for his being handed over has come (Mt 26:45). Judas arrives with an armed band provided by the Sanhedrin and greets Jesus with a kiss, the prearranged sign for his identification (Mt 26:47–49). After his arrest he rebukes a disciple who has attacked the high priest's servant with a sword (Mt 26:51–54), and chides those who have come out to seize him with swords and clubs as if he were a robber (Mt 26:55–56). In both rebukes Jesus declares that the treatment he is now receiving is the fulfillment of the scriptures (Mt 26:55, 56). The subsequent flight of all the disciples is itself the fulfillment of his own prediction (cf. 31). In this episode, Matthew follows Mark with a few alterations.

q. [26:36–46] Mk 14:32–42; Lk 22:39–46.

* [26:36] Gethsemane: the Hebrew name means "oil press" and designates an olive orchard on the western slope of the Mount of Olives; see note on Mt 21:1. The name appears only in Matthew and Mark. The place is called a "garden" in Jn 18:1.

r. [26:36] Jn 18:1.

s. [26:37–39] Heb 5:7.

* [26:37] Peter and the two sons of Zebedee: cf. Mt 17:1.

t. [26:38] Ps 42:6, 12; Jon 4:9.

* [26:38] Cf. Ps 42:6, 12. In the Septuagint (Ps 41:5, 12) the same Greek word for sorrowful is used as here. To death: i.e., "enough to die"; cf. Jon 4:9.

u. [26:39] Jn 4:34; 6:38; Phil 2:8.

* [26:39] My Father: see note on Mk 14:36. Matthew omits the Aramaic 'abba' and adds the qualifier my. This cup: see note on Mk 10:38–40.

* [26:41] Undergo the test: see note on Mt 6:13. In that verse "the final test" translates the same Greek word as is here translated the test, and these are the only instances of the use of that word in Matthew. It is possible that the passion of Jesus is seen here as an anticipation of the great tribulation that will precede the parousia (see notes on Mt 24:8; 24:21) to which Mt 6:13 refers, and that just as Jesus prays to be delivered from death (Mt 26:39), so he exhorts the disciples to pray that they will not have to undergo the great test that his passion would be for them. Some scholars, however, understand not undergo (literally, "not enter") the test as meaning not that the disciples may be spared the test but that they may not yield to the temptation of falling away from Jesus because of his passion even though they will have to endure it.

* [26:42] Your will be done: cf. Mt 6:10.

v. [26:42] 6:10; Heb 10:9.

w. [26:45] Jn 12:23; 13:1; 17:1.

THE BETRAYAL AND ARREST OF JESUS.

47[x] While he was still speaking, Judas, one of the Twelve, arrived, accompanied by a large crowd, with swords and clubs, who had come from the chief priests and the elders of the people. **48** His betrayer had arranged a sign with them, saying, "The man I shall kiss is the one; arrest him." **49** Immediately he went over to Jesus and said, "Hail, Rabbi!"[*] and he kissed him. **50** Jesus answered him, "Friend, do what you have come for." Then stepping forward they laid hands on Jesus and arrested him. **51** And behold, one of those who accompanied Jesus put his hand to his sword, drew it, and struck the high priest's servant, cutting off his ear. **52** Then Jesus said to him, "Put your sword back into its sheath, for all who take the sword will perish by the sword. **53** Do you think that I cannot call upon my Father and he will not provide me at this moment with more than twelve legions of angels? **54** But then how would the scriptures be fulfilled which say that it must come to pass in this way?" **55**[*] At that hour Jesus said to the crowds, "Have you come out as against a robber, with swords and clubs to seize me? Day after day I sat teaching in the temple area, yet you did not arrest me. **56**[y] But all this has come to pass that the writings of the prophets may be fulfilled." Then all the disciples left him and fled.

---

x. [26:47–56] Mk 14:43–50; Lk 22:47–53; Jn 18:3–11.

[*] [26:49] Rabbi: see note on Mt 23:6–7. Jesus is so addressed twice in Matthew (Mt 26:25), both times by Judas. For the significance of the closely related address "teacher" in Matthew, see note on Mt 8:19.

[*] [26:55] Day after day...arrest me: cf. Mk 14:49. This suggests that Jesus had taught for a relatively long period in Jerusalem, whereas Mt 21:1–11 puts his coming to the city for the first time only a few days before.

y. [26:56] 26:31.

JESUS BEFORE THE SANHEDRIN.*

57[7] Those who had arrested Jesus led him away to Caiaphas* the high priest, where the scribes and the elders were assembled. **58** Peter was following him at a distance as far as the high priest's courtyard, and going inside he sat down with the servants to see the outcome. **59** The chief priests and the entire Sanhedrin* kept trying to obtain false testimony against Jesus in order to put him to death, **60**[a] but they found none, though many false witnesses came forward. Finally two* came forward **61** who stated, "This man said, 'I can destroy the temple of God and within three days rebuild it.'" **62** The high priest rose and addressed him, "Have you no answer? What are these men testifying against you?" **63**[b] But Jesus was silent.* Then the high priest said to him, "I order you to tell us under oath before the living God whether you are the Messiah, the Son of God." **64**[c] Jesus said to him in reply, "You have said so.* But I tell you:
From now on you will see 'the Son of Man
seated at the right hand of the Power'
and 'coming on the clouds of heaven.'"

65 Then the high priest tore his robes and said, "He has blasphemed!* What further need have we of witnesses? You have now heard the blasphemy; **66** what is your opinion?" They said in reply, "He deserves to die!" **67**[*d] Then they spat in his face and struck him, while some slapped him, **68** saying, "Prophesy for us, Messiah: who is it that struck you?"

* [26:57–68] Following Mk 14:53–65 Matthew presents the nighttime appearance of Jesus before the Sanhedrin as a real trial. After many false witnesses bring charges against him that do not suffice for the death sentence (Mt 26:60), two came forward who charge him with claiming to be able to destroy the temple…and within three days to rebuild it (Mt 26:60–61). Jesus makes no answer even when challenged to do so by the high priest, who then orders him to declare under oath…whether he is the Messiah, the Son of God (Mt 26:62–63). Matthew changes Mark's clear affirmative response (Mk 14:62) to the same one as that given to Judas (Mt 26:25), but follows Mark almost verbatim in Jesus' predicting that his judges will see him (the Son of Man) seated at the right hand of God and coming on the clouds of heaven (Mt 26:64). The high priest then charges him with blasphemy (Mt 26:65), a charge with which the other members of the Sanhedrin agree by declaring that he deserves to die (Mt 26:66). They then attack him (Mt 26:67) and mockingly demand that he prophesy (Mt 26:68). This account contains elements that are contrary to the judicial procedures prescribed in the Mishnah, the Jewish code of law that dates in written form from ca. A.D. 200, e.g., trial on a feast day, a night session of the court, pronouncement of a verdict of condemnation at the same session at which testimony was received. Consequently, some scholars regard the account entirely as a creation of the early Christians without historical value. However, it is disputable whether the norms found in the Mishnah were in force at the time of Jesus. More to the point is the question whether the Matthean-Marcan night trial derives from a combination of two separate incidents, a nighttime preliminary investigation (cf. Jn 18:13, 19–24) and a formal trial on the following morning (cf. Lk 22:66–71).

z. [26:57–68] Mk 14:53–65; Lk 22:54–55, 63–71; Jn 18:12–14, 19–24.

* [26:57] Caiaphas: see note on Mt 26:3.

* [26:59] Sanhedrin: see note on Lk 22:66.

a. [26:60–61] Dt 19:15; Jn 2:19; Acts 6:14.

* [26:60–61] Two: cf. Dt 19:15. I can destroy…rebuild it: there are significant differences from the Marcan parallel (Mk 14:58). Matthew omits "made with hands" and "not made with hands" and changes Mark's "will destroy" and "will build another" to can destroy and (can) rebuild. The charge is probably based on Jesus' prediction of the temple's destruction; see notes on Mt 23:37–39; 24:2; and Jn 2:19. A similar prediction by Jeremiah was considered as deserving death; cf. Jer 7:1–15; 26:1–8.

b. [26:63] Is 53:7.

* [26:63] Silent: possibly an allusion to Is 53:7. I order you…living God: peculiar to Matthew; cf. Mk 14:61.

c. [26:64] Ps 110:1; Dn 7:13.

* [26:64] You have said so: see note on Mt 26:25. From now on…heaven: the Son of Man who is to be crucified (cf. Mt 20:19) will be seen in glorious majesty (cf. Ps 110:1) and coming on the clouds of heaven (cf. Dn 7:13). The Power: see note on Mk 14:61–62.

* [26:65] Blasphemed: the punishment for blasphemy was death by stoning (see Lv 24:10–16). According to the Mishnah, to be guilty of blasphemy one had to pronounce "the Name itself," i.e., Yahweh; cf. Sanhedrin 7, 4.5. Those who judge the gospel accounts of Jesus' trial by the later Mishnah standards point out that Jesus uses the surrogate "the Power," and hence no Jewish court would have regarded him as guilty of blasphemy; others hold that the Mishnah's narrow understanding of blasphemy was a later development.

* [26:67–68] The physical abuse, apparently done to Jesus by the members of the Sanhedrin themselves, recalls the sufferings of the Isaian Servant of the Lord; cf. Is 50:6. The mocking challenge to prophesy is probably motivated by Jesus' prediction of his future glory (Mt 26:64).

d. [26:67] Wis 2:19; Is 50:6.

PETER'S DENIAL OF JESUS.

69[e] Now Peter was sitting outside in the courtyard. One of the maids came over to him and said, "You too were with Jesus the Galilean." **70**[*] But he denied it in front of everyone, saying, "I do not know what you are talking about!" **71** As he went out to the gate, another girl saw him and said to those who were there, "This man was with Jesus the Nazorean." **72** Again he denied it with an oath, "I do not know the man!" **73**[*] A little later the bystanders came over and said to Peter, "Surely you too are one of them; even your speech gives you away." **74** At that he began to curse and to swear, "I do not know the man." And immediately a cock crowed. **75**[f] Then Peter remembered the word that Jesus had spoken: "Before the cock crows you will deny me three times." He went out and began to weep bitterly.

e. [26:69–75] Mk 14:66–72; Lk 22:56–62; Jn 18:17–18, 25–27.

* [26:70] Denied it in front of everyone: see Mt 10:33. Peter's repentance (Mt 26:75) saves him from the fearful destiny of which Jesus speaks there.

* [26:73] Your speech…away: Matthew explicates Mark's "you too are a Galilean" (Mk 14:70).

f. [26:75] 26:34.

MATTHEW CHAPTER 27

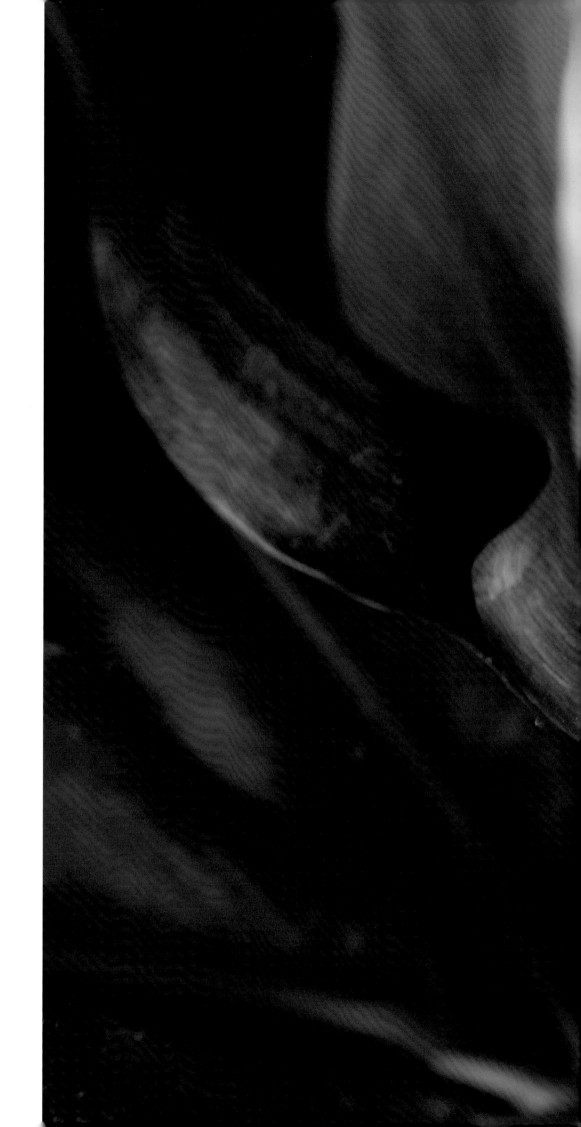

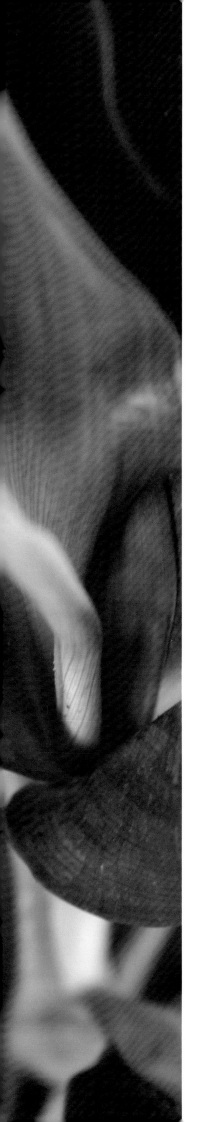

JESUS BEFORE PILATE.

1[*] When it was morning,[a] all the chief priests and the elders of the people took counsel[*] against Jesus to put him to death. **2** They bound him, led him away, and handed him over to Pilate, the governor.

* [27:1–31] Cf. Mk 15:1–20. Matthew's account of the Roman trial before Pilate is introduced by a consultation of the Sanhedrin after which Jesus is handed over to…the governor (Mt 27:1–2). Matthew follows his Marcan source closely but adds some material that is peculiar to him, the death of Judas (Mt 27:3–10), possibly the name Jesus as the name of Barabbas also (Mt 27:16–17), the intervention of Pilate's wife (Mt 27:19), Pilate's washing his hands in token of his disclaiming responsibility for Jesus' death (Mt 27:24), and the assuming of that responsibility by the whole people (Mt 27:25).

a. [27:1–2] Mk 15:1; Lk 23:1; Jn 18:28.

* [27:1] There is scholarly disagreement about the meaning of the Sanhedrin's taking counsel (symboulion elabon; cf. Mt 12:14; 22:15; 27:7; 28:12); see note on Mk 15:1. Some understand it as a discussion about the strategy for putting their death sentence against Jesus into effect since they lacked the right to do so themselves. Others see it as the occasion for their passing that sentence, holding that Matthew, unlike Mark (Mk 14:64), does not consider that it had been passed in the night session (Mt 26:66). Even in the latter interpretation, their handing him over to Pilate is best explained on the hypothesis that they did not have competence to put their sentence into effect, as is stated in Jn 18:31.

3[b] Then Judas, his betrayer, seeing that Jesus had been condemned, deeply regretted what he had done. He returned the thirty pieces of silver[*] to the chief priests and elders,[c] **4** saying, "I have sinned in betraying innocent blood." They said, "What is that to us? Look to it yourself." **5**[*] Flinging the money into the temple, he departed and went off and hanged himself. **6** The chief priests gathered up the money, but said, "It is not lawful to deposit this in the temple treasury, for it is the price of blood." **7** After consultation, they used it to buy the potter's field as a burial place for foreigners. **8** That is why that field even today is called the Field of Blood. **9** Then was fulfilled what had been said through Jeremiah the prophet,[*] "And they took the thirty pieces of silver, the value of a man with a price on his head, a price set by some of the Israelites, **10**[d] and they paid it out for the potter's field just as the Lord had commanded me."

b. [27:3–10] Acts 1:18–19.

[*] [27:3] The thirty pieces of silver: see Mt 26:15.

c. [27:3] 26:15.

[*] [27:5–8] For another tradition about the death of Judas, cf. Acts 1:18–19. The two traditions agree only in the purchase of a field with the money paid to Judas for his betrayal of Jesus and the name given to the field, the Field of Blood. In Acts Judas himself buys the field and its name comes from his own blood shed in his fatal accident on it. The potter's field: this designation of the field is based on the fulfillment citation in Mt 27:10.

[*] [27:9–10] Cf. Mt 26:15. Matthew's attributing this text to Jeremiah is puzzling, for there is no such text in that book, and the thirty pieces of silver thrown by Judas "into the temple" (Mt 27:5) recall rather Zec 11:12–13. It is usually said that the attribution of the text to Jeremiah is due to Matthew's combining the Zechariah text with texts from Jeremiah that speak of a potter (Jer 18:2–3), the buying of a field (Jer 32:6–9), or the breaking of a potter's flask at Topheth in the valley of Ben-Hinnom with the prediction that it will become a burial place (Jer 19:1–13).

d. [27:10] Zec 11:12–13.

THE DEATH
OF JUDAS.

JESUS QUESTIONED BY PILATE.

11[e] Now Jesus stood before the governor, and he questioned him, "Are you the king of the Jews?"[*] Jesus said, "You say so." **12**[f] And when he was accused by the chief priests and elders,[*] he made no answer. **13** Then Pilate said to him, "Do you not hear how many things they are testifying against you?" **14** But he did not answer him one word, so that the governor was greatly amazed.

e. [27:11–14] Mk 15:2–5; Lk 23:2–3; Jn 18:29–38.

* [27:11] King of the Jews: this title is used of Jesus only by pagans. The Matthean instances are, besides this verse, Mt 2:2; 27:29, 37. Matthew equates it with "Messiah"; cf. Mt 2:2, 4 and Mt 27:17, 22 where he has changed "the king of the Jews" of his Marcan source (Mk 15:9, 12) to "(Jesus) called Messiah." The normal political connotation of both titles would be of concern to the Roman governor. You say so: see note on Mt 26:25. An unqualified affirmative response is not made because Jesus' kingship is not what Pilate would understand it to be.

f. [27:12] Is 53:7.

* [27:12–14] Cf. Mt 26:62–63. As in the trial before the Sanhedrin, Jesus' silence may be meant to recall Is 53:7. Greatly amazed: possibly an allusion to Is 52:14–15.

THE SENTENCE OF DEATH.

15 *g Now on the occasion of the feast the governor was accustomed to release to the crowd one prisoner whom they wished. **16*** And at that time they had a notorious prisoner called [Jesus] Barabbas. **17** So when they had assembled, Pilate said to them, "Which one do you want me to release to you, [Jesus] Barabbas, or Jesus called Messiah?" **18*** For he knew that it was out of envy that they had handed him over. **19*** While he was still seated on the bench, his wife sent him a message, "Have nothing to do with that righteous man. I suffered much in a dream today because of him." **20**^h The chief priests and the elders persuaded the crowds to ask for Barabbas but to destroy Jesus. **21** The governor said to them in reply, "Which of the two do you want me to release to you?" They answered, "Barabbas!" **22*** Pilate said to them, "Then what shall I do with Jesus called Messiah?" They all said, "Let him be crucified!" **23** But he said, "Why? What evil has he done?" They only shouted the louder, "Let him be crucified!" **24***^i When Pilate saw that he was not succeeding at all, but that a riot was breaking out instead, he took water and washed his hands in the sight of the crowd, saying, "I am innocent of this man's blood. Look to it yourselves." **25** And the whole people said in reply, "His blood be upon us and upon our children." **26** Then he released Barabbas to them, but after he had Jesus scourged,* he handed him over to be crucified.

* [27:15–26] The choice that Pilate offers the crowd between Barabbas and Jesus is said to be in accordance with a custom of releasing at the Passover feast one prisoner chosen by the crowd (Mt 27:15). This custom is mentioned also in Mk 15:6 and Jn 18:39 but not in Luke; see note on Lk 23:17. Outside of the gospels there is no direct attestation of it, and scholars are divided in their judgment of the historical reliability of the claim that there was such a practice.

g. [27:15–26] Mk 15:6–15; Lk 23:17–25; Jn 18:39–19:16.

* [27:16–17] [Jesus] Barabbas: it is possible that the double name is the original reading; Jesus was a common Jewish name; see note on Mt 1:21. This reading is found in only a few textual witnesses, although its absence in the majority can be explained as an omission of Jesus made for reverential reasons. That name is bracketed because of its uncertain textual attestation. The Aramaic name Barabbas means "son of the father"; the irony of the choice offered between him and Jesus, the true son of the Father, would be evident to those addressees of Matthew who knew that.

* [27:18] Cf. Mk 14:10. This is an example of the tendency, found in varying degree in all the gospels, to present Pilate in a relatively favorable light and emphasize the hostility of the Jewish authorities and eventually of the people.

* [27:19] Jesus' innocence is declared by a Gentile woman. In a dream: in Matthew's infancy narrative, dreams are the means of divine communication; cf. Mt 1:20; 2:12, 13, 19, 22.

h. [27:20] Acts 3:14.

* [27:22] Let him be crucified: incited by the chief priests and elders (Mt 27:20), the crowds demand that Jesus be executed by crucifixion, a peculiarly horrible form of Roman capital punishment. The Marcan parallel, "Crucify him" (Mk 15:3), addressed to Pilate, is changed by Matthew to the passive, probably to emphasize the responsibility of the crowds.

* [27:24–25] Peculiar to Matthew. Took water...blood: cf. Dt 21:1–8, the handwashing prescribed in the case of a murder when the killer is unknown. The elders of the city nearest to where the corpse is found must wash their hands, declaring, "Our hands did not shed this blood." Look to it yourselves: cf. Mt 27:4. The whole people: Matthew sees in those who speak these words the entire people (Greek laos) of Israel. His blood...and upon our children: cf. Jer 26:15. The responsibility for Jesus' death is accepted by the nation that was God's special possession (Ex 19:5), his own people (Hos 2:25), and they thereby lose that high privilege; see Mt 21:43 and the note on that verse. The controversy between Matthew's church and Pharisaic Judaism about which was the true people of God is reflected here. As the Second Vatican Council has pointed out, guilt for Jesus' death is not attributable to all the Jews of his time or to any Jews of later times.

i. [27:24] Dt 21:1–8.

* [27:26] He had Jesus scourged: the usual preliminary to crucifixion.

MOCKERY BY THE SOLDIERS.

27^j Then the soldiers of the governor took Jesus inside the praetorium[*] and gathered the whole cohort around him. **28** They stripped off his clothes and threw a scarlet military cloak[*] about him. **29**^k Weaving a crown out of thorns,[*] they placed it on his head, and a reed in his right hand. And kneeling before him, they mocked him, saying, "Hail, King of the Jews!" **30**^l They spat upon him[*] and took the reed and kept striking him on the head. **31** And when they had mocked him, they stripped him of the cloak, dressed him in his own clothes, and led him off to crucify him.

j. [27:27–31] Mk 15:16–20; Jn 19:2–3.

* [27:27] The praetorium: the residence of the Roman governor. His usual place of residence was at Caesarea Maritima on the Mediterranean coast, but he went to Jerusalem during the great feasts, when the influx of pilgrims posed the danger of a nationalistic riot. It is disputed whether the praetorium in Jerusalem was the old palace of Herod in the west of the city or the fortress of Antonia northwest of the temple area. The whole cohort: normally six hundred soldiers.

* [27:28] Scarlet military cloak: so Matthew as against the royal purple of Mk 15:17 and Jn 19:2.

k. [27:29] 27:11.

* [27:29] Crown out of thorns: probably of long thorns that stood upright so that it resembled the "radiant" crown, a diadem with spikes worn by Hellenistic kings. The soldiers' purpose was mockery, not torture. A reed: peculiar to Matthew; a mock scepter.

l. [27:30] Is 50:6.

* [27:30] Spat upon him: cf. Mt 26:67 where there also is a possible allusion to Is 50:6.

THE WAY OF THE CROSS. *

32[m] As they were going out, they met a Cyrenian named Simon; this man they pressed into service to carry his cross.

* [27:32] See note on Mk 15:21. Cyrenian named Simon: Cyrenaica was a Roman province on the north coast of Africa and Cyrene was its capital city. The city had a large population of Greek-speaking Jews. Simon may have been living in Palestine or have come there for the Passover as a pilgrim. Pressed into service: see note on Mt 5:41.

m. [27:32] Mk 15:21; Lk 23:26.

THE CRUCIFIXION.

33[n] And when they came to a place called Golgotha (which means Place of the Skull), **34**[o] they gave Jesus wine to drink mixed with gall.[*] But when he had tasted it, he refused to drink. **35**[p] After they had crucified him, they divided his garments[*] by casting lots; **36** then they sat down and kept watch over him there. **37** And they placed over his head the written charge[*] against him: This is Jesus, the King of the Jews. **38** Two revolutionaries[*] were crucified with him, one on his right and the other on his left. **39**[*q] Those passing by reviled him, shaking their heads **40**[r] and saying, "You who would destroy the temple and rebuild it in three days, save yourself, if you are the Son of God, [and] come down from the cross!" **41** Likewise the chief priests with the scribes and elders mocked him and said, **42** "He saved others; he cannot save himself. So he is the king of Israel![*] Let him come down from the cross now, and we will believe in him. **43**[*s] He trusted in God; let him deliver him now if he wants him. For he said, 'I am the Son of God.'" **44** The revolutionaries who were crucified with him also kept abusing him in the same way.

n. [27:33–44] Mk 15:22–32; Lk 23:32–38; Jn 19:17–19, 23–24.

o. [27:34] Ps 69:21.

* [27:34] Wine…mixed with gall: cf. Mk 15:23 where the drink is "wine drugged with myrrh," a narcotic. Matthew's text is probably an inexact allusion to Ps 69:22. That psalm belongs to the class called the individual lament, in which a persecuted just man prays for deliverance in the midst of great suffering and also expresses confidence that his prayer will be heard. That theme of the suffering Just One is frequently applied to the sufferings of Jesus in the passion narratives.

p. [27:35] Ps 22:19.

* [27:35] The clothing of an executed criminal went to his executioner(s), but the description of that procedure in the case of Jesus, found in all the gospels, is plainly inspired by Ps 22:19. However, that psalm verse is quoted only in Jn 19:24.

* [27:37] The offense of a person condemned to death by crucifixion was written on a tablet that was displayed on his cross. The charge against Jesus was that he had claimed to be the King of the Jews (cf. Mt 27:11), i.e., the Messiah (cf. Mt 27:17, 22).

* [27:38] Revolutionaries: see note on Jn 18:40 where the same Greek word as that found here is used for Barabbas.

* [27:39–40] Reviled him…heads: cf. Ps 22:8. You who would destroy…three days; cf. Mt 26:61. If you are the Son of God: the same words as those of the devil in the temptation of Jesus; cf. Mt 4:3, 6.

q. [27:39] Ps 22:8.

r. [27:40] 4:3, 6; 26:61.

* [27:42] King of Israel: in their mocking of Jesus the members of the Sanhedrin call themselves and their people not "the Jews" but Israel.

* [27:43] Peculiar to Matthew. He trusted in God…wants him: cf. Ps 22:9. He said…of God: probably an allusion to Wis 2:12–20 where the theme of the suffering Just One appears.

s. [27:43] Ps 22:9; Wis 2:12–20.

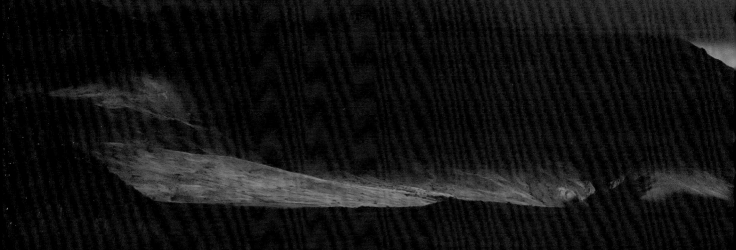

THE DEATH OF JESUS.

45[*][t] From noon onward,[u] darkness came over the whole land until three in the afternoon. **46**[v] And about three o'clock Jesus cried out in a loud voice, *"Eli, Eli, lema sabachthani?"*[*] which means, "My God, my God, why have you forsaken me?" **47**[*] Some of the bystanders who heard it said, "This one is calling for Elijah." **48**[w] Immediately one of them ran to get a sponge; he soaked it in wine, and putting it on a reed, gave it to him to drink. **49** But the rest said, "Wait, let us see if Elijah comes to save him." **50**[*] But Jesus cried out again in a loud voice, and gave up his spirit. **51**[x] And behold, the veil of the sanctuary was torn in two from top to bottom.[*] The earth quaked, rocks were split, **52**[y] tombs were opened, and the bodies of many saints who had fallen asleep were raised. **53** And coming forth from their tombs after his resurrection, they entered the holy city and appeared to many. **54**[*] The centurion and the men with him who were keeping watch over Jesus feared greatly when they saw the earthquake and all that was happening, and they said, "Truly, this was the Son of God!" **55** There were many women there, looking on from a distance,[*] who had followed Jesus from Galilee, ministering to him. **56**[z] Among them were Mary Magdalene and Mary the mother of James and Joseph, and the mother of the sons of Zebedee.

---

[*] [27:45] Cf. Am 8:9 where on the day of the Lord "the sun will set at midday."

t. [27:45–46] Mk 15:33–41; Lk 23:44–49; Jn 19:28–30.

u. [27:45] Am 8:9.

v. [27:46] Ps 22:2.

[*] [27:46] Eli, Eli, lema sabachthani?: Jesus cries out in the words of Ps 22:2a, a psalm of lament that is the Old Testament passage most frequently drawn upon in this narrative. In Mark the verse is cited entirely in Aramaic, which Matthew partially retains but changes the invocation of God to the Hebrew Eli, possibly because that is more easily related to the statement of the following verse about Jesus' calling for Elijah.

[*] [27:47] Elijah: see note on Mt 3:4. This prophet, taken up into heaven (2 Kgs 2:11), was believed to come to the help of those in distress, but the evidences of that belief are all later than the gospels.

w. [27:48] Ps 69:21.

[*] [27:50] Gave up his spirit: cf. the Marcan parallel (Mk 15:37), "breathed his last." Matthew's alteration expresses both Jesus' control over his destiny and his obedient giving up of his life to God.

x. [27:51] Ex 26:31–36; Ps 68:9; 77:19.

[*] [27:51–53] Veil of the sanctuary…bottom: cf. Mk 15:38; Lk 23:45. Luke puts this event immediately before the death of Jesus. There were two veils in the Mosaic tabernacle on the model of which the temple was constructed, the outer one before the entrance of the Holy Place and the inner one before the Holy of Holies (see Ex 26:31–36). Only the high priest could pass through the latter and that only on the Day of Atonement (see Lv 16:1–18). Probably the torn veil of the gospels is the inner one. The meaning of the scene may be that now, because of Jesus' death, all people have access to the presence of God, or that the temple, its holiest part standing exposed, is now profaned and will soon be destroyed. The earth quaked…appeared to many: peculiar to Matthew. The earthquake, the splitting of the rocks, and especially the resurrection of the dead saints indicate the coming of the final age. In the Old Testament the coming of God is frequently portrayed with the imagery of an earthquake (see Ps 68:9; 77:19), and Jesus speaks of the earthquakes that will accompany the "labor pains" that signify the beginning of the dissolution of the old world (Mt 24:7–8). For the expectation of the resurrection of the dead at the coming of the new and final age, see Dn 12:1–3. Matthew knows that the end of the old age has not yet come (Mt 28:20), but the new age has broken in with the death (and resurrection; cf. the earthquake in Mt 28:2) of Jesus; see note on Mt 16:28. After his resurrection: this qualification seems to be due to Matthew's wish to assert the primacy of Jesus' resurrection even though he has placed the resurrection of the dead saints immediately after Jesus' death.

y. [27:52] Dn 12:1–3.

[*] [27:54] Cf. Mk 15:39. The Christian confession of faith is made by Gentiles, not only the centurion, as in Mark, but the other soldiers who were keeping watch over Jesus (cf. Mt 27:36).

[*] [27:55–56] Looking on from a distance: cf. Ps 38:12. Mary Magdalene… Joseph: these two women are mentioned again in Mt 27:61 and Mt 28:1 and are important as witnesses of the reality of the empty tomb. A James and Joseph are referred to in Mt 13:55 as brothers of Jesus.

z. [27:56] 13:55.

THE BURIAL OF JESUS. *

57[a] When it was evening, there came a rich man from Arimathea named Joseph, who was himself a disciple of Jesus.[b] **58** He went to Pilate and asked for the body of Jesus; then Pilate ordered it to be handed over. **59** Taking the body, Joseph wrapped it [in] clean linen **60** and laid it in his new tomb that he had hewn in the rock. Then he rolled a huge stone across the entrance to the tomb and departed. **61** But Mary Magdalene and the other Mary remained sitting there, facing the tomb.

*
[27:57–61] Cf. Mk 15:42–47. Matthew drops Mark's designation of Joseph of Arimathea as "a distinguished member of the council" (the Sanhedrin), and makes him a rich man and a disciple of Jesus. The former may be an allusion to Is 53:9 (the Hebrew reading of that text is disputed and the one followed in the NAB OT has nothing about the rich, but they are mentioned in the LXX version). That the tomb was the new tomb of a rich man and that it was seen by the women are indications of an apologetic intent of Matthew; there could be no question about the identity of Jesus' burial place. The other Mary: the mother of James and Joseph (Mt 27:56).

a. [27:57–61] Mk 15:42–47; Lk 23:50–56; Jn 19:38–42.

b. [27:57] Is 53:9.

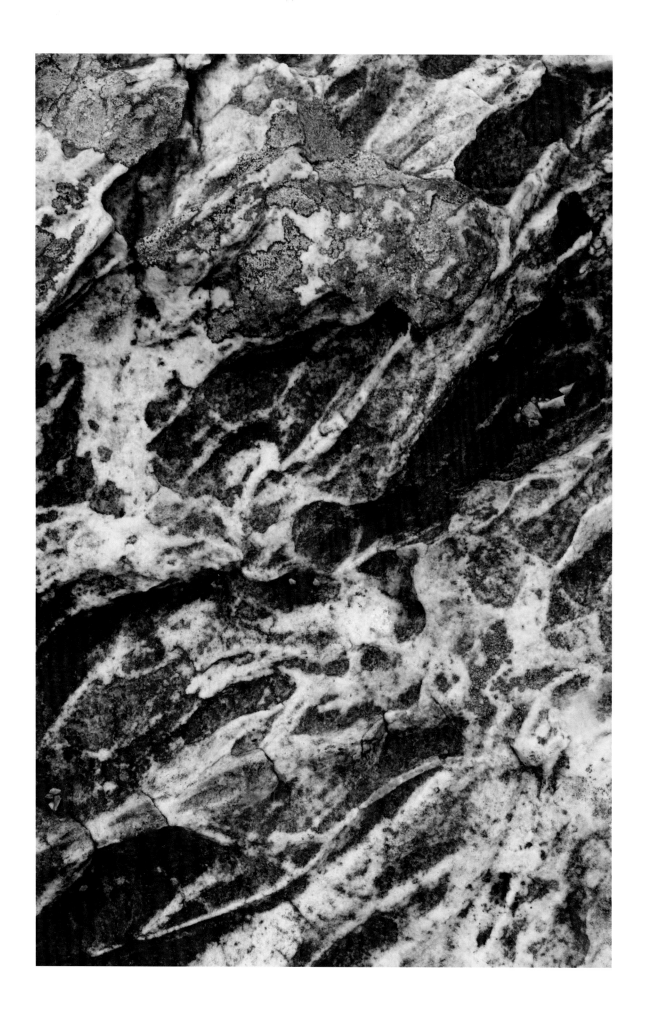

THE GUARD AT THE TOMB.*

62 The next day, the one following the day of preparation,* the chief priests and the Pharisees gathered before Pilate **63**[c] and said, "Sir, we remember that this impostor while still alive said, 'After three days I will be raised up.' **64** Give orders, then, that the grave be secured until the third day, lest his disciples come and steal him and say to the people, 'He has been raised from the dead.' This last imposture would be worse than the first."* **65** Pilate said to them, "The guard is yours;* go secure it as best you can." **66** So they went and secured the tomb by fixing a seal to the stone and setting the guard.

* [27:62–66] Peculiar to Matthew. The story prepares for Mt 28:11–15 and the Jewish charge that the tomb was empty because the disciples had stolen the body of Jesus (Mt 28:13, 15).

* [27:62] The next day...preparation: the sabbath. According to the synoptic chronology, in that year the day of preparation (for the sabbath) was the Passover; cf. Mk 15:42. The Pharisees: the principal opponents of Jesus during his ministry and, in Matthew's time, of the Christian church, join with the chief priests to guarantee against a possible attempt of Jesus' disciples to steal his body.

c. [27:63] 12:40; 16:21; 17:23; 20:19.

* [27:64] This last imposture...the first: the claim that Jesus has been raised from the dead is clearly the last imposture; the first may be either his claim that he would be raised up (Mt 27:63) or his claim that he was the one with whose ministry the kingdom of God had come (see Mt 12:28).

* [27:65] The guard is yours: literally, "have a guard" or "you have a guard." Either the imperative or the indicative could mean that Pilate granted the petitioners some Roman soldiers as guards, which is the sense of the present translation. However, if the verb is taken as an indicative it could also mean that Pilate told them to use their own Jewish guards.

MATTHEW CHAPTER 28 [*]

[*] [28:1–20] Except for Mt 28:1–8 based on Mk 16:1–8, the material of this final chapter is peculiar to Matthew. Even where he follows Mark, Matthew has altered his source so greatly that a very different impression is given from that of the Marcan account. The two points that are common to the resurrection testimony of all the gospels are that the tomb of Jesus had been found empty and that the risen Jesus had appeared to certain persons, or, in the original form of Mark, that such an appearance was promised as soon to take place (see Mk 16:7). On this central and all-important basis, Matthew has constructed an account that interprets the resurrection as the turning of the ages (Mt 28:2–4), shows the Jewish opposition to Jesus as continuing to the present in the claim that the resurrection is a deception perpetrated by the disciples who stole his body from the tomb (Mt 28:11–15), and marks a new stage in the mission of the disciples once limited to Israel (Mt 10:5–6); now they are to make disciples of all nations. In this work they will be strengthened by the presence of the exalted Son of Man, who will be with them until the kingdom comes in fullness at the end of the age (Mt 28:16–20).

THE RESURRECTION OF JESUS.

326

1[a] After the sabbath, as the first day of the week was dawning,[*] Mary Magdalene and the other Mary came to see the tomb. **2**[*b] And behold, there was a great earthquake; for an angel of the Lord descended from heaven, approached, rolled back the stone, and sat upon it. **3**[c] His appearance was like lightning and his clothing was white as snow. **4** The guards were shaken with fear of him and became like dead men. **5** Then the angel said to the women in reply, "Do not be afraid! I know that you are seeking Jesus the crucified. **6**[*] He is not here, for he has been raised just as he said. Come and see the place where he lay. **7**[d] Then go quickly and tell his disciples, 'He has been raised from the dead, and he is going before you to Galilee; there you will see him.' Behold, I have told you." **8** Then they went away quickly from the tomb, fearful yet overjoyed, and ran to announce[*] this to his disciples. **9**[*e] And behold, Jesus met them on their way and greeted them. They approached, embraced his feet, and did him homage. **10** Then Jesus said to them, "Do not be afraid. Go tell my brothers to go to Galilee, and there they will see me."

a. [28:1-10] Mk 16:1-8; Lk 24:1-12; Jn 20:1-10.

* [28:1] After the sabbath...dawning: since the sabbath ended at sunset, this could mean in the early evening, for dawning can refer to the appearance of the evening star; cf. Lk 23:54. However, it is probable that Matthew means the morning dawn of the day after the sabbath, as in the similar though slightly different text of Mark, "when the sun had risen" (Mk 16:2). Mary Magdalene and the other Mary: see notes on Mt 27:55-56; 57-61. To see the tomb: cf. Mk 16:1-2 where the purpose of the women's visit is to anoint Jesus' body.

* [28:2-4] Peculiar to Matthew. A great earthquake: see note on Mt 27:51-53. Descended from heaven: this trait is peculiar to Matthew, although his interpretation of the "young man" of his Marcan source (Mk 16:5) as an angel is probably true to Mark's intention; cf. Lk 24:23 where the "two men" of Mt 24:4 are said to be "angels." Rolled back the stone...upon it: not to allow the risen Jesus to leave the tomb but to make evident that the tomb is empty (see Mt 24:6). Unlike the apocryphal Gospel of Peter (9:35—11:44), the New Testament does not describe the resurrection of Jesus, nor is there anyone who sees it. His appearance was like lightning...snow: see note on Mt 17:2.

b. [28:2] 25:51.

c. [28:3] 17:2.

* [28:6-7] Cf. Mk 16:6-7. Just as he said: a Matthean addition referring to Jesus' predictions of his resurrection, e.g., Mt 16:21; 17:23; 20:19. Tell his disciples: like the angel of the Lord of the infancy narrative, the angel interprets a fact and gives a commandment about what is to be done; cf. Mt 1:20-21. Matthew omits Mark's "and Peter" (Mk 16:7); considering his interest in Peter, this omission is curious. Perhaps the reason is that the Marcan text may allude to a first appearance of Jesus to Peter alone (cf. 1 Cor 15:5; Lk 24:34) which Matthew has already incorporated into his account of Peter's confession at Caesarea Philippi; see note on Mt 16:16. He is going...Galilee: like Mk 16:7, a reference to Jesus' prediction at the Last Supper (Mt 26:32; Mk 14:28). Matthew changes Mark's "as he told you" to a declaration of the angel.

d. [28:7] 26:32.

* [28:8] Contrast Mk 16:8 where the women in their fear "said nothing to anyone."

* [28:9-10] Although these verses are peculiar to Matthew, there are similarities between them and John's account of the appearance of Jesus to Mary Magdalene (Jn 20:17). In both there is a touching of Jesus' body, and a command of Jesus to bear a message to his disciples, designated as his brothers. Matthew may have drawn upon a tradition that appears in a different form in John. Jesus' words to the women are mainly a repetition of those of the angel (Mt 28:5a, 7b).

e. [28:9-10] Jn 20:17.

11 While they were going, some of the guard went into the city and told the chief priests all that had happened. 12 They assembled with the elders and took counsel; then they gave a large sum of money to the soldiers, 13 telling them, "You are to say, 'His disciples came by night and stole him while we were asleep.' 14 And if this gets to the ears of the governor, we will satisfy [him] and keep you out of trouble." 15 The soldiers took the money and did as they were instructed. And this story has circulated among the Jews to the present [day].

* [28:11–15] This account indicates that the dispute between Christians and Jews about the empty tomb was not whether the tomb was empty but why.

THE REPORT OF THE GUARD. *

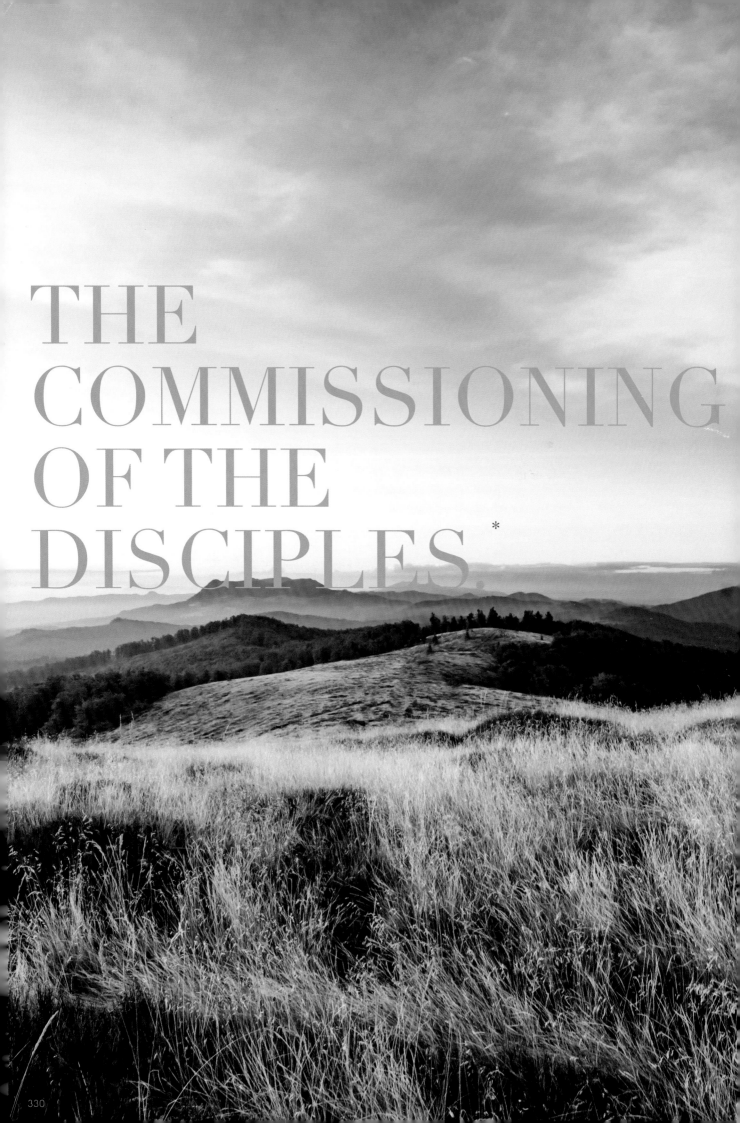

THE COMMISSIONING OF THE DISCIPLES.*

16[f] The eleven[*] disciples went to Galilee, to the mountain to which Jesus had ordered them. **17**[*] When they saw him, they worshiped, but they doubted. **18**[*][g] Then Jesus approached and said to them, "All power in heaven and on earth has been given to me. **19**[h] Go, therefore,[*] and make disciples of all nations, baptizing them in the name of the Father, and of the Son, and of the holy Spirit, **20**[i] teaching them to observe all that I have commanded you.[*] And behold, I am with you always, until the end of the age."

[*] [28:16–20] This climactic scene has been called a "proleptic parousia," for it gives a foretaste of the final glorious coming of the Son of Man (Mt 26:64). Then his triumph will be manifest to all; now it is revealed only to the disciples, who are commissioned to announce it to all nations and bring them to belief in Jesus and obedience to his commandments.

f. [28:16–20] Mk 16:14–16; Lk 24:36–49; Jn 20:19–23.

[*] [28:16] The eleven: the number recalls the tragic defection of Judas Iscariot. To the mountain…ordered them: since the message to the disciples was simply that they were to go to Galilee (Mt 28:10), some think that the mountain comes from a tradition of the message known to Matthew and alluded to here. For the significance of the mountain, see note on Mt 17:1.

[*] [28:17] But they doubted: the Greek can also be translated, "but some doubted." The verb occurs elsewhere in the New Testament only in Mt 14:31 where it is associated with Peter's being of "little faith." For the meaning of that designation, see note on Mt 6:30.

[*] [28:18] All power…me: the Greek word here translated power is the same as that found in the LXX translation of Dn 7:13–14 where one "like a son of man" is given power and an everlasting kingdom by God. The risen Jesus here claims universal power, i.e., in heaven and on earth.

g. [28:18] Dn 7:14 LXX.

h. [28:19] Acts 1:8.

[*] [28:19] Therefore: since universal power belongs to the risen Jesus (Mt 28:18), he gives the eleven a mission that is universal. They are to make disciples of all nations. While all nations is understood by some scholars as referring only to all Gentiles, it is probable that it included the Jews as well. Baptizing them: baptism is the means of entrance into the community of the risen one, the Church. In the name of the Father…holy Spirit: this is perhaps the clearest expression in the New Testament of trinitarian belief. It may have been the baptismal formula of Matthew's church, but primarily it designates the effect of baptism, the union of the one baptized with the Father, Son, and holy Spirit.

i. [28:20] 1:23; 13:39; 24:3.

[*] [28:20] All that I have commanded you: the moral teaching found in this gospel, preeminently that of the Sermon on the Mount (Mt 5–7). The commandments of Jesus are the standard of Christian conduct, not the Mosaic law as such, even though some of the Mosaic commandments have now been invested with the authority of Jesus. Behold, I am with you always: the promise of Jesus' real though invisible presence echoes the name Emmanuel given to him in the infancy narrative; see note on Mt 1:23. End of the age: see notes on Mt 13:39 and Mt 24:3.